Praise for **LAUNCH**

"This is a GREAT book about launching products and growing businesses, but it's about so much more. It's about creating a movement, making an impact, and delivering huge value into the marketplace—and it's based on experience and results. If you want to bring your product, business, or movement into the world in a big way, then LAUNCH is your recipe book."

— **Daniel G. Amen, M.D.**, author of *Change Your Brain, Change Your Life* and eight other *New York Times* bestsellers

"I've personally used Jeff Walker's methodologies to start from scratch and launch five brands, each of which hit one million dollars in revenue in less than 12 months. This book is invaluable, and Jeff is the modern marketing savant the world has been waiting for."

— **Brendon Burchard**, #1 *New York Times* best-selling author of *The Millionaire Messenger*

"What Jeff Walker teaches in LAUNCH is vital for modern marketing success. You don't need more tactics or tools; you need smart strategy, and that's exactly what this book delivers."

— **Marie Forleo**, #1 *New York Times* best-selling author of *Everything Is Figureoutable*

"Jeff Walker's LAUNCH is the how-to guide for persuasive marketing, delivered with integrity and authenticity. This is the ultimate primer for new and established marketers alike."

— **Mike Michalowicz**, author of *Profit First* and *Get Different*

"This book is a must-read for everyone trying to influence and change people's lives in a positive way. It's a GREAT business book, but it's also much more than a business book. I plan to get a copy for every Hay House author."

— **Reid Tracy**, CEO, Hay House, Inc.

"The careers of thousands of successful online entrepreneurs have already been launched by Jeff's extraordinarily practical concepts, structures, strategies, tools, and processes. LAUNCH is a must-read for all marketers—the go-to handbook for making money selling anything on the Internet."

— **Dan Sullivan**, president and founder of The Strategic Coach

"When it comes to Internet marketing, Jeff Walker is a bona fide genius. Now with LAUNCH, he maps out exactly how you can successfully market any product or service online. A must-read for all serious entrepreneurs."

— **Randy Gage**, author of the *New York Times* bestseller *Risky Is the New Safe*

"This book isn't just for people who want to make a lot of money in their businesses really fast. This is for people who want to live their best life, doing what they were born to do, and serving the world. I highly recommend this book to anyone who wants to make a bigger impact along with a much bigger income."

— **Christian Mickelson**, CEO of CoachesWithClients.com

"Wow! What can you say about Jeff Walker? This guy owns the launch space. Believe me—if you're looking to launch a product, business, or even a book, then pick up this book and read it NOW. I guarantee you won't regret it."

— **Eric T. Wagner**, founder and CEO of Mighty Wise Academy, writer on Forbes

"If I could say one word about Jeff Walker and LAUNCH, it would be: IMPACT. If you are looking for a huge positive impact on your business, your family, or in life, then LAUNCH is a must-read. Don't walk to get a copy . . . run, and let Jeff Walker help you create a great legacy for those around you."

— **JB Glossinger**, founder of MorningCoach.com

"In the early days of Web marketing, it was complete freaking chaos online. We knew we had unprecedented access to vast global audiences, but we lacked a simple, elegant way of introducing new products and closing sales. Enter Jeff Walker . . . who arrived well-versed in old-school direct marketing, coupled with a unique early-adopter's grasp of the potential online. . . . The launch formula he perfected produced results for us far beyond any of our other online marketing efforts . . . time after time after time. It was stunning. And fun. And elegant in its simplicity. Jeff codified the way online launches will be conducted for generations to come."

— **John Carlton**, legendary copywriter and author of *The Simple Writing System* and *The Entrepreneur's Guide to Getting Your Shit Together*

"I've known Jeff Walker for several years—I've watched the way he does business. It's 100 percent based on building value, and that's exactly what this book does. . . . Jeff teaches from experience, and he teaches with huge heart and great humility. His strategies are both revolutionary and incredibly effective."

— **Janet Bray Attwood**, *New York Times* best-selling co-author of *The Passion Test*

LAUNCH

LAUNCH

How to Sell Almost Anything Online, Build a Business You Love, and Live the Life of Your Dreams

JEFF WALKER

HAY HOUSE, INC.
Carlsbad, California • New York City
London • Sydney • New Delhi

Published in the United States by: Hay House, Inc.: www.hayhouse.com® •
Published in Australia by: Hay House Australia Pty. Ltd.: www.hayhouse.com.au •
Published in the United Kingdom by: Hay House UK, Ltd.: www.hayhouse.co.uk •
Published in India by: Hay House Publishers India: www.hayhouse.co.in

Cover design: Alan Dino Hebel • *Interior design:* Joe Bernier • *Indexer:* J S Editorial, LLC

Cataloging-in-Publication Data is on file at the Library of Congress

Hardcover ISBN: 978-1-4019-6023-0
Tradecover ISBN: 978-1-4019-7473-2
E-book ISBN: 978-1-4019-6024-7
Audiobook ISBN: 978-1-4019-6025-4

10 9 8 7 6 5 4 3 2 1
1st edition, July 2021
2nd edition, September 2023

Printed in the United States of America

This product uses paper and materials from responsibly sourced forests. For more information, please go to: bookchainproject.com/home.

Dedicated to my wife, Mary, and my incredible children, Dan and Joan, who have been with me for this whole crazy ride (and giving me unwavering support every step of the way). I love each of you with all my heart.

CONTENTS

PREFACE TO THE UPDATED EDITION

When I published the first version of this book in 2014, my launch formula was already well proven. I had been teaching it for more than 10 years, and I had thousands of successful students who had launched uncountable products, services, online courses, membership sites, and entire businesses.

What remained to be seen was whether I could teach the formula in a book and replicate that success . . . and do so for the much broader market that a book would reach. Well, the results are in—and they have surpassed my wildest dreams. I continually hear from readers who tell me about their successes. Here's a rather outsize example from a review that was left on Amazon by Tiffany Aliche. With her permission, I've condensed the review for length.

★★ It LAUNCHED me into an 8-figure/year business! ★★

5 years ago I had an idea for a new business. An online school that taught women how to take their finances and lives to the next level, the Live Richer Academy.

I had no idea how to introduce my new business to my audience, then a friend suggested I read Launch.

Not only did I read Launch, *but I also followed it to a T. I did every-single-step.*

The results were amazing! Within the first thirty minutes of launching my school, I'd made $30,000. That was around what I used to make a year when I was a preschool teacher.

The week-long launch grossed me around $70,000. That was more money than I'd ever imagined.

With the 3rd launch, I dusted the book off again and did ALL of the steps. This time, I grossed around $250k during launch week!

The last launch I did about a year ago made $560k in the launch week!

And I can proudly say that as of this year (2020), this former preschool teacher now runs an 8-figure/year business!

Launching is NOT easy. It's A LOT OF WORK. What I like about this book is that it lays out ALL of the work, step-by-step.

If you're not sure how to share your new product or service with your audience, I highly suggest Launch. *It helped to change the trajectory of my business and life.*

Tiffany "The Budgetnista" Aliche
. . . former preschool teacher, and
now a financial educator and the
author of *Get Good with Money.*

That's one example, one story, one review out of thousands. And it's certainly not typical or average or what you should expect. Any time you hear an example like that, you need to understand that there was a lot of work involved, and undoubtedly some sleepless nights. But it's a very real story, and it came from someone who built her business based on what she learned in this book.

And that, dear reader, is why you should take what I'm about to share with you very seriously. This book isn't full of fantasies or fairy tales or magic tricks. It contains a proven formula that works, and it's packed with examples of real people who have built real businesses using that formula—and you can go look those people up on Google if you like.

WHAT'S NEW IN THIS EDITION, AND WHAT HASN'T CHANGED

The first edition of *Launch* got lots of results for readers. The core formula is unchanged and continues to work. But I keep refining the formula, and we keep getting new tools to use, so it was time for an updated edition. Here's what's new and updated:

I've added chapters on using social media in your launches, on Live Launches (using live broadcasts to deliver some or all of your launch content), and using paid traffic (i.e., advertising) in your launches.

Also, since the first edition was published, we've greatly advanced the art of the Open Cart, so I've added new content to Chapter 8.

And, of course, I've refreshed the entire book; there are changes throughout. I also expanded the Glossary and added an Index.

What's not changed is the core formula—because it's working better than ever. The results are light-years beyond what they were when I first developed the formula in the late 1990s, better than when I first started teaching them to clients in 2003, and significantly stronger than when I published the first edition of this book in 2014.

The formula keeps working because it's based on human psychology that's been part of us for thousands of years and will still be with us in another thousand years. In our fast-paced digital world, it's fashionable to assume that any work will be outdated in a couple of years (or even a couple of months). But if you're reading this book 70 years after I write these words, my prediction is that the formula will still work—because it uses strategies that are rooted in how our brains function. How the formula is delivered will surely change, but it is still going to work.

One final note before we get going: Earlier I shared Tiffany's review of the book. She built an eight-figure business (in other words, a business with more than $10 million in annual sales) from scratch with what she learned in these pages, and she left a five-star review.

Right next to her review was a one-star review that said "Useless, I really don't understand the hype about this method or the book. The author does not say anything valuable."

Now, I've spent enough time in the public eye to know that I won't appeal to everyone. I know I'm not everyone's cup of tea. And I know some people won't believe me or the examples I give of my students throughout the book. (Even though they can go online and look up all the people I feature!)

But I would also suggest that the difference between Tiffany's $10 million business and that one-star review is as much about the reader's willingness to suspend disbelief and get to work as anything else. And I would humbly suggest that if you approach this book and this formula with a belief in the possibilities it holds for you, then your results may surpass what you can imagine.

A NOTE TO THE READER

This book will build your business—fast. Whether you've already got a business or you're itching to start one, this is a recipe for getting more traction.

Think about it—what if you could launch like Apple or the big Hollywood studios? What if your prospective customers eagerly counted down the days until they could buy your product? What if you could create such powerful positioning in your market that you all but eliminated your competition? And you could do all that no matter how humble your business or budget?

There's a process—a formula, if you will—that can get you there. I've created and honed that formula over the last 25 years, and I'm going to share it with you in these pages.

There's no theory in this book. Everything I'm going to teach you is based on real-world results. This formula was created through trial and error, testing, and hard-won experience.

I've personally done dozens of wildly successful launches of my own products (and I've also had a few that were not so successful . . . that's often where the biggest learnings come from!). But what's far more important than my results is my students' success—they've collectively done thousands of launches in countless markets and niches. You're going to meet some of those students in this book, because I'm a big fan of teaching from (and by) example. You will note that these are NOT hypothetical scenarios. I've read lots of business books that use fictional case studies to explain their methods, but this isn't one of those books.

As I said, I'm going to give you real-world examples throughout the book. And if you want to go deeper—I've got additional audio and video case studies you can get (for free) from the member site that goes along with this book. I've also got training videos and additional resources at the site, which you can access here: http://thelaunchbook.com/member.

I love sharing the stories of my students' launches. I do it primarily because it's instructive, but also because they're my heroes. I believe that entrepreneurs are the future of humanity. They're the ones who are driving human progress, creating jobs, and building real value in the world. And that's one of the reasons I'm so passionate about my business—it's all about helping entrepreneurs and would-be entrepreneurs.

I also believe that we are living in the greatest time in history for entrepreneurial growth and opportunity. It's never been easier to get started, and it's never been easier to grow a business. The ability to reach tightly niched markets on a global basis is simply unprecedented. For instance, the first sale I ever made was in a tiny niche market to a gentleman in Switzerland . . . and I did it from the basement of my home in Colorado.

Of course, that's not to say that it's easy. There's plenty of hard work involved, just like in any human accomplishment. This is definitely NOT a get-rich-quick book. But the formula has been proved over and over—it's the road map to a fast start for your product or business. After all, if you're going to put in the work, it's nice to know that you're using a proven, tested system.

The results have been staggering. I started my businesses from the humblest beginnings imaginable, and I've gone on to sell tens of millions of dollars' worth of my products. More to the point, my students and clients have dwarfed my own success—they've sold well over a billion dollars' worth of their own products and services.

The funny thing is, as I reflect back, it all happened accidentally. I didn't set out to reinvent marketing or to become a leader in the industry. You see, when I started out, I had zero sales and marketing experience. And, to a large extent, that's why I succeeded.

QUICK CLARIFICATION: PRODUCT LAUNCH FORMULA VERSUS THE PLF COACHING PROGRAM

In this book I'll be teaching you the core of the Product Launch Formula®. This is the formula that I started developing in 1996 and that I've been teaching since the early 2000s. It's been used by thousands of my students in hundreds of markets around the world. Many of them have launched using this book and only this book. I already told you about Tiffany Aliche, who launched a $10 million business with this $20 book.

In the interest of full disclosure, I want to tell you that I also have a high-end training program called the Product Launch Formula Coaching Program (or PLF Coaching Program, for short). This is an additional, paid program that I offer, and it is not inexpensive. You can think of this book as something like a college textbook, and the PLF Coaching Program as the college course that goes along with the book. Plenty of my readers have launched with nothing more than this book, and I also have tens of thousands of students who have gone through my coaching program. Either way, I just want to see you get launched.

Here's an important point: Throughout this book, when I write "Product Launch Formula" or "PLF," please know that I'm referring to the methodology. If I want to refer to my training program, I'll use "PLF Coaching Program" or "Product Launch Formula Coaching Program."

If you're interested in the PLF Coaching Program, you can learn more at ProductLaunchFormula.com. That's the only plug I'll give for my program in this entire book.

Please note that if you join my email list either at this book's member site (thelaunchbook.com/member) or at ProductLaunchFormula.com, then you'll eventually get to see me do a launch. I typically do only two or three a year, but if you're following my emails and you're patient enough, you'll get to see me take you through the entire process. If you watch how I follow the formula, it just might be one of the best marketing lessons of your life.

CHAPTER 1

From Stay-at-Home Dad to Six Figures in Seven Days

It was just another click . . . just like the hundreds or even thousands of clicks or taps we make every day. But this was a really important click for me, and I hesitated. My finger hovered over that button before I clicked. Five seconds, ten seconds, and still I waited. The truth is, I was terrified. I had months of planning and years of hopes and dreams riding on that click. In fact, it felt like the future of my family was hanging in the balance.

Little did I know that click was going to start a cascade of events that would literally change the very face of marketing and business on the Internet. As I sat there at the homemade desk I had shoved into a corner of my dimly lit basement, there were no grand thoughts of changing the world. I was using a beat-up old computer, an old-school dial-up Internet connection, and I hadn't held a job in more than seven years. Humble beginnings indeed.

But the real reason I hesitated over that click came down to one word: *desperation*. I was desperate for a change. I needed a success. I needed to make some money. I needed to turn my life around. And I had been waiting for (and working toward) this moment for too long . . .

You see, this whole journey started when my wife, Mary, walked through the front door in tears—a moment etched in my memory forever. She had left work in the middle of the workday, and now she was standing in front of me, in tears from the pressure of supporting our family. Mary could no longer stand having to leave for work every morning before our two young kids even woke up and coming home at night when it was almost time to tuck them into bed.

I had been home taking care of our babies. The politically correct term these days is "primary care provider" or "stay-at-home dad," but back then we just called me "Mr. Mom," and it was a whole lot less socially acceptable than it is now. Several years before, I had quit my corporate job, a job most people would probably consider a good one, in operations management. But I was the proverbial square peg in a round hole. I just didn't fit in the corporate world. I didn't understand the politics, and I felt like I was forever swimming upstream when I tried to get things done. I saw myself as a corporate failure. So when my son was about a year old and my wife graduated from the University of Colorado and landed a job with the U.S. Bureau of Reclamation, I walked away from my corporate career.

I didn't have a plan. I didn't know what I was going to do. I just knew I couldn't keep living in the corporate world.

The whole Mr. Mom thing went on for longer than I expected. Soon we had a second baby, which meant I was caring for two small children. As anyone who has been in that role knows, my days were busy. But I needed to make a change. I needed to figure out a way to support my family, to give my wife a break, and to relieve all the pressure that was crushing down on our family.

And that's what that click was all about—changing our lives, creating a new and more prosperous future. It was about launching a product and launching a business. It was about creating an income and changing my family's fortunes. Never in my wildest dreams did I think it would change the world.

GO AHEAD AND QUIT YOUR DAY JOB

When I finally built up the nerve to click the button, the reaction was breathtaking—like stomping on the gas pedal of a Porsche 911 Twin Turbo.

That click sent an email from my computer.

The email went to a server based just outside Green Bay, Wisconsin.

And that triggered an email broadcast that went out to the people who had subscribed to my simple email newsletter.

Within seconds, that email broadcast landed in the inboxes of my subscribers.

The email was very short, containing less than 50 words. But at the end of the email there was a link to an order form on my website where people could buy a product that I had just created. The product was an upgraded version of my newsletter about the stock market and what I thought was going to happen in the market in the near future.

(Actually, to be more accurate, I hadn't even created the product yet, but I'll get to that later, when I teach you about the Seed Launch®.)

Of course, all that took just a few seconds, but every single second after I clicked the Send button seemed to drag on for an eternity. I felt like I held my breath the entire time. I needed to know . . . would anyone buy my new product?

After 30 seconds I optimistically checked to see if anyone had bought yet. Nothing.

Forty seconds. Nothing.

Fifty seconds. Nothing.

Fifty-nine seconds . . . and the FIRST SALE came in!

A few seconds later, another order. And then another, and another, and then three more. Every time I clicked Refresh, there were more orders!

Within an hour, the total sales were over $8,000. By the end of the day, sales had gone beyond $18,000. And by the end of the week my humble little offer had made over $34,000—almost as much as I had ever made in an entire YEAR back in my corporate job.

That was the launch that brought Mary home. It wasn't my first-ever launch (that's a crazy story I'll get to a little later), but it was the one that convinced me that my little, fledgling business could support my family. Within a few months Mary had left her job and come home to stay. We were ecstatic. (We joke that she "retired," but nothing could be further from the truth. In addition to being a full-time mom, she quickly took over back-office operations in the business.)

You know, money is a funny thing. For some people, $34,000 is a crazy amount—an almost unbelievable number (and for me, it was life changing). For others, it might not be big enough to get them excited. But no matter what group you're in, if you stick with me throughout this book, I've got some pretty amazing results to share with you.

Because I didn't know it at the time, but I was just getting started. As hard as it was to believe as I sat in my basement at a homemade desk, I was creating something that would literally change thousands of lives.

HOW I GOT RICH HELPING THOUSANDS OF OTHERS GET RICH

Let's get clear on one thing right from the start: This is not a get-rich-quick book.

Yes, what I'm about to share with you has created amazing riches and abundance in my life and in the lives of many of my students. But that money, wealth, and influence didn't magically appear overnight.

There is a formula behind all the amazing success. And that's what this book is all about: taking you behind the curtain and showing you that formula.

Along the way, I'm going to introduce you to a world that most people don't know exists, a world where ordinary people are creating extraordinary businesses. A world where people are starting businesses with almost no investment or capital, often launching those businesses from a spare bedroom or their kitchen table. And a world where those people are going from start-up to profits in a remarkably short time.

And then there are those who are applying this formula to a business they already own and seeing a breathtaking increase in their sales.

This isn't the world of high-flying, high-tech start-ups where a few geeky programmers get together, work 20 hours a day, try to "get funded" by some venture capitalists, then sell to Google for $100 million. (Or, more likely, go bust amid a pile of greasy old pizza boxes and empty Red Bull cans.) If you want to go down that road, I wish you the best of luck. But this isn't the book for you.

What I'm talking about is creating a business (or growing an existing one) and generating profits right out of the gate. A business with low overhead, low start-up costs, and minimal or no staff. A business that is highly profitable and gives you great flexibility in your life. And, last but not least, a business that creates great value in the world and allows you to "do good" at whatever level you choose.

I know, it all sounds like the land of milk and honey, right? All beauty and grace? Can't possibly be true, right?

I know, I know.

In fact, I wouldn't believe it if I hadn't seen it for myself, over and over again. The reality is this: The Internet and our entire digital media world have completely changed the game for anyone who wants to have his or her own business. It's now easier, faster, and cheaper to start and run a business than at any time in history.

And if you already have your own business, the Internet gives you the power to grow it more quickly and easily than ever before.

And I say all that from experience. I started my first online business in 1996, in the Internet's Dark Ages, and I've been profitable every year since then. Right through the dot-com crash, right through the Great Recession, right through every Google update and Facebook algorithm change, right through a global pandemic. I've sold tens of millions of dollars' worth of my products online in four distinctly different markets, and along the way, I've taught thousands of online entrepreneurs how to start and grow their businesses. My students and clients have done well over a billion dollars in sales (and counting).

Though I'd rather talk about my students' success than my own, I think it's safe to say that I'm widely regarded as one of the top digital marketing experts and leaders (or at least the longest tenured—as I write this, I've been teaching my formula for more than 15 years).

However, as you're going to learn, it wasn't always that way. I wasn't born with any type of marketing superpowers. Before I started my first online business, I had never run a business before. I had absolutely zero sales training and no marketing skills. In fact, I was always the kid who couldn't sell more than two bags of doughnuts for the Boy Scouts fundraiser every year (and one was the bag that my parents bought).

THE RULES HAVE CHANGED

The world is clearly in the midst of a huge transition. The very nature of our communications and daily lives has changed radically in just the last two decades. We live in a more transparent world, a world with a seamlessly connected client base that can instantly pull up thousands of reviews about hundreds of competitors. A world with an ever-increasing level of competition for your prospects' attention. A world where the "marketing fog" grows thicker with each passing day. A world that puts ever greater value on authenticity and congruency.

The rules of business and marketing have changed, and those changes have killed many businesses. But the changes have also created enormous opportunity for thousands of others. If you understand the new playing field, grabbing your future customer's attention and building a relationship with him or her has actually gotten a lot simpler in many ways. And that's what this book is all about.

So whether you're in a time of transition and desperately want to start a business . . .

Or you're running a department or a profit center at a major corporation . . .

Or you're a solo practitioner or service provider (such as a lawyer, massage therapist, or Ayurvedic astrologer) and you're sick of the dollars-for-hours shuffle . . .

Or you've got a promising side hustle that you think could grow into something bigger . . .

Or you already have a successful online business, but your sales are stagnant and you need to inject some momentum into it . . .

Or you're even an artist (such as a painter, author, or jeweler) struggling to get noticed in a very crowded digital world . . .

The fact is that you need to launch. Every successful product, business, and brand starts with a successful launch. You can't afford to show up slowly. You need momentum and cash flow, because they are the very lifeblood of every successful business.

MILLION-DOLLAR DAYS

After that $34,000 launch, after Mary quit her job and came home to stay, my business just kept on growing. My launches got better and better, and my results got better and better, until I had one that did more than $106,000 in seven days—all from my home, all with no staff, all with almost zero costs.

These were the "quiet years." There were lots of great things about my business, and I loved my business and my life. I was making more money than I had ever dreamed of, Mary could stay home with the kids and be a full-time mom, and we were able to move to my dream hometown of Durango, Colorado, where I could pursue my passion for all kinds of outdoor sports like mountain biking, whitewater kayaking, and skiing.

That all changed, however, when I went to an Internet marketing seminar in Dallas in February 2003.

When I got off the plane in Dallas for that seminar, I didn't think my business was all that special. I figured there must be a lot of people with online businesses who were doing launches the same way I was. The success I was having was breathtaking for me, but I didn't know that making six figures in seven days in a one-person business was the type of thing that would stop people in their tracks. I mean, it was really cool and I still had a hard time believing I had pulled that off, but I was going to a seminar with a bunch of fancy experts. I figured they must all be doing stuff like this.

In the next three days at that marketing seminar, as I met lots of new people (and forged some friendships I value and enjoy to this day), I realized that no one else was doing the stuff I was doing. They definitely weren't doing launches the way I was or getting the results I was getting. In fact, I was shocked when I realized that I had basically invented a new way of marketing—an approach that would eventually come to be known as the Product Launch Formula.

One of the people I met at that seminar was a man named John Reese. He's one of those guys you realize are brilliant the moment you meet them, but at that time he was mostly flying under the radar. He was a true Internet marketing expert, but few people knew it at the time.

We stayed in touch after the event and became friends, and I shared my launch "secrets" with him. In 2004 John put my techniques to work on two launches. The first one was for a three-day seminar he put on. It did almost $450,000 in sales and proved to me that my techniques would work outside my little business teaching people about the stock market.

John's next launch was for a training course on how to generate traffic for one's website, and this launch was a game changer. It generated $1,080,000 in sales in just 24 hours—a million-dollar day! What makes that number even more shocking is that his business was a tiny micro-business he ran from home with almost no staff or team whatsoever. (I think John had one person helping with the launch and a part-time customer service assistant.)

I was stunned that this new marketing approach I had invented could generate such insane results. But at the time I was still publishing my financial newsletters, and even though I was starting to get regular calls from people looking for help with their launches, I was largely still behind the scenes in the bigger Internet business world. I had a wonderful life—living in Durango, running a great business, going skiing and mountain biking with my kids. I was happy behind the scenes and not looking for a spot in the limelight.

But after John publicly thanked me for my help with his launches, the cries for me to consult on launches kept getting louder. And after urging from John and several others (especially Yanik Silver, another prominent leader in the early online business industry, and one who I had helped with a launch), I decided it was time to publish my work—to start teaching others my Product Launch Formula.

THE DAY MARKETING CHANGED

I suppose the real test came on October 21, 2005. I had decided to launch my Product Launch Formula training course, and my reputation (and my business future) were on the line. After all, the proof really was going to be in the pudding. If I claimed to be an expert on product launches, I'd better do an outstanding job on MY launch, right?

But even though I had done plenty of successful launches— and helped others do the same—there was an extra challenge this time. I was creating an entirely new business, starting from scratch. All my previous success had come from teaching about the stock market. Now I was going to be teaching people how to launch products and businesses online. I didn't have an email list of prospects in this new market, and my old list of stock market investors wouldn't do me any good at all. I didn't have "expert positioning" in the market; I was largely unknown except to the few people I had helped with their launches. But that didn't slow me down, because I knew how to get around such limitations. (I'll show you how when I teach you about JV Launches.)

So the pressure was on, but by this time I was experienced. My launch was a crazy success. In the first week I sold just over $600,000 worth of my new Product Launch Formula training program. And with that launch, I instantly created a new business (in a new market) and developed hundreds of new clients and a list of thousands of new prospects.

The proof was in the pudding, indeed. ☺

Since then it's been a wild ride. Over the years I've continually updated and revised my PLF training so that it has evolved into a complete coaching program. In fact, the Product Launch Formula Coaching Program has arguably gotten more results than any other digital marketing training product ever.

I have thousands of Product Launch Formula Owners, and many of them have enjoyed jaw-dropping success. It's hard to quantify their total results, but I know that my students and clients have done more than a billion dollars in sales, and that number goes up every day.

Remember, most (but not all) of those PLF Owners are small, even micro-sized businesses. This isn't like Google doing another billion dollars in sales. These are mostly tiny businesses, and the impact of those sales are absolutely huge. I've had many PLF Owners equal my "six figures in seven days" success, and many have had million-dollar launches.

People have used PLF in every type of market and niche you can think of and realized tremendous success. In fact, it's almost become a hobby of mine to keep track of many of those markets. Here's just a partial list of some of the markets:

dating advice	*pet care*
Photoshop tutorials	*dog agility training*
becoming an Amazon seller	*tennis instruction*
college admissions	*yoga*
mixed martial arts	*youth soccer coaching*
cake decorating	*hand analysis*
knitting	*brain science*
mutual fund investing	*barbecue*
dressage	*adventure travel*
learning guitar	*surface pattern design*
learning piano	*test preparation*
health food	*calligraphy*
massage therapy	*juggling*
personal training	*baseball*
fiction writing	*corset making*

writing children's books
crocheting
trading (forex, futures, stocks, etc.)
real estate investing
training doctors to read ultrasounds
business coaching (around the world)
raw food
romance (writing love letters)

medicinal herbs
meditation
marching band accessories
treating fetal alcohol syndrome
officiating weddings
songwriting
indoor bicycle training
becoming a great parent
self-defense
how to draw
spiritual growth

Remember, in the interest of brevity, I gave just a partial list—there are dozens and dozens more examples. Don't make the mistake of thinking PLF won't work for your business or market.

It's also been used all over the world—I haven't heard from anyone in Antarctica yet, but it's worked on all the other continents. I have successful PLF students in dozens of countries, and it's worked in more languages than I can keep track of.

And it works with all kinds of products and businesses, such as:

online courses
physical widgets
online services
estate sales
coaching
consulting
B2B business system sales
board games
real estate
software
home study courses

online membership sites
offline services (dentists, tax services, etc.)
ebooks
mastermind and networking groups
artwork (paintings, jewelry, etc.)
nonprofit fundraisers
getting people to church
travel packages
apps

Again, this is only a partial list. But here's the takeaway: Product Launch Formula and my PLF students have completely redefined the way stuff is sold online.

ENOUGH ABOUT ME. WHAT ABOUT YOU?

Now you know the story behind the Product Launch Formula, but what does all this have to do with you? Can this formula work for you? Can you start an online business using my Product Launch Formula? Or if you already have a business, can it help you grow it?

In my experience, unless you're selling a commodity (like gasoline or sand) or you're someone who offers an emergency service (like a locksmith or bail bondsman), then the answer is an emphatic YES. I've seen so many PLF Owners have so much success in so many different fields that almost nothing surprises me anymore.

In this book, I'll be sharing some of their stories. You'll meet people from many different walks of life, people with wildly different products and businesses. Folks like Amy Small, who sells hand-spun yarn. She started using PLF to help her struggling business, and she's completely transformed every aspect of it. And John Gallagher, who sells products about foraging for edible and medicinal herbs and plants. John was on food stamps when he did his first launch, and now he has a seven-figure business. And Will Hamilton, who sells tennis instruction products and has used his launches to create a strong enough brand so that he now partners with top-level tennis pros. And Anne LaFollette, who started her online business in her 60s after being downsized out of the corporate world. She teaches about surface pattern design, and her business reached well into six figures in sales in only her second year in business.

All of this might sound like magic, or complicated, or just plain unattainable. Well, stick with me and you'll see that it's not complicated, that it just plain works, and how and why it can work for you.

I've organized this book to follow a logical progression:

In the first five chapters I'll give you the foundational material, including an overview of the PLF process, along with email lists, mental triggers, and the Sideways Sales Letter®. In the next three chapters I'll dive deep into the formula itself. I'll walk you through the full launch process, including the Pre-Prelaunch, the Prelaunch, and then the Open Cart. In the next five chapters I'll show you the details of putting the formula to work—including the Seed Launch (this is how you start from scratch), the JV Launch (how you can do those big mega-launches), and Live Launches, as well as social media and paid traffic. The final four chapters are about fitting PLF into your business and your life.

Now just to be clear, I'm not saying that PLF is easy or automatic. There is definitely work involved. Like I said at the beginning, this is NOT a get-rich-quick scheme. But the reality is thousands of people are creating these types of small, underground, highly profitable online businesses. And with Product Launch Formula they are putting together super-powerful product launches (or entire BUSINESS launches) that are creating nearly instant sales and momentum for their businesses.

Sound good? Are you ready to roll?

In the next chapter I'm going to walk you through the basic structure of the Product Launch Formula, and then we'll move forward from there. Along the way you're going to see why it's so completely revolutionary, why it works in so many different markets, and why it works for so many different types of businesses and products.

And soon I'll get to the crazy story of how I made more than a million dollars in sales in a single hour. ☺

↑

CHAPTER 2

The Product Launch Formula Explained

John Gallagher was a busy man. He had a wife and two young kids, he was going to school to become an acupuncturist, and he worked nearly full time at the Wilderness Awareness School, a non-profit that he helped start. When you meet John, you're quickly struck by his earnestness and his passion and energy—he's not the kind of guy who sits around idle. But there wasn't a lot of time or money to go around (many nonprofits don't pay so well), so John relied on food assistance to help feed his family. He never thought he would have to do that—he wasn't a "food stamps" kind of guy. But he did what he had to do to get by. Besides, he was sure it would be a temporary situation, because John had big plans. He had the entrepreneurial itch and what seemed like a great idea for a business.

John's passion is foraging for and preparing edible and medicinal plants and herbs, and he had created an educational board game with his wife that taught kids all about herbs. The game would be called Wildcraft: An Herbal Adventure Game, and it was time to bring the game to market.

Of course, if you're going to create a board game, there are some big up-front costs—the minimum quantity you must order from a manufacturer is quite large. But John pushed ahead, borrowing nearly $20,000 from his dad and placing an order for 1,500 games. Like so many entrepreneurs before him, he was willing to go deeper into debt to get his business started. Even though this seemed like a step backward, he knew once the sales started to roll in he would be able to climb out of debt.

Then came the big day when the games arrived at his home, and he started to realize just what 1,500 games looked like. As pallet after pallet was unloaded from the semi-truck, his excitement started to turn to worry. The boxes filled the entire garage. Then the spare bedroom. Then the second bathroom, even the shower stall.

But John put his worry aside, because it was time to bring the game out into the world. It was a beautiful game. He knew it would provide hours of entertainment and education to a lot of families—and that it was the ticket out of debt and into prosperity for his family.

So John planned a launch party and invited his friends and acquaintances and extended community. He wasn't sure what to expect, but there was one scenario he wasn't prepared for: total heartbreak.

John Gallagher with some of his inventory of Wildcraft games.

THE ENTREPRENEURIAL LAND OF BROKEN DREAMS

Unfortunately, it takes a lot more than a great idea to start a business. In fact, this story is a lot like thousands of other entrepreneurial stories that end with a soul-crushing defeat. We see it all the time: A new store in the mall, a new restaurant downtown, suddenly empty with a For Rent sign in the window. A beautiful new blog that is started with enthusiasm but quickly becomes a ghost town, with no visitors, no comments, no new articles. It's absolutely heartbreaking, because that's not just a business going down in flames—that's someone's dream. It represents hundreds of hours and thousands of dollars invested in a big vision—a big vision that has failed catastrophically.

In John's case, the picture was especially dismal. He sold only 12 games at his launch party, leaving him with 1,488 more to sell. John faced a monumental low point in his life. Not only did he feel like he had failed, he was literally surrounded by his failure. He and his family lived in a home stuffed floor to ceiling with unsold games. Those games seemed to stare at him every minute of the day, all day long. Even worse, he didn't know what to do next. He had just dug himself into a huge hole of debt, and he had no idea how to even begin to climb out of it.

Like so many other would-be entrepreneurs, John had seen his dreams nearly smashed to pieces on the rocks of what I call "Hope Marketing." He created his product and hoped it would sell. And if you know many entrepreneurs, you've probably heard a very similar story before. However, John's story has a different ending.

SNATCHING VICTORY FROM THE JAWS OF DEFEAT

At his wife's urging, John went to Google and searched for help about launching a product—which is where he found the Product Launch Formula Coaching Program. And then, since my PLF program is not inexpensive, he went to his dad and borrowed even more money. (Note: I do NOT advise borrowing money to buy any of my training materials. It worked out for John, but it's not a practice I recommend.)

John dove headfirst into PLF, and he intuitively saw that it would be a perfect match for his board game. Within a few weeks he had a new plan for his product launch and was ready to put it in place. It's worth noting that John spent almost nothing on his PLF-style launch. PLF is all about the method, not sinking a lot of money into the launch. John counted down the hours to his new launch with huge anticipation, wondering if it could possibly meet his newly heightened expectations.

He didn't have to wait long. The results were staggering—and an incredible contrast to his first, failed launch. In just the initial launch period, John sold 670 games, bringing in right around $20,000! Even more remarkable, since he had spent almost nothing on his launch, nearly the entire amount could go toward paying off the cost of getting the games manufactured.

For those keeping score at home, that's 12 sales for Hope Marketing and 670 sales for Product Launch Formula. That's an increase of 55 times. The game sold for about $30, and translated into dollars, the contrast looks even more dramatic: $360 in sales versus $20,100. Now, just to be crystal clear, John didn't spend anything on advertising during his PLF-style launch. He didn't have any new promotional partners. He didn't get any media coverage. He used the same resources and assets he already had, and since his family was on food stamps he clearly didn't have a lot of resources. In fact, he actually started out with a borrowed laptop computer and used the free Internet connection at the local library.

John's success with that first launch was truly remarkable, but he was just getting started. He's now sold more than 150,000 copies of his Wildcraft game, and he's launched many other products, including one of the most popular membership sites in his niche (HerbMentor.com). In fact, what he's done since that first launch makes his initial success seem modest in comparison. I'll tell you more of his crazy story a little later, because it's such a great illustration of how one well-executed launch can set you up in business nearly overnight. For now let's just say that in the first edition of this book, he was the guy who went "from food stamps to a six-figure income," but that needs a little updating. Now John is the man who went from food stamps to a seven-figure business.

One more note before we temporarily leave John's story: The one asset John had in his launch was a small email list—a list of people who had requested that he stay in touch with them via email. I'll get to the magic of having an email list in the next chapter. But the quick story is that when you combine a list with PLF, it's almost like having a license to print money.

A WARNING ABOUT THOSE BIG NUMBERS

In the last chapter I threw some crazy numbers at you, like how I started from scratch, ran a business out of my basement, and eventually made $106,000 in a single week (with no employees, no physical store, no inventory—nothing but a computer and an Internet connection). Then I told you about how I taught one friend my Product Launch Formula and he sold $1,080,000 in 24 hours—again with almost no staff, no office, etc. Next I slipped in that part about my business growing to the point where I did more than $1 million in sales in a SINGLE HOUR (when I was still working out of my home and running things by the seat of my pants).

After that I explained how my students and clients have done over $1 billion (!) in product launches in all types of markets, selling all kinds of different products, and that many of those students were running micro-businesses with almost no overhead. And now I've shared the story of John Gallagher, who started when his family was on food stamps and went on to build a seven-figure business.

In fact, the numbers are all so crazy that I worry I might lose you. I understand that when you're just getting started, it can be hard to imagine numbers this big. But please remember two things: First, the numbers are all real. And second, my first launch did $1,650 and I was shocked by those results. I was a complete newbie when I started out; so was John Gallagher, and so were many of my other students.

If you're like me when I began my business, then the odds of you coming right out of the gate and doing a million-dollar launch are probably lower than winning the lottery. It's not going to happen when you first start out. But you need to know this: you can absolutely start from scratch just like I did, quickly build up your business, and quickly grow your results.

I'm going to walk you through my formula for how to do exactly that, but first I have to introduce you to this "hidden world" where ordinary people are building extraordinary businesses—and building them quickly, with nearly zero up-front investment.

A "SECRET" WORLD AND THE EVOLUTION OF MARKETING

Back when I started in the mid-1990s and early 2000s, I found a "secret" world of business that most people had never heard of—a world of colorful characters, real-world rags-to-riches stories, and nearly unbridled opportunity. That world might not be so secret anymore, but to a large degree it still exists.

It's a world where businesses can be created from the ether—start with an idea and you could be in business in a matter of days, often with almost no financial investment.

It's a world where a seat-of-the-pants business that you run from home with a skeleton staff (or no staff at all) can become a multimillion-dollar company.

It's a world that's not limited by time and space. You can run your business on your own schedule, and you can pick it up and move it to Bali if you like (or the mountains of Colorado, like I did).

It's a world where you don't need to invest large sums of money to get started, where you can bootstrap your way to success without having to raise any capital.

And it's a world that scales—these businesses can grow independent of the time you put into them. That means you break free from trading your precious time for dollars. Your income becomes leveraged. It's a world where regular people can start from scratch and actually get rich.

This is the world of the entrepreneurial direct marketing online business, and I was lucky enough to stumble into it back in 1996, during its earliest days. This world has transformed my life, and I've watched it transform the lives of thousands of other people. The history and evolution of that world is a crazy story, and maybe someday I'll write that book, because it's a story I experienced from the beginning. But more to the point of this book, I need to bring you into this world to give you a full understanding of the Product Launch Formula and how you can put the power of PLF to work in your business and your life.

Make no mistake: No matter what the size or type of your business (or your business dreams), this world offers something for you.

You see, back when I started in 1996, the Internet was expanding like crazy. The growth rate was exponential. Every month the number of users grew by a faster rate. The word *Internet* was starting to enter the collective consciousness, and suddenly everyone was talking about it, even if they didn't quite understand what it was. But no one had really figured out how to use the Internet for business, and the question from every business-minded person was "Can I make any money from it?"

The big corporations certainly didn't have a plan. For the most part, the Internet was more like the Wild West than a normal business environment. And that's not the type of arena the big corporations like to play in. But that's exactly the type of environment the "little guy" (and by that I mean both men and women, because MANY of these early start-ups were run by women) can thrive in. And thrive they did.

The Internet offered the perfect opportunity for the little guy to start a new business. These businesses cost very little to start, there were no set hours (since a website is always online), and they were independent of physical location. Furthermore, there was no big, entrenched competition, there was almost no regulation, you could have an instant global reach, and the Internet was growing every day.

These businesses focused mostly on providing "information" that fell into two categories: information that solved a problem (such as learning to play guitar or installing crown molding) or content that provided entertainment (such as jokes, photos, or games).

It's impossible to say how many profitable online businesses were in existence when I started mine in 1996, but there weren't very many. My guess is that they numbered in the dozens, or possibly hundreds, but by any count it was a pretty small universe. However, that universe quickly expanded as people learned that starting an Internet business could be quick and easy. Of course, the Internet didn't reverse the laws of entrepreneurship—the great majority of those initial businesses didn't last very long. But the sheer volume of start-ups meant a lot of those businesses would actually make it.

And it would be those businesses that pioneered much of the commercial, for-profit Internet world. For instance, I can remember when Jeff Bezos came on a discussion list I was part of to ask about creating an affiliate program for his new online bookstore, Amazon.com.

This was the primordial soup of the Internet business world, and that's where I started to piece together what would become known as the Product Launch Formula.

THE FORMULA THAT LAUNCHED A THOUSAND BUSINESSES

By now you're probably wondering, "What exactly IS the Product Launch Formula?" And, more important, "Will it work for me?"

Here's the big picture: The Product Launch Formula is a system to get your target market so engaged with your product (or business) that they almost beg you to sell it to them. And this all happens before you even release the product.

PLF works in all kinds of markets and with all kinds of products, and it's remarkably adaptable to just about any situation where you're releasing a new product or starting a new business. This is the system that I've been using and developing since 1996 and have been teaching to clients since 2005. The proof is in the results—the formula just keeps working.

Let's start with a fact we all know to be true: the growth of the Internet and all digital media since the late 1990s has changed the world in a fundamental way. It's a very different world, and we're never going back to the old ways of doing things. Nowhere is this more true than in business. And in that arena, we're going to focus on three factors that have changed the way business is done.

1. Speed of communication: This might seem so obvious now that you don't even think about it, but it's a lot easier and faster to communicate with your market than ever before. Within just a few minutes, you can write an email and broadcast it to your list of prospects and clients. They can be reading your message within seconds of when you press the Send button. Within a few more seconds you can update your social media followers, and they can see your update immediately. A few short years ago, the total time from original thought to creation to publication to consumption would be measured in days or weeks or months. Now it can be compressed to minutes.

2. Cost of communication: The cost to send an email or make a post to your social media followers is extremely low. The barriers to entry in the publishing game have been removed. What does it cost to become a publisher? Someone can create a Facebook page, Instagram account, or Twitter profile for free and start publishing instantly. A decade or two ago even the most inexpensive ways to start broadcasting or publishing would have set you back thousands of dollars.

3. Interactivity: When your followers respond to your message, you have all kinds of tracking data. This gives you nearly instant feedback on how your message is resonating with your target market. Compare that with a few years ago, when publishing was almost like shouting into the wilderness. Depending on the terrain and other conditions, you might hear a faint echo some time after your shout. More likely, you would get no feedback whatsoever.

Perhaps you've never thought about these changes before, or maybe by now you take them for granted. Either way, they have huge implications in many areas of our human experience—from politics to entertainment to medicine to interpersonal relationships. But what we're going to focus on here is business. Because those three factors—speed of communication, cost of communication, and interactivity—changed the way business and marketing worked, they created a world where nimble entrepreneurs can generate shockingly successful results in their businesses. And as you'll see, all of a sudden those crazy numbers I've been sharing with you will start to make sense.

TURNING YOUR MARKETING INTO AN EVENT

Have you ever noticed how Hollywood tries to build buzz before a movie is released? First there's the trailer, six months (or even a year) before the movie. Then there are TV ads leading up to the movie. Then the actors head out on a tour of the talk shows. And of course there's the social media campaign right around the release date.

How about when Apple releases a product? The company always creates a massive campaign leading up to the release date. In the months before a new product release, all the Apple fan sites are full of breathless rumors about when the release will be, the actual product to be released, and what new features to expect.

Those types of campaigns create a huge amount of buzz and excitement BEFORE THE PRODUCT IS EVER RELEASED. In fact, sometimes the release becomes an event in and of itself. Huge anticipation surrounds the launch, and people are genuinely engaged and paying attention.

Now contrast that to a normal marketing campaign, what I called Hope Marketing earlier. That's where you create a product or open a business or roll out a new ad campaign, and you hope it does well.

Now, *hope* is an uplifting word and can be truly wonderful in many areas of our lives. If you're shipwrecked at sea—to give an extreme example— hope can keep you alive while you wait to be rescued. But in business, *hope* is an ugly, nasty word. A soul-sucking word. You need to take control of your success; to the best of your ability, you want to take chance out of the equation. Don't bank the future of your business on hope.

Clearly, it would be better to engineer your product releases, your business launch, and your promotions so that your prospects are eagerly anticipating your launch, right? That's what's behind those big Hollywood releases and the Apple launches. Wouldn't you love to have instant momentum for your business? Imagine how that type of a start would change your business. Think about how creating massive anticipation for your product—before it's even released—would be a complete game changer.

Of course, there's only one problem. You probably don't have a budget of millions of dollars for your promotion or a hotshot creative team. And unless you have the resources and talent of Apple or, say, Universal Studios, it seems like you're stuck with Hope Marketing.

Well, hang on, because this is where the Product Launch Formula has changed the game. Remember those three game-changing factors I mentioned earlier—the decreased cost of communications, the increased speed of communications, and the greatly enhanced interactivity? Those are your keys to the kingdom. They're the reason why tiny online businesses, run by ordinary folks like you and me, have built an entirely new playing field—a playing field with unprecedented opportunity.

YOUR MARKET IS A CONVERSATION

Let's start with a nearly universal truth: people find conversations a lot more interesting than monologues or lectures. The evolution of the Internet has basically been one long movement toward increased conversation. Never before in history has it been easier to communicate and converse with more people around the world.

Sure, sometimes when you look at the comments on YouTube, those "conversations" may make you question the future of humanity. Nevertheless, we're clearly conversing with one another more now than at any time in history. And that conversation has carried over into business and marketing.

People are no longer interested in being shouted at by a TV commercial touting whatever features a product has. Actually, they were never interested in that, but now they have more choices, and it's a lot easier to tune you out when you start shouting at them, "Buy my stuff, buy my stuff, BUY MY STUFF!"

So instead of shouting at your prospects, what if you engaged them in a conversation? For instance, imagine you're a beginning guitar player, and an expert guitar teacher you're following online says something like this:

Hey, I've got this really cool new technique I can use to teach anyone to play one new song each week, and I just had this idea to put together a course that teaches my "secret" method. (Actually, I don't know if it's a secret, but I've never seen anyone else use this method. I showed it to a few friends, and it works really well—like, I can't believe the results my students are getting.) In any case, before I create the course, I want to make sure I cover everything. So can you help me out and tell me what your #1 challenge is when you're trying to learn to play an entire song?

It's so simple, but asking that question starts a conversation. It definitely doesn't shout out "BUY MY STUFF" to your followers.

Opening a dialogue with your potential clients is an example of what I call "the shot across the bow," and it's a great way to start your Prelaunch campaign. And that simple question, modified for hundreds of different markets, has been the start of countless successful PLF-style product launches.

SEQUENCES, STORIES, AND TRIGGERS

Okay, I just gave you a little example of the start of the PLF-style Prelaunch. It might not look all that powerful or special, but you'll see soon enough how that inauspicious start can build into something that almost takes on a life of its own.

At its heart, Product Launch Formula is made up of sequences, stories, and triggers. We'll cover sequences first.

The level of information that each of us is subject to every day is staggering. We've got email, voice mail, texts, messaging, social media, TV, advertising everywhere (on my airline seatback tray . . . really?), etc., etc., etc. The volume of information and data is only expanding and will continue to do so. And the number of marketing messages we see every day is growing just as rapidly.

Of course, our ability to absorb and comprehend those messages has NOT expanded. That means we're all working harder and harder to filter them out. We're all actively trying to avoid them, to tune them out. We use technology to filter what we can, and then we simply ignore most of the stuff that slips through those filters.

The military uses the term "the fog of war" to describe the uncertainty that happens on a fast-changing battlefield. Well, as a businessperson or marketer, you're competing in an environment that I call the "communication fog." You have to find some way to cut through that fog or your business will perish. It's that simple.

You can't rely on one single marketing message; instead you need to think in sequences. Instead of relying on a single communication to make your point, you use a sequence of communications that build on each other. Our product launches use a series of sequences—the Pre-Prelaunch, the Prelaunch, the Open Cart, and the Post-Launch.

Think about the whole phenomenon of the Harry Potter books. Which book release got more attention, the first book or the final one? The answer is the final book, because each book in the sequence gathered more attention and more fans—and those fans were rabidly anticipating each new book in the series.

So let's take a quick look at the primary sequences in PLF:

Pre-Prelaunch: This is where you begin. You use it to start building anticipation among your most loyal fans (and I understand that you might not have any loyal fans yet—I'll get to that in Chapter 3). The Pre-Prelaunch is also used to judge how receptive the market will be to your offer and to figure out some of the primary objections people will have. (Objections are the concerns that a prospect has about a potential purchase—about buying your product.) Surprisingly enough, the Pre-Prelaunch can even be used to tweak your final offer.

Prelaunch: This is the heart and soul of your sequencing, where you gradually romance your market with three pieces of high-value Prelaunch Content. You use your Prelaunch to activate mental triggers such as authority, social proof, community, anticipation, and reciprocity, and you do all that while answering the objections of your market. Typically, you release your Prelaunch Content over a period of 5 to 12 days. The format for that content can vary widely, from videos to podcasts to email to written PDF reports to webinars to live broadcasts (and I'm sure we'll invent a few more formats as the years go by).

Open Cart: This is the big day you've been building up to, the day you actually send the offer for your product or service out into the world and start taking orders. I call this "Open Cart" because you're "opening the shopping cart." Your launch is actually a sequence as well, and a very powerful one at that. It starts with the email that basically says, "We're open, you can finally buy now," and continues for a finite amount of time, usually anywhere from 24 hours to seven days, when you finally shut it down.

Post-Launch: This is the cleanup sequence, where you follow up with both your new clients and the prospects who didn't buy from you. The Post-Launch isn't as exciting as the other sequences, but it's important because that's where you deliver value and build your brand. And if you do it right, the Post-Launch starts to set up your next launch.

It all sounds pretty simple, right? Well, it is. And it's also pure gold when you mix in the power of story.

STORY: HOW HUMANS COMMUNICATE

Stories are powerful. They are how humans have passed down wisdom, knowledge, and culture for as long as we've been around. Think back to some of your earliest memories from school, and it's likely that the lessons you actually remember were based in stories. Think of all the world's religions, and you will realize that the vast majority of their teachings are delivered through story.

I'm a rational person, and I love knowledge and facts. That's the world I naturally live in. In this book, I would love nothing more than to give you data, theory, examples, and more data. But look how I started the first two chapters of this book, with my story in Chapter 1 and then with John Gallagher's in this chapter. And guess what you'll remember from these chapters a week from now? I'm willing to bet that it will be "Mr. Mom doing six figures in seven days" and "food stamps to seven figures." That's the power of story.

If you want to make your business and your marketing memorable, then your marketing needs to tell a story. That doesn't mean you have to become a novelist, but you need to tell an engaging story about your products and services and why they matter to your prospects. And you need to communicate that story to your prospects.

There is no better way or better place to tell your story than in your launch sequence. This is one of the hidden weapons of PLF, because the most powerful way to communicate your message is with a story, and the serial nature of your Prelaunch Sequence is a perfect place to tell that story.

It's no accident that most Prelaunch Sequences have three pieces of content. Most movies or novels naturally break down into three parts, and no doubt you've heard of the three-act play. We're dealing with a structure that has been proven over time immemorial, so why not use that structure in your marketing and base your sequences around it? Even the launch itself has three primary sequences: Pre-Prelaunch, Prelaunch, and launch.

Again, this might seem simple, but it's incredibly powerful stuff. And when you start to layer sequences and the power of story together, then you're creating a powerhouse structure.

THE FINAL PIECE OF THE PUZZLE: MENTAL TRIGGERS

Humans are funny creatures. We all like to think that we make rational, logical decisions. But it's really not that way. In fact, the vast majority of our decisions and behaviors are based in emotion and mental programming—and then we use our precious logic to justify those decisions.

There are a number of mental triggers that influence our decisions and behaviors. These triggers are always working just below our consciousness, and they exert enormous influence over how we act. For instance, if we perceive something as being scarce, we will naturally give it more value. If we view someone as an authority figure, we are almost automatically more influenced by that person than by others. And if we consider ourselves part of a community, we will overwhelmingly act in accordance with how we think the people in that community are supposed to act.

Those are just three mental triggers: scarcity, authority, and community. There are many more, however, and I'll cover them a little later. Here's the thing to understand right now: These triggers create enormous influence over our actions. They are timeless, and they are universal. They will not lose their power of persuasion anytime soon, and they work in any language, in any country, and just about any business.

At the end of the day, no matter what business you're in, you are really in the business of influencing your prospects and your clients. Your launch sequence gives you the ultimate opportunity to activate those mental triggers that will influence your prospects and clients.

PUTTING IT ALL TOGETHER

This chapter has been a quick whirlwind tour through the Product Launch Formula. What I've given you here is just an overview; I'll cover all of this in much greater detail in the following chapters. For now, you can just start thinking about combining your sequences, the power of story, and mental triggers.

You layer these mental triggers, one on top of another, so you're not dependent on any one trigger but combining them to create a powerfully influential message. You embed those mental triggers into a compelling and memorable story that cuts through the marketing fog, a story that connects your offer to the hopes, dreams, fears, and aspirations of your future customer. And you deliver that story in a tight sequence that turns your launch into a big event that captures your prospects' imaginations and builds anticipation toward your launch day.

Now you've got a formula for an incredible launch.

This is the formula that John Gallagher used to sell 670 games instead of the 12 he sold with traditional, old-world-style Hope Marketing. And it's the formula he's gone on to use over and over to build a serious business in a small niche.

Now, before we get into the nitty-gritty of the Product Launch Formula, I have one more critical piece of the puzzle for you. And this one will grow to become your personal "money machine." I think of it as a metaphorical printing press that I use to legally print money on demand. And you can have one as well.

I'm talking about your email list, and that's what we'll cover in the next chapter.

If you would like to see a case study I did with John Gallagher that examines his launches in detail (and shows how he built a seven-figure business), you can see it here: http://thelaunchbook.com/john.

CHAPTER 3

Income on Demand: Your List

I've already told you about a few launches in this book. As you continue, you'll hear about "clicks" and "Send buttons" and "pushing Send." This all might lead you to wonder if there's some magical "Launch" button you push to start your launch. And if so, where do you get one of those buttons?

Well, it's not magical, but there really is something you click to start your launch—and sometimes the results can seem magical. It's the click that will send an email out to all your email subscribers, and it's the fuel that drives your launch.

Of course, if you're starting from scratch, then you won't have a list. That's okay. Everyone starts off with no list, including me. This chapter will get you started. If you already have a list, or you have a group of past clients, then you're way ahead of the game, and you're that much closer to launching.

But make no mistake, once you start to build a list, and you combine it with the launch formula in this book, then you'll have the ability to make sales on demand. Your email list is your metaphorical "Launch" button. It may sound a little cheesy (and there will always be work involved), but having an email list is the closest thing you can have to a printing press that will print money for you.

Let me give you a real-world example from my life. When my wife and I decided to move out of the Denver area, the timing wasn't ideal. My business was just starting to really take off, and Mary had recently quit her job to be home with the kids and help me grow the business. We wanted to move to the mountains, specifically to Durango, a beautiful town in southwest Colorado. However, we thought we would take some time before we made the move; we wanted to adjust to Mary being home. And we were still a little nervous about my business being the sole source of income for the family.

But you know what they say about the best-laid plans. Just a couple of months after Mary left her job, we took a weekend trip down to Durango and found the home we wanted to live in. It was our dream home in a dream community. It was available immediately, and we knew it wouldn't stay on the market very long.

The problem was timing. We wanted the kids to finish out the school year in their current school, which meant we would have to buy the home in Durango several months before we sold our home in Denver. To do that, I needed a bunch of money quickly— something like an extra $70,000—for the down payment on the new home.

Now, at that point a lot of people would start thinking about borrowing money, either from a bank or possibly from a friend or family member. But that isn't what I was thinking. My first thought was "What can I launch? What type of offer can I make to my email list to raise that kind of money quickly?"

That's the power of the list. It means that you have the ability to create a big payday on demand. And that's exactly what I did. I looked at all the interactions and feedback I'd had with the people on my list, and I sat down and mapped out an offer that I knew they would want. I also made sure it was a product that I could create quickly and easily. And then I put together a launch for that product.

That's the backstory behind my first six-figure launch—the first "six in seven" that I mentioned in Chapter 1. The result of that launch was that I did $106,000 in a single week, and of that about \$103,000 was profit. Just that quickly, I had the down payment for our house. That's the power of the list (and, of course, a well-orchestrated Product Launch Formula–style promotion).

But again, I'm not some magician. I don't have any superpowers. It took a lot of effort to create that email list—but you can do the same thing. Think about what it would be like to have that kind of an asset in your business and your life. Think about how it would transform every aspect of your life.

That's what this chapter is about: building the kind of responsive email list that gives you tremendous power in your life.

THE GOLDEN STRATEGY

List building is one of the core strategies I always focus on in every business I own.

If you take NOTHING else from this book but an obsessive focus on building your list of clients and prospects, the book will still be worth 10,000 times what you paid for it.

What exactly am I talking about when I say "list"? This is really simple—it's a list of people who have asked to subscribe to your emails. Typically, you'll have an opt-in form on your website, and people will be able to enter their email address in that form to subscribe to your emails. I'm sure you've joined plenty of email lists over time, perhaps to hear from someone about a topic you're interested in or to get updates from an online retailer.

Of course, you have to give people a reason to subscribe to your email list. It might be to receive a newsletter or get regular updates about something. It could be to learn about special deals or find out about new content that you've created. But no matter what the promise is, the promise is the reason they are joining your email list.

For example, I'm an avid skier, so in the winter I get daily snow updates from two ski areas near me. Every morning I receive a short email from each that tells me whether they got any new snow overnight. I'm also a guitar player, so I'm on a couple of lists to get notices of new guitar tutorials. And I use a Mac computer, so I'm on a list that sends me updates about new Mac software. Those are just a few examples; I'm on lots of other email lists. I'm sure you're on several as well.

Make no mistake—once you start to build an email list for your business, you've taken a huge step toward controlling your financial destiny, and this is true no matter what type of business you're in. A list or database of prospects and loyal clients is always one of the most important assets in any business.

If you own a dry cleaning store, the clients who come in regularly are your bread and butter. If you run a restaurant, the customers who come in every week or every month are the people who keep you in business. However, the online world tends to speed up and intensify everything, and that's definitely the case with your list. In the online world, your list is everything.

EVERYTHING.

In fact, it really is hard to fathom the power of an email list until you have a list and you push that Send button . . . and then within seconds you start to see people responding and clicking through to your website. That power is breathtaking, and once you experience it, you will realize that your life has changed forever.

Of course, since there is so much data tracking online, you get to see the results in real time. For larger lists (say, those with more than 10,000 subscribers), it can actually take several minutes before your email list server delivers to all of them. But once the email starts going out, you'll typically start to see the response within seconds. For really large lists (I have well over 300,000 subscribers, and there are far larger lists out there), you sometimes have to take extra precautions so that whatever website you are sending people to doesn't crash. For example, when I published my first blog post at JeffWalker.com, I sent an email to my list to tell them about it. That email sent so much traffic to the blog that it crashed the server.

Now, I don't want to get too technical on you too early in this discussion, and I don't want to intimidate you. If you're just starting out in your list-building endeavors, you're a long way from having to worry about crashing servers. I just mention it to show you the power of having a list.

We have a saying in the business that sums it up in four words: "Push Send, make money." That's why having a list is like having a license to print money at will. This, of course, is why I wasn't worried about saving for my kids' college education—because I had a list.

WHAT ABOUT SPAM?

Before we go any further, I just want to be super-clear about one thing. When I talk about email lists, I am NOT talking about sending spam email. I'm talking about building a legitimate list of people who have asked to receive your emails.

There are many definitions of spam out there, and what is regarded as spam has changed quite a bit over time. (The laws regarding spam continue to evolve as well.) But for our purposes, spam can be defined as unsolicited commercial email. I've been publishing online since 1996, and I have never sent a single spam message. In fact, everything I do (and teach) is the very antithesis of spam.

The reality is that spamming is a very quick way to put yourself out of business. Don't do it. Send email only to people who have requested it.

YOUR LIST IS NOT JUST ANOTHER STRATEGY, IT'S *THE* STRATEGY

As I mentioned above, list building has been a core strategy for me since the beginning. In fact, it was the ONLY strategy I had when I started out. I actually began my list building efforts before I even had a website (and that was long before social media profiles existed).

I can't remember exactly why I was so focused on list building from day one, but I quickly realized just how powerful lists were. Those lists have become the cornerstone of everything that I do in my business. Of course, over the years plenty of other people have figured this out as well. But there's another thing that set me apart from most other people who were building lists back then, and that is summed up in one word:

Relationship.

That might sound like a funny word when we're talking about your email going out to thousands of people, but the reality is that your message is landing in a lot of individual inboxes. Every subscriber on your list is an individual, a unique person. I know I'm stating the obvious, but many list owners seem to forget this. I hear them talk about sending a "blast" to their email list—their term for an email broadcast. But think about it: Does anyone like to get blasted?

Remember that your email is landing in a very personal place—the inbox of your reader's computer. If you doubt how private this space is, just think about letting a stranger browse through your own inbox—not a very pleasant thought for most people. Most of us feel very protective of our inboxes, and because every email you send is landing in your subscriber's inbox, you have a lot of power.

Lots of times I'll go to a conference and people will come up to me (people I've never met) and start talking to me like I'm a long-lost friend. Sometimes I'll wonder if they actually ARE an old friend I've somehow forgotten. They'll start asking me about the stuff I've shared from my personal life in my emails—about how the skiing or the mountain biking season has been, about how my kids are doing, about how my guitar playing is going. And that's a GOOD THING, because I want my readers to feel like they have a personal connection with me. That connection is what gets them to open my emails, read my emails, and ultimately click on the links in my emails.

You see, it doesn't matter how many people are on your list if the emails sit unopened in your subscribers' inboxes. If they don't actually open your emails and read them, then you might as well not bother building a list.

What I'm talking about is how responsive your list is, and the responsiveness of lists varies dramatically. There are lists out there where 60 percent or more of the people on the list open the email. That's on the super-responsive end of the spectrum. And there are other lists where less than 1 percent of the people on the list open the email, which, of course, is on the dismally unresponsive end.

Obviously, you want a responsive list. It's better to have a list of 100 people where 60 percent open your emails (i.e., 60 people) than to have a list of 1,000 where only 1 percent do (i.e., 10 people).

So how do you build and maintain a responsive list? Well, there's a lot of strategy (and some tactics, and a little art) in the process, but it really comes down to "relationship." And the easiest way to increase the responsiveness of your list is to increase the connection and relationship you have with the people on your list. Remember:

1. The size of your list is not nearly as important as how responsive the list is, so your list relationship—which encourages response—is extremely important.

2. The entire PLF process you are about to learn is one of the best ways to build your relationship with the people on your list.

WHAT ABOUT SOCIAL MEDIA?

Of course, there are other types of lists in addition to email. You can also build a list of followers on social media sites such as Instagram, Snapchat, YouTube, or Twitter. Building a following on social is in many ways simpler than building an email list. It's seemingly effortless: post a few updates or videos and you'll gain some followers. You don't need to create a lead magnet, or an opt-in page, or find a list host (more on all these in the pages ahead). What could be easier?

But as of right now, email still has considerably more power when it comes to driving clicks and sales. As I type this, an email subscriber is at least 20 times more powerful in my business than a follower on social media. In other words, I would rather have an email list of 1,000 people than a Facebook following of 20,000. Of course, results will vary dramatically due to many factors, including platform and engagement. But studies in the industry confirm my experience: in general, an email subscriber will out-perform a social media follower in terms of pure response rates (both clicks and sales), and the results aren't even close.

My message here isn't that you should ignore social media; just don't use it as an excuse for not building your email list. You will regret it if you do.

Better yet, use your social media presence to build your email list. Social is a great place to reach your future customers—they're already gathering and having conversations there, so you should be there as well. Take part in the conversation, add value to it, and then invite them over to join your email list. I'll have more on this in Chapter 12, "Using Social Media in Your Launch."

SOCIAL MEDIA + EMAIL = A WINNING COMBINATION

Despite my continued focus on building your email list, there are some amazing things about social media. And when you use social media in conjunction with your email list, it can be a pow-erful tool to improve the overall performance of any promotion. Your people are already on social media, and when you're sending to them via email and also on their favorite social media sites, the ability to reach them increases.

Basically, you can coordinate your promotions between your email list and your social media advertising. The mechanics of this vary by social media platform and are constantly chang-ing (and I'll cover them in the chapters on social media and paid traffic), but know this: it's entirely possible to run ads on social sites that reach just the people on your email list. So on the morning that you send an email to drive people to your Prelaunch Content, you can also be running social media ads to those same people to send them there as well. This is an additive approach, and it gets results. In this case, social media is truly a force multiplier.

The thing to remember here is this: email is still central to your list building, but whether someone clicks on an email or clicks from their favorite social media site, you're still getting them to click through to your content. It all starts by bringing them into your universe by getting them to join your list.

Later on, in Chapters 12 and 13, I'll give specifics on how social media and paid traffic can fit into your overall launch strategy.

A PROSPECT LIST VERSUS A BUYER LIST

There are several types of lists, and it's important to understand the differences. Lots of times when people talk about lists, they just throw out a number: "I've got a 30,000-person list!" Well, a statement like that doesn't mean much. So let's peel this onion a little bit.

So far we've talked about two types of lists: email and social media. I also mentioned that as of right now, email lists are much more powerful than social media lists, but a combination of the two of them is the most powerful.

Another critical distinction is between "prospect" lists and "customer" lists. The definition is pretty simple. A prospect is someone who has NOT bought anything from you yet (you can think of your prospect as a "future customer"). A customer (or client, or buyer) is someone who HAS bought something from you. In your business you will have both types of lists. The important thing to remember is that a list of customers (or buyers) is a lot more valuable than a list of prospects. In my personal experience, a person on your buyer list is worth 10 to 15 times what a person on your prospect list is worth.

This leads to a couple of key points. First, you want to try to move people from your prospect list to your buyer list (and incidentally, a PLF-style product launch is the best way I've found to do that).

Second, you will treat the two lists differently. You want to maintain a great relationship with both, but if you're going to spend extra time and effort on your list relationship, then the place to spend it is on your buyer list. That usually means putting in the time and effort to send them some cool content or a bonus of some kind. I remember ordering from an e-commerce store that would often (but not always) include a little bit of hard candy or some other treat in their packages. I'm sure their cost to do that was just a few pennies, but I still remember getting those extras—and it's been several years since I ordered from them. A little surprise bonus or personal touch can really go a long way. For example, we always send out a handwritten thank-you post-card via snail mail to our new Product Launch Formula Owners. That's a simple way to stand out and build a relationship.

With an online business, it's really easy to create and send content-based bonuses, like an extra training video or report. This obviously works great for information-based businesses (such as one that teaches clients to play the guitar), but it will also work well for other businesses.

For example, a website that offers guitar courses could include an extra video lesson on playing movable chords or some other topic. But let's say you have an e-commerce store that sells guitars. Well, you could send that same video about movable chords. Or you could send a video about the care and maintenance of a guitar.

You could simply put the bonus video online—this will cost almost nothing other than the time to shoot and edit the video. Then you can send a link to the bonus video in your email—a great way to condition people to open your emails and click on your links. After all, if you occasionally send them cool bonuses in your emails, they'll always be looking forward to your next one.

LIST GETTING: HOW TO BUILD YOUR LIST

Okay, now that I've been going on for a while about how awesome lists are, hopefully I've got you sold on the idea that you should get a list as soon as you possibly can. Here's how to do it.

First off, this is going to be a hyper-abbreviated lesson on list building. I could write an entire book on the topic. And I've actually created an entire course on list building, because it's a rich and deep topic and so important. If you want to take this topic further (and you should!), you can get my List Building Blueprint for free at http://thelaunchbook.com/list.

The first thing to do is get clear on who your prospect is; I use the term *avatar*. Think of your avatar as your typical prospect, the typical person you're trying to reach. If you're teaching about golf, you generally aren't trying to reach all golfers; you might be going after school-age golfers who are trying to get a college scholarship. Or you might be going after 45- to 55-year-old women who are just starting to golf after their kids have gone off to college. Or you could be going after men with handicaps under 10 who want to improve their short game.

I don't really know the golf market, so I just made all those up. But you get the idea—everything about your marketing will be completely different depending on which of those three groups you are targeting.

This is the deal: Your list building is the very sharp end of your marketing efforts. It's the first place where people have contact with you, so you have to get it right. And the very first step in getting it right is understanding to whom you are selling, who your avatar is. You have to get this right because we're going to create a "squeeze page," which I will explain in a moment. That squeeze page will have a "lead magnet"— something of value (a video, a special report, a short e-course, a profile quiz) that you will give to your website visitors if they join (or subscribe to) your list. Your squeeze page and your lead magnet will be the keys to your list building efforts.

As I just mentioned, it's important to get this first piece of your marketing right. In fact, it's critical. This is your lead element in the battle for your business. However, you don't have to get it perfect right out of the gate. In fact, no one gets it perfect right away. The good news is that it's really easy to be incremental about this. You get your first squeeze page up, and then you work on improving it.

One of the coolest things about an online business is how much data you get and how easy it is to test things. In the most basic form (and one of the most useful), you create two versions of your squeeze page. Then you use software to alternate which version is shown to your site visitors (check my Resource Page at http://thelaunchbook .com/resources) and watch to see which version has the best response rate. After you have a winner, then you use the winner but create another test to see if you can improve it even more, and so on.

This is called split testing, or A:B testing, and it's the key to constantly improving your site's conversion rate. In this case, your conversion is simply the percentage of visitors you get to join your email list.

Again, the important thing to remember is this: Don't worry about perfection when you're starting out. No one gets it right the first time. The important thing is to get the first version done and then improve from there.

HOW TO GET PEOPLE TO JOIN YOUR LIST

So what is a squeeze page? As far as can be determined, this idea was pioneered many years ago by my friend Dean Jackson, and it has proved to be one of the most significant developments in the online marketing world. A squeeze page is a very simple page that gives visitors two options: They can opt in with their email address to get something free (this is your lead magnet). Or they can leave the page.

By forcing your visitors to choose, well, you force them to choose. And you should be clear right from the start that, for most websites, the majority of your visitors will choose to leave. This can be very painful for a new website owner to think about. But the reality is, only one thing on your site is 100 percent guaranteed: EVERYONE will eventually leave it. And you need to understand this: if they leave your site without opting in to your list or buying something from you, then the odds of their coming back are extremely slim. And when I say "extremely slim," what I really mean is "almost no chance at all."

If you doubt this, just think about your own actions online. How many times do you return to a website that you visited randomly? Even if you bookmark it? Even if a site is really cool? Probably not very often; instead, it's a matter of "out of sight, out of mind." Your visitors will be the same. Once they leave your site, they will likely never think about it again . . . UNLESS you capture their email address. Everything changes if they join your list, because then you can use your emails to drive them back to your site (or any site you want to send them to).

When you think about your list building that way, all of a sudden it starts to make a lot of sense to put up a squeeze page and force people to make a choice when they come to your site. Make them either opt in or leave.

If you're having a hard time wrapping your head around the idea of a squeeze page, here's another way to think about it. Consider the value of a subscriber to your email list. When you're just starting out, this can be a difficult number to calculate, but I will tell you that in many market niches, a general rule of thumb is that a subscriber is worth $1 per month or $12 per year. That's a really rough guesstimate, and I could write for a long time about email list metrics and characteristics. But let's stick with that $12 per year for this example.

Let's say that you do NOT have a squeeze page, but you have some type of form people use to subscribe to your site. Maybe there's an opt-in box in the right-side menu that says "Subscribe to my newsletter." That's not a very powerful way to convert your site visitors into email subscribers, so you might get only 3 percent of your visitors to subscribe to your list. That means that each visitor is worth 36 cents to you in the next year. This is how the math goes: Since each subscriber is worth $12 per year and 3 percent of your visitors subscribe, it's a matter of simple multiplication. In this case, 0.03 x $12 = $0.36.

Now let's say you do have a squeeze page. You are forcing your visitors to make a choice—either subscribe to your email list or leave your site. With a squeeze page, you're very likely to get a higher rate of conversion to your list. In this case, let's assume you get a 20 percent opt-in rate, a number that is quite realistic. That means each visitor is worth $2.40 in the next year. (Here's the math: 0.20 x $12 = $2.40.)

This means that for every visitor you have, you are losing $2.04 by not having a squeeze page. You are getting only 36 cents instead of $2.40 per visitor. Now, of course, this is hypothetical, and there are all kinds of factors and variables at play here. But the fact is that in many cases, putting a squeeze page on your site is an instant win in terms of website profitability.

One of the most important things that make a squeeze page work is having a really strong opt-in offer (this is the lead magnet that I mentioned earlier). Basically, this is the honey that you offer your visitors on your squeeze page to convince them to subscribe.

So what's the lead magnet? It all depends on your avatar. What do they really want? What are their greatest fears? Their biggest desires? What keeps them awake at night? Going back to golf, if your avatar is an average male duffer who plays one round of golf a week with his buddies, then maybe he just wants to drive the ball farther than his friends, especially on the first tee. If that's the case, then a great lead magnet might be a video tutorial on how to completely crush your drive on the first tee, every single time. Or maybe instead of a video, it could be a written PDF report.

Getting your squeeze page right is really about getting the lead magnet right. And it doesn't have to be perfect the first time out, since this is another thing you can test very easily. But at the end of the day, the effectiveness of your squeeze page is very much dependent on the quality of your lead magnet and how closely it aligns with your avatar's hopes, dreams, and desires.

Okay, enough theory. Let's take a look at some examples of squeeze pages.

The Launch Masterclass at ProductLaunchFormula.com

Anne LaFollette: From Doodles to Dollars

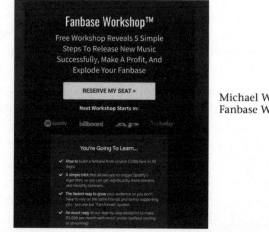

Michael Walker:
Fanbase Workshop

Cathy Hay: Tailor Your Sleeves Like a Pro

So far we've covered:

1. Defining your avatar.
2. Creating your squeeze page.
3. Creating your opt-in lead magnet.

Now the only thing left to do to get your list rolling is drive some traffic to your squeeze page. Of course, driving traffic is another one of those huge topics that I could write a book or two about. And it's a topic that is constantly changing, which means if I did write those books, they would probably be out of date by the time you read them. But here's a big-picture overview.

There are a number of ways to drive traffic. The first things that most people think of are the search engines, such as Google. These will bring you "natural search" traffic—meaning traffic that comes from people finding your site in the search engines. Getting your site to rank on Google (and by "rank" I mean appear near the top of the search listings) is part science and part art, and people devote entire careers to it. One important thing to remember is that it's VERY hard to get a squeeze page to rank well on Google. Nevertheless, natural search is something that I always build into my business at some level.

Another way to drive traffic is through "paid traffic." This is the advertising you see on Google, Facebook, Instagram, and other sites. These ads are basically sold on an auction basis, available to the highest bidder. It's actually more complicated than that, but that's a close enough explanation for now. In any case, paid traffic can be expensive, but it's great for testing squeeze pages because you can start driving traffic literally in minutes. I'll cover paid traffic in depth in Chapter 13.

Another way to send traffic to your site is through social media, such as YouTube, Twitter, and Instagram. Again, this is a big topic—far too big to cover in any real depth here—but I would have loved to have something like Facebook available when I started out. You can create a Facebook presence in minutes and start gathering followers there almost immediately. You already know that my preference is always going to lean toward building an email list first, but you can use your social media presence to drive traffic to your squeeze page. In other words, you can use your social media following to build your email list. I'll have more on using social media to build your list in Chapter 12.

There are many other ways to drive traffic to your squeeze page, such as creating great content that attracts word-of-mouth traffic (this has always been one of my personal favorites), other forms of advertising, and online forums.

And, of course, there's my personal all-time favorite source of traffic, which is affiliates and Joint Venture partners. This is when other people with lists send you tons of traffic, and it doesn't cost you a single penny up front—you pay them out of the sales that are generated by that traffic. This is the ultimate shortcut to building a big list fast. In fact, I've personally added more than 50,000 people to my list in a matter of days using this method. But this is an advanced strategy, and we're not ready to talk about that one yet—I'll go into all the gory details a little later.

THE LAUNCH LIST

Up above I told you about two types of lists—the prospect list and the buyer list. The difference between these two is really important. In some ways, the entire goal of your business is to move people from your prospect list to your buyer list, since it's so much easier to sell to someone who has already bought from you. There's one more type of list that's important to understand: the Launch List.

A Launch List consists of people who are specifically interested in following your launch. When you're first starting out and building your list toward a specific launch (likely a Seed Launch, covered in Chapter 9), you can assume everyone on your list is going to be interested in your launch. That means your entire list is basically a Launch List.

However, after you've been building your list for a while, you'll have people who have joined it over time, and likely for a variety of reasons. They've become accustomed to you sending emails of a certain type and at a certain frequency. As you head into a launch, your emails and their subject matter are likely to change somewhat, and you're probably going to be sending a lot more of them. In this case, it's smart to use a Launch List strategy.

For example, maybe you've built a list of people who are interested in mindfulness, a big list that you've assembled over a couple of years. Now you want to launch a product about the treatment of trauma. This is a related topic, and many of your "mindfulness" people will be interested. But not all of them. This is the time for a Launch List.

So you'll put together an opt-in page inviting everyone to register to get your launch content—in this case it might be a video series about the treatment of trauma. Then you'll email your list and tell them about this upcoming video series (in other words, you send them your Prelaunch Content). You'll send several emails to your full list to try and encourage people to opt in for your new video series (i.e., for your new launch).

Then, as you get into your launch, you'll send your launch emails only to your Launch List instead of your full list. Only the people who are interested in the treatment of trauma will get the emails.

It might sound counterintuitive to email only a portion of your readers, but in the long run this is a winning strategy. You'll be mailing to the people who are interested in your launch, and you won't be irritating those who don't want to hear about it. You'll build your relationship with the people who've opted-in for your Launch List, and you'll maintain your relationship with the rest of the people, who just want to hear about mindfulness.

THE SECRET TO HAVING A LIST IS TO JUST GET STARTED

Okay, by now I hope I've got you convinced of the power of lists and the absolute necessity of list building in your business. It drives me nuts that there are still people out there who don't do this. The bottom line is that this is all about your bottom line. Your lists of prospects and clients are the biggest assets in your business. In fact, I could argue that they're almost the ONLY true asset for most online businesses.

Since I've started teaching the Product Launch Formula, the number one question I get is "What if I don't have a list?" Sometimes people just whine about it: "Jeff, that's great for you because you have a big list, but I don't have one."

The truth is, that's exactly where I began: with ZERO people on my list. But I went to work building it—slowly, methodically, diligently. Some days I would get a single new subscriber, some days I would get none. My efforts gradually started to pick up momentum, and I would get three or four subscribers a day. I kept at it, and soon I was getting 30 subscribers a day . . . and 30 subscribers a day starts to add up. That's 900 subscribers in a month or 10,800 in a year.

And guess what? In many markets you can make hundreds of thousands of dollars a year with a list of 10,000 subscribers.

The bottom line is that if you want to build a viable business online, you NEED to focus on list building. That's why I put this chapter so early in the book—it's a core principle. And it's part of the Product Launch Formula story, because there is no better way to maximize the results you get from your list than with a product launch.

And here's an advanced secret: there is no better way to build a list quickly than with a product launch. Remember John Gallagher and the launch of his board game? Well, he had a very small list that he used in that launch. You'll remember that his first launch (before he got PLF) had 12 sales, and that after he applied PLF, he had 670 sales. The one thing I didn't tell you is that in addition to all those sales he made, he added more than 1,000 new subscribers during that launch.

That's what usually happens in a properly structured PLF-style launch. It's one of the best ways to build your list. But I'm starting to get ahead of myself.

CHAPTER 4

The Sideways Sales Letter: How to Sell Your Stuff without Being "Salesy"

Way back in 1996, when I started my first online business and I didn't have a clue about sales or marketing, I stumbled my way through all kinds of things. And I made one "mistake" that has made all the difference. In fact, that mistake became the core strategy that's made me millions of dollars, made my clients over a billion dollars in sales, and changed the way stuff is sold online. That strategy is the Sideways Sales Letter.

Back when I started, not only did I have no clue about how to sell stuff, but I didn't even know there were entire schools of thought about selling. I didn't know there were all kinds of sales theory and sales training. I just had no idea.

So I gradually made up my own way of selling. And it turns out that what I created was perfectly tuned to the new way of doing business online. As people have become exponentially more connected due to the Internet, the entire game of selling stuff has changed. And my approach to business was completely aligned with our newly connected digital lives.

Think about it. When you buy almost any type of hard goods, you can instantly pull up real user reviews on Amazon.com. You're about to go on vacation, you can quickly look at reviews on Tripadvisor.com. You're looking for an entertaining movie to go to, you can check out the ratings, well, pretty much everywhere.

And with greater connectivity, people have become more highly attuned to authenticity. They're more skeptical. It's like everyone is walking around with a giant, supersensitive "BS detector" that's always on full alert.

People have learned to see a pitch coming from a thousand miles away, and they've learned to distrust it. It's just a side effect of our uber-connected world. That's why, in most cases, the traditional old way of selling doesn't work so well anymore—or at least not nearly as well as the Sideways Sales Letter does.

Before I can explain the Sideways Sales Letter, I need to give you some context. There's been a traditional tool in direct marketing going back many decades simply called the "sales letter" (also known as the "long-form sales letter"). Basically, this is a lengthy printed advertisement written in the form of a letter. These sales letters can be 8 pages, 12 pages, 24 pages, or even longer. When most people first encounter a long-form sales letter, they have one of two reactions. If it's a topic they are interested in and it's a good letter that's been written by a pro copywriter, they'll start reading and soon get sucked right into the narrative of the letter. On the other hand, if it's a topic they don't care about or the letter is poorly written, they'll wonder why ANYONE would ever read such a long and boring advertisement.

The important thing for you to remember is that these long-form sales letters have been used for decades, and they have generated billions of dollars in sales for all kinds of products. The development of the long-form sales letter was one of the most significant advances ever in sales and marketing. It was, to borrow an old phrase from advertising legend Albert Lasker, "salesmanship in print." You could effectively make a complicated sale without being face-to-face with your future customer.

AN OLD TOOL FOR NEW PROFITS

What happened to the sales letter when the Internet came along? Well, it made the jump to the online world pretty easily. In fact, within a few years sales letters had become really popular online, and they got even longer on the Internet because you didn't need to pay for printing. It didn't cost any more to use a 40-page sales letter than a 12-page letter, so many of them got longer.

In the last few years, another change has been the use of video. The long sales letter has morphed into a long sales video. Think of it as a 20- or 30-minute commercial.

You've probably been to a website with a long-form sales letter. These sites are very simple—there's generally only a single page on the site, a very long page of sales copy for one product. There are no links on the site other than a Buy It Now button or an Add to Cart button. You either buy the product or you leave.

Alternatively, the page might have a sales video instead. Again, the page will be very simple, with a video that lasts anywhere from 15 minutes up to an hour or more. Again, the only link on the page is the Add to Cart button.

As e-commerce and online sales started to get rolling around 1998 and 1999, the use of the long-form sales letter really started to proliferate, especially among small, bootstrapping entrepreneurs, and definitely in the information marketing world.

As a bit of ancient history, this was back when the big online brands were in the middle of the dot-com bubble. They weren't focused on conversion, and they didn't even care much about profits. They worried about "user acquisition" and how "sticky" their site was—those were the things that drove crazy valuations on Wall Street. It's hard to believe, but revenue and profit weren't really on their radar for those dot-com businesses. It was the scrappy little solopreneurs and micro-businesses who worried about that type of stuff. And it was those tiny businesses that pioneered the direct marketing techniques that really drive online commerce to this day.

In any case, when the long-form sales letter was adopted in the online marketing world, it just plain worked. Many sites that started using this old-school direct marketing tool instantly saw their conversions and profits increase dramatically. But even as those sites proliferated, their days were numbered.

ENTER THE SIDEWAYS SALES LETTER

The secret of the Sideways Sales Letter that I stumbled on to was this: Instead of taking 8 or 12 or 20 pages to tell the story in a long, vertical sales letter, I flipped the sales process on its side. Instead of pages, I used days. Instead of a 10-page sales letter, I used a 10-day sequence. Instead of one superlong letter, I split it up into a series of contacts over a number of days. I call those contacts Prelaunch Content or PLC.

Instead of hoping that I could somehow weave magically spellbinding sales copy that could keep people reading for page after page, I used great sequential content and the power of story to pull the prospect into my sales message. Instead of delivering the equivalent of a superlong monologue, I turned the whole process into a conversation—a Launch Conversation. Instead of betting everything on one point of contact when the prospect landed on the sales page, I used the power of multiple "touches" and a sequence to drive my prospects wild with anticipation and turn my marketing into an event.

At its core, the Sideways Sales Letter is a sequence of Prelaunch Content followed by a sales message. The typical sequence will have three pieces of content that you share with your prospects over a period of up to 12 days. In the years I've been using and teaching this formula, the format of the content has varied widely, but the strategy has remained the same. These days, the content is often online video, but it can take any number of forms, such as email or blog posts or PDF reports. The Prelaunch Content is structured so that it's compelling and valuable and naturally leads into the sale of your product. At the end of the Prelaunch Sequence, you Open Cart by sending your prospects to a sales page to close the sale.

I want to emphasize that part about VALUABLE content—this isn't just about taking a sales pitch and stretching it out over a couple of weeks. That's not going to grab and hold anyone's attention. Through this process you deliver real value to your future customers.

Now, that was a hyper-condensed version of the Sideways Sales Letter and the launch process, and I'll be going into much greater detail on how you do this. The important thing to get right now is that the results are dramatic. Let's take a look at an example.

HOW ONE MAN STOPPED TRADING HOURS FOR DOLLARS

Barry Friedman is a professional juggler and a highly accomplished one at that. He started juggling when he was 15 and quickly became extremely passionate about it. Barry decided he wanted to make a living as a juggler and entertainer, even though his high school guidance counselor told him he would probably be broke and homeless within a few years. That prediction didn't pan out, and Barry has achieved great success, including appearing on *The Tonight Show* with the iconic Johnny Carson at the age of 23 and performing at the White House.

In addition to his juggling skills, Barry also became highly skilled at the business end of his profession. He was able to get high-paying gigs, many of them in the corporate world. Life was good, and Barry was making a great living.

Then came the day that Barry had a nasty mountain biking accident. As he lay in the hospital recuperating from surgery to repair his shoulder and collarbone, he wondered just how he was going to make a living. His career depended on being able to fly around the country to various gigs and performing onstage. Now he was facing six months of recovery, and even then it was unclear whether he would be able to juggle with his surgically repaired body. His income was based on his health and his ability to keep getting up onstage.

Of course, in that regard Barry was no different from almost anyone else. His financial security was tied to his ability to continue working. Even though being onstage and performing was a lot more glamorous than driving to work and sitting in front of a computer in a cubicle, he was still trading his time for dollars. Even though he worked for himself, and even though every show brought a large payday, he was still selling his time for money. If he didn't show up, he didn't get paid.

Barry Friedman

That was when Barry started to put together another plan—an alternate way to make a living that would completely sidestep the "dollars for hours" way of making money. He was about to step onto what I call the leverage train, where his income wasn't tied to the number of hours or days he worked. Barry knew that many of his fellow entertainers really struggled with the business end of things. They didn't market themselves well, and booking gigs never came easy. That was something Barry was very good at; in addition to being a world-class juggler, he had always been great at getting gigs, especially high-paying corporate ones. He knew how to sell his services and get paid top dollar.

Barry decided to start teaching those skills. He had seen a lot of online training programs, and it seemed like a perfect way for him to teach entertainers how to land more high-paying gigs. Barry had also discovered Product Launch Formula, and he had gone through the PLF Coaching Program. He created an online membership site called "Get More Corporate Gigs" where his clients could get ongoing training for a monthly subscription fee of $37.

Product Launch Formula works really well for membership sites like Barry's, but I want to focus on the launch of Barry's next product. He decided to create a high-end coaching group where he would work a lot more closely with clients for a much higher fee.

Barry had seen high-end online coaching programs, and he knew how powerful they could be. So he created an offer for the Showbiz Blueprint. This would be a 10-week, small-group program where his clients would have access to weekly group coaching calls. There would also be "hot seats" for each participant (where Barry gave feedback on their business challenges), a private community site, weekly "office hours," and a number of other benefits. In order to ensure that everyone got enough individual attention, the offer would be limited to 15 participants. The price was $2,000 if paid in full up front, and slightly more if clients used his payment plan.

The Showbiz Blueprint obviously offered a much higher level of training, coaching, and interactivity than Barry's membership site, and it was aimed at the premium end of his market. This type of premium offer is ideally suited to a PLF-style launch, because buying something like this is a big decision and a big commitment. The Sideways Sales Letter gives you the luxury of time to communicate the true value of your offer.

Barry went into this launch with a list of fewer than 1,000 people. He used his first piece of Prelaunch Content, a video, to quickly build rapport with his subscribers and demonstrate that he really understood their pain. In fact, he more than understood their pain; he had actually lived it.

He knew his target audience was really good at getting free (or very low-paying) gigs like library events, festivals, birthday parties, and the like, but they didn't know how to properly market to clients who had money! And they weren't even aware that the marketing they were using to land the low-paying shows was actually driving away potential high-paying gigs.

The real pain point that Barry addressed in his Prelaunch (i.e., his Sideways Sales Letter) was that the average entertainer is terrified of being forced to get a real job. It's a nightmare for someone who is a talented magician, ventriloquist, comedian, or juggler to think they might end up waiting tables or driving a truck—and possibly even worse, having to acknowledge that their parents or teachers or friends were right: they couldn't make a living as an entertainer!

So Barry's first piece of Prelaunch Content showed his prospects that he really understood them, because he had the same hopes, dreams, and fears as they did. And then the video went on to paint the opportunity for them to build a serious business (and income) with their skills. The basic theme of the video was this:

"I'm a lot like you. I found a passion for juggling when I was a kid, but was told I couldn't do it for a living. My high school guidance counselor, Mr. Pavliga, said that if I continued to pursue a career as a juggler, by the time I was 22 I would be broke and probably homeless. Right then, I swore to myself that I would prove him wrong.

"A few years later, I had just turned 23 when I performed on my first *Tonight Show*. I was standing behind the curtain and thinking, 'I hope Mr. Pavliga is watching.' It was all I could think about while I heard Johnny Carson introducing my partner and me. I was told I'd never make it as a professional juggler, but I didn't listen, and now I've been on over 100 television shows . . . and you can do that too! And in this free training, I'm going to show you how."

Of course, there was a lot more to the video, but that gives you the overall tone. Basically, Barry was establishing his credibility, he was creating a connection with his prospects, and he was delivering a very inspirational message. He was also delivering real value, because he was showing his viewers that it really was possible to get great, high-paying gigs. It showed that selling yourself as a highly paid entertainer was a learnable skill. Finally, the video showed entertainers that they had the opportunity to take the same skills they already had and get paid a lot more money for them. Nowhere in the video was there any hint of a sales message or an offer. You can see Barry's first Prelaunch video at this link: http://thelaunchbook.com/barry.

One really important part of the Sideways Sales Letter is what I call the Launch Conversation, because when you post your Prelaunch Content, you will generally do it on a blog or website where there's a place to leave comments below the video. (As I mentioned above, your Prelaunch Content can take many forms, but as I type this, it's most often delivered via video or live video broadcasts.) At the end of your videos you ask your viewers to respond in some way, such as by submitting questions or making comments. Barry did exactly that, then took part in the discussion that developed in the comments. He answered questions and engaged with his prospects. When you do that, you begin to change your launch from a monologue into a conversation, and conversations are almost always a lot more interesting to your prospects than monologues.

Those comments also give you some incredible insight into what your prospects are thinking and feeling. Their questions will help you identify the biggest objections, which gives you a chance to answer those objections, both in your comments and in your subsequent pieces of Prelaunch Content.

In Barry's second Prelaunch video, he revisited the potential pain of failing at the business, then really focused on teaching. The overall basic message was this:

"What if this all falls apart and your parents were right? What if you can't make it as an entertainer? If you want to succeed in this business, you need to treat it like a business. You've spent hundreds of hours working on your craft, but that's only part of the equation. It's not enough to be able to put on a great show. You also need to work on mastering the business. You need to master how to market and promote yourself.

"I've figured out how to do both—put on a great show and build a great business. Here's what I did to build my hugely successful career as a juggler. Here's what works and what doesn't work. And if you're making these common mistakes, here's how you fix them." And at that point Barry started teaching his audience the fundamental principles and methods of marketing themselves as entertainers.

Lots of times people worry about giving away too much of the "good stuff" during their Prelaunch. They worry that if they reveal too much, their prospects won't need to buy their products. However, in my experience this is rarely a problem. The mistake I see far more often is not giving away enough high-quality content. In this case, Barry's launch was for a super-premium offer; no one else in the market was charging anywhere near $2,000. If you're going to sell at the premium end, the best way to attract high-end clients is to deliver massive value up front. And that's exactly what Barry did.

Remember, even though Barry was a very accomplished juggler, and even though he had traveled the world with his business and had even appeared on TV and at the White House, he was still selling primarily to people who had never heard of him. He had no official credentials when it came to teaching people about business. He had no letters after his name. He had no degrees or certifications. He was going to be relying on his own experience (which, of course, makes for the best teachers), but the fact remained he was a complete stranger to most of his prospects.

Still, by sharing great content in his Prelaunch videos, he established the authority he needed. He showed that he had the experience to teach his prospects how to get high-paying clients and build their business.

And just like with his first video, there was no hint of a sale in his second piece of Prelaunch Content. Just solid, great information. Barry was building his authority, and he was building great reciprocity with his audience. (I just jumped ahead a little bit. In the next chapter I'll show you the magic of the mental triggers, which build enormous influence with your audience. Authority and reciprocity are two of the critical and super-powerful mental triggers I'll cover in that chapter.)

Before I leave the question of possibly giving away too much of the good stuff in your Prelaunch, let me say this: If you're worried that lots of people won't buy after they watch your Prelaunch, then you're absolutely right. Most of your prospects won't buy. In fact, in almost all launches the vast majority of your prospects won't buy. That's just the way the math works. That's how direct marketing works. However, the ones who do buy make all the difference—after all, how many $2,000 sales did Barry need to make a serious impact on his life? The answer is: not that many.

In his third Prelaunch video, Barry reviewed his launch story and stepped up the teaching even more. He actually reviewed the websites of various entertainers, discussed the mistakes they were making, and showed how those mistakes could be easily fixed.

And then Barry started to make a pivot to the sale. He talked about how he was going to personally guide 15 people through his Showbiz Blueprint, the exact promotional system that helped him land the highest-paying gigs in the industry (and also got him invitations to perform on the *Tonight Show* and at the White House). This was the first mention of an upcoming product, the first hint that there was a sale coming.

Making the pivot to the sale in the final piece of Prelaunch Content is critical, and leaving out that pivot is a mistake a lot of people make. Often people get so caught up in delivering great content that they don't want to talk about the sale in that final Prelaunch video.

When I interviewed Barry for the case study about his launch, I asked him about this, and sure enough, he told me he didn't want to put that pivot in there. He was loving the teaching, and his prospects were loving Barry for all of the great content that he was giving them. He didn't want to mess with all those good vibes by talking about his upcoming product. Still, "I decided to just follow PLF," Barry said, "and you told me to put that in there, so I did and the formula worked."

The three videos were delivered over a period of six days. And when Barry opened up registration, he sold out all 15 spots almost immediately for a total of $29,955 in sales. His costs were almost nonexistent—basically just the fees to process the credit card orders. What's more, between the buzz that the launch built up and the results that his clients got, Barry had enough momentum to fill another entire class after he finished the first one. That meant his total sales were $59,910, and he did that with an email list of fewer than 1,000 people.

That means his revenue was more than $59 for every person on his email list!

But it didn't end there. Barry has rerun the very same launch with the very same videos four more times. Each time he has put between 15 and 18 people into his class. After a few launches, Barry stopped offering individual coaching calls for the people who signed up. That meant he took another big step up in terms of leveraging his time. He reduced his price to $997 when he did this, but it meant that each additional sale took absolutely no extra time to fulfill. He was now making sales for no extra work. He had left the "trading hours for dollars" world and jumped aboard the leverage train.

If you do the math, he has now sold out six classes with 15 to 18 people per class. The majority of those people paid $2,000, and the rest paid $997 for the version without any personal coaching calls. That means Barry has done more than $100,000 in sales with very minimal costs. He has done all this while selling a product that provides enormous value to his clients . . . and he hasn't had to travel to any shows to do it.

That's the power of a PLF-style launch, and that's the power of the Sideways Sales Letter. In Chapter 7 I'll give you the formula for what you should put in each piece of Prelaunch Content. The key takeaway for now is that the Sideways Sales Letter gives you the time and space to connect with your future customers and deliver real value. It lets you cut through the marketing fog and set yourself apart from any competition. It creates a deadly effective sales machine without requiring you to be a great salesperson, and you won't feel like you need to take a shower after you make the sale. ☺

(You can see the full case study with Barry Friedman here: http://thelaunchbook.com/barry.)

CHAPTER 5

Tools of Mass Influence: The Mental Triggers

When I first released my Product Launch Formula training back in 2005, two things happened.

First, people started to use the formula and get amazing results—to the extent that people in the business were completely stunned. The results were 2 times, 5 times, 10 times, even 50 times what they were used to seeing.

Second, many "experts" in the market almost immediately started to predict that all that success would immediately start to die off once the tactics became widespread. They said that PLF was a fad and that people would soon stop responding to the launches. Once everyone had seen one of these launches, the bloom would be off the rose, and the results would quickly fade.

Of course, that didn't happen; the results my students are getting today are even better than back when I first started teaching the Product Launch Formula. This was true when I wrote the first edition of this book in 2014, and it was still true as I worked on this second edition in 2021. In fact, we just saw two of the biggest-ever launches happen simultaneously, in one of the most competitive, launch-crazy markets there are. The verdict is still the same: PLF-style launches haven't gone away. They've just gotten better as we've refined the model.

Here's what those self-styled experts missed back in 2005, and here's what some of them continue to miss to this day: A big part of the reason the model keeps working is that we've continued to evolve the tactics. (For instance, when I started doing these launches, online video didn't exist. Online live broadcasts didn't exist. Even social media didn't exist. Those things are all tactics that we now use in our launches.) An even bigger reason is that the success of this product launch model is due to the integral STRATEGIES that we use, and those strategies are timeless. You see, PLF is solidly rooted in the very core of our psyche. That might seem like a big statement in a book about marketing and entrepreneurship, but that's what we've got in store for you in this chapter.

I've already teased you with a little introduction to the mental triggers—those things that directly influence how we act and make decisions. They're incredibly powerful, and they act at a subconscious level. These mental triggers have roots that go back thousands of years, and they are present in all of us to varying degrees. And unless there is a fundamental change in the way our brains work (highly unlikely!), these triggers will continue to exert massive influence over our actions.

Part of the power of the Product Launch Formula is that it gives you a canvas on which to activate these mental triggers as you move through your launch. The mental triggers (along with your sequences and your launch story) form the very cornerstone of your successful product launch. Hit these triggers over and over in your Prelaunch Sequence and your Launch Sequence, and you can create a nearly hypnotic spell over your prospects (and even your entire market).

WITH GREAT POWER COMES GREAT RESPONSIBILITY

Before I give you the details of these mental triggers, I have to warn you: this is powerful stuff, and unfortunately it can be used for evil as well as good. Frankly, I know this knowledge will fall into the hands of some people who will use it unethically. But I also know, from years of working with my PLF Owners, that the vast majority of them are really cool people who have applied this knowledge ethically to create tremendous value in the world.

My sincerest wish is that you do exactly that—create something amazing and use this knowledge to share your gifts with the world.

Okay, let's get started. Here are nine of my favorite mental triggers:

1. Authority

People tend to follow others in positions of authority. Think about doctors in their white coats. Most of us become deferential as soon as we see that white coat walk into the examination room. We listen to what the doctor has to say and take any advice seriously. We probably feel at least a little intimidated, reluctant to disagree with anything the person in that white coat says.

This isn't unusual. We often look for others to help guide our decisions. Like so many other mental triggers, the authority trigger helps us shortcut the decision-making process. As we move through our everyday lives, we have thousands and thousands of tiny decisions to make. Every action we take requires some level of thought and choice. Following people with authority is a way in which our brain has evolved to make those decisions more efficiently.

If you want to be more influential in your business and marketing, it pays to be seen as an authority. The good news is that it can be shockingly easy to create authority. When I was a teenager in high school, I learned a very important lesson about authority. Three of my friends and I were driving home after a school football game—just like several hundred other people—and got stuck in a traffic jam in the parking lot. There were so many cars trying to get out the exit that no one was moving at all. One of my friends, who understood a lot more about authority than I did, found a flashlight rolling around on the floor of the car and immediately knew what to do. He jumped out of the car, turned on the flashlight, and started directing traffic. Actually, he didn't really direct traffic; he mostly just walked in front of our car and waved us forward through the congestion. Seeing the flashlight's beam, other drivers made way for our personal "traffic director," and we drove right out of the parking lot. The only authority he had to direct traffic came from the flashlight. But people saw that flashlight, and they assumed he was in charge. And I learned a big lesson that night: It just doesn't take very much to create authority.

The Product Launch Formula is a perfect tool for establishing authority. As we move through the Prelaunch and share high-quality content with our prospects, we create authority almost automatically. When Barry Friedman mentioned being on *The Tonight Show* and performing at the White House, that gave him instant authority. And since he talked about those accomplishments within the context of wanting to help his clients, it didn't come off as empty bragging but instead helped him bond with his prospects.

2. Reciprocity

Reciprocity is the idea that if someone gives something to us, we will feel some obligation to give them something in return. This is a very important mental trigger—and again, something that goes back thousands of years. In fact, reciprocity is the very basis from which humans were able to create commerce and trade. For trade to occur, there has to be some amount of trust that when we give a product or service to someone, they will complete the trade by holding up their end of whatever agreement we have made.

Reciprocity is a very powerful trigger. For example, in my family we celebrate Christmas, and a very strong part of the Christmas tradition is the idea of giving gifts. Surely one of the worst feelings in the world is when a friend or neighbor shows up at your house with a gift for you and you don't have one for them. Whether you celebrate Christmas or not, I'm sure you can relate to this feeling.

When someone gives you a gift and you don't have a way to recip-rocate, that triggers something deep inside you. You want to make it right, and you look for a way to give something back.

During a PLF-style launch, you spend the entire Prelaunch giving to people. That's what the whole Prelaunch is about—giving out great, free content. When you give out that content, you're creating a large reciprocity imbalance. The greater the value of your Prelaunch Content, the greater that imbalance. In the end, when you ask for something back, your prospect will have a greater tendency to want to reciprocate. And at the end of the launch, that reciprocation often equates to a sale.

During a Prelaunch there will be several cycles of giving and receiving before you even get to asking for the order. Make no mistake—reciprocity is an extremely powerful mental trigger, and you'll be activating this trigger throughout your entire launch.

3. Trust

Building trust is the ultimate shortcut to becoming influential in someone's life. I'm sure you can think of many times when a trusted friend or parent or teacher told you something that you believed without question because of your relationship with that person—something that, if a stranger had told you the same thing, you absolutely wouldn't have believed. That's the power of trust.

Obviously, if you want to influence someone, it's much easier if they trust you. If you want to get someone to do something, it's much easier if they trust you. If you want to convince someone to buy something from you, it's much easier if they trust you.

Of course, in business it can be difficult to earn someone's trust. Especially in the current marketing environment, where everyone is inundated with marketing messages all day long. Your prospect is getting thousands and thousands of messages. Cutting through that marketing fog is hard enough. Trying to actually cre-ate trust in that environment is even harder.

One of the easiest ways to create trust is through time. Maybe you once had a neighbor who seemed a bit different or even strange. You didn't consider him to be a friend and probably didn't even know him all that well. But after you lived next door for a period of time, and after he proved to be reliable and honest, you developed a sense of trust in him. Time makes it much easier to trust people.

That's one of the luxuries that the Product Launch Formula and the Sideways Sales Letter give you: time. Compared with a normal "drive-by" advertisement or sales pitch, these tools give you time for repeated interaction with your prospects. They make building a trust relationship with your prospect much easier than with the old way of marketing.

4. Anticipation

Another super-powerful mental trigger is anticipation, and this is a critical part of the Product Launch Formula. In fact, when I started teaching PLF, many people referred to it as "anticipation marketing."

Anticipation is one of the triggers that allow you to cut through the marketing fog. It lets you grab your market's attention and not let go. Think back to when you were a child and you looked forward to some special day. Maybe it was your birthday. Maybe it was Christmas morning. Maybe it was your last day of school before summer vacation. Time seemed to slow down as the big, anticipated day approached. It was all you could think about. You couldn't wait for that day.

Well, here's a news flash: all of us are really just big kids. We haven't gotten over anticipating those special days. And if you do it right, your launch can be almost like mixing together your prospect's birthday and summer vacation all in one bundle.

Anticipation is closely related to scarcity, which is another super-powerful trigger I'll get to in just a minute, but basically it's the idea that people will want something more if there's less of it available. Anticipation is also closely tied to the "event" trigger, where you're circling a date on the calendar and focusing all your attention on it. If you use anticipation right, people will put the date of your launch on their calendar and look forward to it. It's like you're putting your prospects into your story line. They can't wait for the next installment, they can't wait to see what's going to happen, they can't wait to get your product.

As with all the mental triggers, when you mix anticipation with the other mental triggers, the power is magnified and the impact is often breathtaking.

5. Likability

Likability is a mental trigger that you have certainly experienced in your life. The simple fact is that we enjoy doing business with people we know, like, and trust. We are more influenced by people we like than those we don't like.

So how do you become more likable? At the risk of stating the obvious, you become more likable by doing likable things. When you're seen being gracious, kind, generous, and honest . . . well, people will like you more. And the more likable you are, the more influence you will have.

People generally like to do business with other people more than with a large, faceless corporation. If you look around, you'll see even the biggest corporations are starting to realize this, and they're doing their best to humanize their message. In an age of ever-increasing digital communication, we're all looking for increased connection and authenticity.

If you look at what I've already shared with you about the power of the Prelaunch Sequence, you'll see that a well-constructed sequence will inherently make you more likable. You're giving people great free content, you're interacting with them, you're responding to their questions and comments. All of these actions make you more likable. You're building a strong connection with your market and your clients, and that makes you more influential.

6. Events and Ritual

When you turn your marketing into an event (which is what running a well-executed PLF-style launch is all about), then your marketing becomes magnetic. People love events, and they get pulled in by them. It makes them feel as though they are part of something bigger than themselves. This is one of the reasons that sports fans get so caught up in the fate of a team. In reality, the people on "their" team are usually a bunch of complete strangers. But watching them compete becomes an important event in fans' lives.

A big part of this trigger is the idea of ritual. When people go through an event together, that's what it becomes. Rituals pull people together and create some of the most powerful experiences we as human beings can have. In fact, ritual is a cornerstone of nearly all religion. In our modern world, we can sometimes feel starved for ritual (which, again, explains why sporting events are so important to so many), and that's why this type of thing can be a peak experience for us.

Now, this isn't a manual on how to start a religion or build a sports franchise, but this is powerful stuff that you can tap into quickly and easily. Turn your marketing into an event, and you will transform your results.

7. Community

Community is a very powerful mental trigger. We act in accordance with how we think the people in our community are supposed to act. Where I grew up, in the American Midwest, almost everyone worked hard to have a green lawn in front of their home. The amount of time, effort, and money it took to create and maintain a lush, green lawn was considerable. I think it's safe to assume that not everyone who was working so hard on those lawns did so because they loved growing grass. But the social norm of the community was that the residents had well-cared-for lawns in front of their homes, so they tended them very carefully.

If you reflect on your own life, I bet you can think of many communities you're part of. These might be work communities, social communities, communities of friends, even online communities. And all of them have norms that govern how members are expected to act (even if they are not explicitly stated). These norms can be wildly different from community to community, but they are very powerful within each.

Here's something exciting you might not know. While communities may seem large and established and difficult to get going, that's not always true. You can actually build your own online community right in the midst of your launch. Once you get people interacting with you, with your marketing, and with one another, you're on your way to forming a community—which means, of course, that you can create your own community norms. Those norms could include actions like helping spread the word about your Prelaunch Content, making comments on your launch blog, or "liking" your posts in social media. Or even buying your product.

8. Scarcity

Scarcity is one of the most powerful mental triggers in existence, period. It's simple—when there is less of something, we want it more. In reality, it's the *perception* of scarcity that motivates us. If you think about it, the power of scarcity shows up in our lives over and over, in all kinds of ways. Why do people value diamonds more than other pretty rocks? Because they're harder to find. They're more difficult to cut. There are fewer of them. And they're very expensive.

It's the same with gold, or Rolexes, or Ferraris.

One of the things that scarcity does is force people to make a decision. The vast majority of people will put off a decision if you give them a choice, especially when it comes to spending money. One of the key objectives you have in your marketing is to push people to make a decision. That's what scarcity does. If something is truly scarce, then a person needs to act quickly before that resource goes away.

To create a well-executed launch, you absolutely need to build scarcity into it. There has to be some negative consequence if people don't take action and buy before the end of the launch (for instance, the price could go up after the launch). If you make sure there's some scarcity built into your launch, it will take your results to a completely different level.

In fact, we often see as many sales in the last 24 hours of a launch as we do during the rest of the launch combined. If you structure your launch correctly, the last-second rush is every bit as predictable as the rush to buy flowers on Valentine's Day. It's almost like a spectator sport. If you have programmed scarcity into your launch, plan on making a big bowl of popcorn and sitting back and watching all the orders pour in on the last evening of your launch.

Read those last three paragraphs again—because the power of scarcity will transform your results. If you implement nothing else in this book but that one tactic and you absolutely INSIST on using that tactic in EVERY launch you do, it will literally pay you back 10,000 times what you invested in this book.

9. Social Proof

Social proof is another super-powerful trigger. While it can be very hard to create in an old-style marketing campaign, social proof is extremely easy to build into your PLF-style product launch.

Social proof is the idea that if we see other people taking action, then we will be inclined to take that action as well. Typically we take cues from the people around us when we're unsure of how to act. We are social creatures, and it's hard to overemphasize just how completely we are influenced by what we see other people around us doing.

For example, consider this scenario: It's 7 p.m. and you drive into a strange town. You're hungry and you're looking for a restaurant. Let's just say the battery in your smart phone is dead and you don't have any way to check restaurant reviews, so you're on your own when it comes to picking a restaurant. You see two restaurants. The one on the right side of the road has no cars in the parking lot, while the one on the left has six cars. Which restaurant are you going to pick? Most people would go to the one with the cars in the parking lot, assuming that all those people must know something, right? That's social proof in action.

And think back to your smart phone. If your battery hadn't been dead and you could check out restaurant reviews, well, you would simply be using another form of social proof. You would be basing your actions on what other people say or do.

Here's one more example. Let's say you want to download a piece of software or an app. You go to an app store or download site and do a search, and 12 different software packages come up in your search. One of them has been downloaded 3.5 million times, one has been downloaded 17,000 times, and the rest have been downloaded just a few hundred times or less. Which one are you going to try first? Most people will start with the one that's been downloaded 3.5 million times. All those other people must know something, right? Again, that's social proof in action.

Here's how social proof applies to your launch: Due to the interactive nature of your launch, you can create all kinds of social proof. When someone new to your site sees other folks making comments on your Prelaunch Content—saying how excited they are about your launch and how they can't wait to buy your product—that is social proof in action, and it's incredibly powerful.

LAYERING AND SEQUENCING: TAKING MENTAL TRIGGERS TO THE NEXT LEVEL

So far this chapter has taken you on a brief tour through the world of mental triggers—the things that, on a very fundamental level, shape our decisions and actions every day. And, more to the point of this book, they shape your prospects' decisions and actions every day.

I've given you just a quick introduction here. In fact, due to space considerations, I've covered only about half of the triggers that I've identified and that I use in my PLF launches. If you want to go deeper on the subject, I've got a video for you at this link: http://thelaunchbook.com/triggers.

One of the important things to remember about these triggers is that they are not isolated. Many of them are closely related, and they work synergistically. When used together, the impact is compounded.

For instance, trust and authority are closely linked. It's easier to establish authority when you have trust, and trust is something that naturally flows from having a position of authority. In fact, there is even a well-worn phrase that combines these two— "trusted authority."

Another example is scarcity and social proof. If something is scarce, it's generally because the demand exceeds supply. And if there's large demand, well, that's social proof right there. So it's almost like social proof and scarcity are two sides of the same coin.

Another key point about mental triggers is that they are more powerful when you sequence them and layer them, one on top of another. And that's where the Product Launch Formula is unparalleled in its power. The way we do launches gives you the time and space to use multiple triggers and to have them build on top of one another.

I'll cover this more when we get to the Prelaunch Sequence and the Launch Sequence, including what triggers you should activate at what point in your sequences, but here's a quick example. Generally at the beginning of your Prelaunch you start with a powerful piece of content that sets up the overall promise and opportunity of the launch. When you share strong, compelling content at the start of your Prelaunch, you instantly develop authority. That authority comes naturally when you publish that content; it's nearly automatic. You will also develop reciprocity when you do this, because you're giving away your great content freely. You have created a need in the receiver to give back to you, which often translates into a sale. You will also have anticipation going for you, as you talk about everything else that's coming up in your Prelaunch.

As you move further through the Prelaunch, you develop social proof as people make public comments about your Prelaunch Content. These comments can be on your blog or in social media—either way, you start to develop strong social proof. And hopefully your interaction throughout the Prelaunch starts to build likability with your prospects (and maybe even a little trust).

Then, as the Prelaunch nears its end and you get close to your Open Cart date, you hit the event and ritual triggers as people start to anticipate your product's arrival. This is a natural time to hit the scarcity trigger, when you start talking about your offer and mention its inherently limited nature.

Bottom line, a PLF-style launch gives you the opportunity to layer the mental triggers so you create an exponentially more powerful effect. That truly is the secret magic here, because not everyone responds to the various triggers in the same way. For example, for some people social proof may be a strong influence, while for others trust and authority may be more important. But when you lay one trigger on top of another throughout your sequences, you build a remarkably irresistible promotion. That's the power of Product Launch Formula, and that's why it's been a complete game changer.

Okay, we've covered a lot of ground. We just wrapped up the mental triggers, and I've already given you a solid grounding in the fundamental parts to the PLF puzzle. Now it's time to press the gas pedal to the floor and get to the hardcore, nitty-gritty details of putting together one of these launches. We're going to start with the part of the launch that's almost completely under the radar—the one component, which no one notices, that sets you up for massive success. It's time for the Pre-Prelaunch.

CHAPTER 6

The Shot across the Bow: Your Pre-Prelaunch

As you go through this book, it will become obvious that there's a significant amount of work and planning that goes into one of these launches. I know, I know . . . I wish it weren't so. But if you want a great launch (and to get everything that it affords), there is always work involved. I figure that if you're still with me, you're not afraid of a little work.

The place where you usually start is with your Pre-Prelaunch Sequence. This is the magic time where your prospects first get an inkling that something cool is coming.

Over the years I've had lots of people try to reverse-engineer the Product Launch Formula process. In other words, they watch a couple of launches and try to figure out how the entire thing is put together. The only problem with reverse-engineering something is that there are often parts hidden "under the hood." Leave out those key ingredients and it screws up the whole thing, making a real mess. And one of the areas that are almost always overlooked is the "Pre-Pre"—because it's the most clandestine. The cool thing is that it's also one of the simplest and easiest parts of the formula.

The whole idea of the Pre-Prelaunch is to begin to activate your tribe—or start building a tribe if you don't have one yet. But you're also doing other important foundational work. You're testing the market's level of interest in your product idea. You're trying to surface potential objections so you can answer them during your Prelaunch. Finally, you're gathering information to help finalize your product offer. As if that weren't enough, you're doing all of this while setting the stage for your Prelaunch Sequence.

I like to call the Pre-Prelaunch the "shot across the bow," which is a naval term for a warning shot fired toward another ship. The idea is to get the other ship's attention without resorting to an overt attack. Your Pre-Prelaunch Sequence is all about grabbing your market's attention without actually trying to sell them anything at all.

Sounds like a big job, right? Well, there's much that will be accomplished in this phase of your launch, which is pretty amazing when you look at how simple and easy the Pre-Prelaunch really is to pull off.

In general, my tool of choice for the Pre-Pre has historically been a simple email or two, although these days social media has also become a big part of the Pre-Pre for many launches. There are times when I've used video, and sometimes I've thrown a survey into the mix.

THE 10 PRE-PRELAUNCH QUESTIONS

When I'm about to head into a launch and I'm thinking about my Pre-Prelaunch, these are the top 10 questions that are running through my mind:

1. **"How can I let people know something is coming without having it feel like I'm trying to sell them something?"**

As soon as people think you're trying to sell something, their defenses go up. When your prospects feel as if there's a sales pitch coming, they instantly believe you less and distrust you more. So the idea here is to begin the conversation about your product WITHOUT overtly selling it.

2. "How can I tease their curiosity?"

Curiosity, which is closely related to anticipation, is another powerful mental trigger. It's a hook that grabs people and doesn't let go. If you can start to engage your prospects' curiosity early on, you'll keep them interested for the entire launch.

3. "How can I get their help in creating this product? How can I make this collaborative?"

This is really important, and it's something most people miss. People will support the things they help create. So if you can get people engaged and make them feel that they're part of the process—possibly even that they're almost co-creators—then you've moved them from prospects to cheerleaders.

4. "How can I figure out what their objections are to this product?"

You can't sell to people until you overcome their objections to the sale. You can't overcome those objections until you discover what they are. You might THINK you know what they are, but you don't really KNOW until you start engaging with your prospects. Unfortunately, most people launch their products without having any real idea of the potential objections. With the Pre-Pre you're going to find out what they are early on—when you still have time to do something about answering and overcoming them.

5. "How can I start to engage my prospects in a conversation about my offer? How can I be engaging and avoid the 'corporate speak' that will kill my launch before it starts?"

This is closely related to the first question, which is about letting your prospects know something is coming without being "salesy." The addition here is the "engagement" piece—starting the conversation and being conversational. In other words, this is where you set the stage for the entire Launch Conversation, where you create a marketing dialogue instead of a monologue.

6. "How can I make this fun and humorous and even exciting?"

Make no mistake. Even though I'm teaching you an incredibly powerful set of tools, your job of keeping people's attention in a crowded market will always be challenging. Think about every second you're engaging them as a ticking "attention bomb." You have only so many seconds to keep them engaged. I'm not trying to intimidate you or be overly dramatic, but the reality is that the people you're selling to have thousands of other things battling for their attention.

Think of humor or surprise as an instant attention reset. Every time you get your prospects to laugh or smile, it resets that ticking attention bomb, and you've gained some precious extra seconds.

7. "How can I stand out in a crowded market? How can I be different?"

This is related to question 6. Standing out is about getting your prospects engaged and keeping them engaged. I never want my marketing to be like other people's marketing. I want to be unique and memorable. There's an old principle that I always keep in mind: In reality, most people (and businesses) are not having much success. At best, they are getting average results. I'm not interested in average results, and you shouldn't be, either. So don't do what the average business is doing; watch what they're doing, and do the opposite.

It's not very hard to stand out in your market and with your prospects. Just do things a little bit differently from how your competitors do them.

8. "How can I figure out how my market wants to be sold to?"

This may sound like a weird question, because you may think that the folks in your market aren't walking around "wanting" to be sold to. You're right; they're not. But they are walking around with problems, and with hopes, dreams, desires, and fears that keep them up at night. They want solutions—and if you have a solution, they certainly want to buy it from you.

9. "How can I figure out my exact offer?"

No matter how much I would like to make Product Launch Formula seem like complete marketing magic, the truth is that you need to create a great offer. In fact, the term that I use for this in PLF is "a crushing offer." It's not really a very technical term, but you get my point.

If your launch is going to be a success, you need a crushing offer. And if you have a crushing offer, you're a long way down the road to having a successful launch. Your Pre-Prelaunch is a key to creating a crushing offer, because if you ask your prospects the right way, they will tell you how to do it.

10. "How can this naturally lead into my Prelaunch Sequence?"

Since your launch (and PLF) is all about sequences, all about creating a greased chute that leads right into your launch day, it's only natural to have your Pre-Prelaunch tie seamlessly into your Prelaunch Sequence.

MY FAVORITE PRE-PRELAUNCH STRATEGY

With those questions running through my head, I looked for an elegant strategy to find the right answers with just an email or two.

Fortunately, I came up with an old standby strategy that works 95 percent of the time, and it will almost certainly work for you. There are many variations on the theme, but even the most basic version is extremely effective.

So let's just jump into an example. This is a Pre-Prelaunch that I created all the way back in 2005 for a product I was launching about trading in the stock market. Now, before you go thinking this is ancient history and won't work anymore, I want to tell you that my students are still having great success using this exact sequence. One more thing: This example is about the stock market, but understand that the strategy has been successfully applied in all kinds of markets. In fact, my students have used it in markets that ranged from "how to learn to play the guitar" to "how to get more clients for your massage practice" to "how to take care of your pet dog."

"QUICK ANNOUNCEMENT AND A FAVOR . . ."

This is so simple and so elegant that the casual reader might miss just how powerful this is, but I'm going to trust that you won't make that mistake. I started this Pre-Pre with a simple email that I sent out to my list. (In recent years, I've done something very similar on Facebook and Instagram.) This is what was in the email:

EMAIL SUBJECT: Quick announcement and a favor...

EMAIL BODY:

Jeff Walker here. We'll be sending your Trading Update in just a little bit. But first I need to ask you a favor.

We're really close to wrapping up our long-awaited trading manual. We will be releasing it in early January. But before we do, I have to ask you a couple of questions. Can you help us out?

You can answer the questions here (and get a little more detail on the trading manual) at this link:

http://www.example.com/

Thanks and best regards,

Jeff

Of course, I gave them a real, live link to the survey . . . but that's it. The start of the Pre-Prelaunch came in a simple email that was only about 80 words long. Just that email alone accomplished quite a bit. But before we walk through it, let's take a look at the page my readers were sent to if they clicked on the link in the email. They landed on a simple web page that said:

Hi,

We're VERY close to finishing our long-awaited Trading Manual.

We have been working on this for more than four years, but we are finally going to wrap it up. We will be releasing it in early January.

This course will be entirely focused on "Support and Resistance." It will include two printed manuals, eight audio CDs, and one video tutorial DVD. It is going to be a complete brain dump of everything that we know about "SUPPORT and RESISTANCE."

We are going to cover all the ways that we use to generate our support and resistance zones, and we are going to show you exactly how we trade those zones.

HOWEVER, we need your help. Before we finalize everything and send it off to the printer, we need to make sure we have covered everything.

That is where you come in. Please take a few minutes to answer this super-short survey—there is really only one thing we want to ask you . . .

What are your two top questions about Support and Resistance that we absolutely NEED to answer in our trading course?

That was it—a super-short email that sent people to a super-short survey. Yes, "audio CDs" and "video tutorial DVD" might sound impossibly quaint, but the same email works today for online courses and membership sites. And years in the future, when "online courses" and "email" sound impossibly quaint, this same type of strategy will still work.

If we go back to the 10 Pre-Prelaunch questions up above, you can see I hit a bunch of them here.

1. "How can I let people know something is coming without having it feel like I'm trying to sell them something?"

Well, I definitely let people know something was coming, and I did it without any hint of an offer. I was simply asking for their help. I wanted their feedback on this project. That truly is what the email was all about, but it also accomplished a lot of other things.

2. "How can I tease their curiosity?"

I did this in a few ways—first just by telling them something was coming that they couldn't get yet. Then, in the email, I told them they could "get a little more detail" by clicking on the link. And then there was the key phrase "We're really close to wrapping up our long-awaited training manual," which I used in the email and repeated in the survey. Just by telling people that the manual was "long-awaited" set the expectation that people were already curious about and eagerly anticipating this product. And this is important, because "buzz," curiosity, and anticipation feed on each other. By introducing that perception early on, I was already setting the stage for the build toward a highly anticipated launch.

Was this product really long-awaited? I don't know. But I do know that I had been dropping hints about it for a long time, and I had built up a list of people who had asked me to create this product. I know that I had been working on the project for a long time, and I was ready to get it launched. That was enough for me to call it long-awaited.

3. "How can I get their help in creating this product? How can I make this collaborative?"

Well, this one is obvious. When my readers clicked through to the survey, I asked them what their top two questions were about the topic. I was including my prospects in the creation of my product by soliciting their feedback. These were the key sentences: "HOWEVER, we need your help. Before we finalize everything and send it off to the printer, we need to make sure we have covered everything."

Remember, people will support that which they help create. I was giving my readers a chance to help create the product.

There was another subtle bit of human psychology going on here. Remember in the last chapter when we covered the reciprocity mental trigger? This might seem counterintuitive, but I was actually engaging the reciprocity trigger here. Now, you might ask, "How can there be reciprocity at play here, since you're asking them for a favor?"

Well, remember that the people reading this were on my email list of subscribers—many of them for a very long time. Just by virtue of my publishing to them every day, they viewed me as an expert or even a "guru." Now, by asking for their opinion, I was giving them my attention—and the key word there is *giving*. By giving my attention, I was building up a little reciprocity in the minds of many of my readers.

Do you see how, with just a short email and a short survey, I was starting to build up a confluence of triggers that would come into play down the road?

4. "How can I figure out what their objections are to this product?"

This one is easy. I was just outright asking them to tell me their objections in the survey. No, I didn't use the word *objections*, because people don't think in those terms. But by indicating their "top two questions," they would tell me what their objections were.

When you do this, you'll always find two or three or maybe even four common themes that keep showing up in the responses. Those themes will contain your prospects' primary objections.

5. "How can I start to engage my prospects in a conversation about my offer? How can I be engaging and avoid the 'corporate speak' that will kill my launch before it starts?"

First of all, look at the email and the survey. No corporate speak there. Right from the start, the subject line was "Quick announcement and a favor . . ." When was the last time a big corporation asked for a favor in their email subject line? And as far as starting the conversation—that's what this entire mini-sequence was about. Asking for their feedback starts the conversation.

6. "How can I make this fun and humorous and even exciting?"

Okay, I'm not sure that I hit this one in this Pre-Prelaunch, other than by letting my readers in on something before it happened. I was letting them into my creative world. It's almost like whispering something to someone in a crowded room—everyone wants to know what you whispered. In this case, I was whispering to my readers before I announced it to the general public.

7. "How can I stand out in a crowded market? How can I be different?"

The key here is that by asking my readers for their feedback before the product was released, I let them become part of the process. And that's absolutely important, because people support what they help create. I gave them a small part to play in the creation of the product, and that's a step toward building an army of people who will support your launch and possibly even buy your product.

8. "How can I figure out how my market wants to be sold to?"

This is what the survey was all about. In addition to gathering the top objections, the survey gave me all kinds of additional data and information.

If you use a survey like this, it's often good to mix up multiple-choice questions with essay questions. You will get a higher response with multiple-choice questions, because it's easier to check a box than to type in an answer. However, essay questions will give you quite a bit more insight. And that insight will often tell you how to construct your Launch Sequence. Often I will literally cut and paste words and phrases directly from this type of survey and use them in my Prelaunch Content.

There is an old saying in the direct marketing world: "You want to enter the conversation that's already taking place in your prospect's mind." The responses you get to a survey give you a shortcut to entering that conversation. It's hard to overstate just how powerful this is.

9. "How can I figure out my exact offer?"

Again, the answer to this question was in the survey responses. Actually, this survey was just the beginning of the answer. If I'm launching an information or knowledge product, it's often possible to continue to tweak the answer all the way up into my launch, so I'll gather data throughout the Pre-Prelaunch and the Prelaunch to help me fine-tune the offer.

Even if you're selling physical products, it's possible to add information-based components to the offer. For example, in this launch we ended up adding some live question-and-answer webinars to the offer. Since these would be delivered after the launch, it took zero effort to add them at this stage. And that same type of bonus can be added to all kinds of launch offers.

10. "How can this naturally lead into my Prelaunch Sequence?"

A few days after I sent that first email, I wrote to my list again. I thanked everyone for the overwhelming response and told them how excited I was to have the project almost complete. That continued the conversation about this upcoming product and did so in a way that was not "salesy." I wasn't screaming, "Buy my stuff, buy my stuff!" at the top of my lungs. Instead, I was asking my list to join me as co-creators.

That Pre-Pre also showed them that I was concerned with making this the best possible product and very interested in what they wanted. I put them in the state of imagining the product as the best possible product for their needs.

$110,000 IN MY BATHROBE

The great thing about the Pre-Prelaunch is that it's a beautiful combination of simplicity and power. It takes some thought and a bit of advanced planning, but the actual execution of your Pre-Prelaunch can be incredibly simple. Take another look at the example I gave—it took one super-short email and a survey. Writing the email and putting together that survey took about an hour. (See my Resource Page for services you can use to create your surveys at http://thelaunchbook.com/resources.)

This is just one example. I've used lots of different techniques for my various Pre-Prelaunches, but this "Top Two Questions Survey" technique is a winner, and I suggest you use it for your first Pre-Prelaunch. It's a great way to let your market know something is coming and gather some quality intelligence about your market at the same time.

This survey gave me some fantastic feedback on what the market was looking for, what my prospects' biggest objections were, and even some of the exact language I would end up using throughout the launch as I built the momentum toward launch day.

That launch was my first time selling a physical product and my first time selling a full training course—and I didn't have a big, fancy publisher behind me. It was just me and my list of email subscribers and a simple little website.

"I made $110,000 in my bathrobe" might sound impossibly cheesy . . . but that's exactly what happened. In fact, I did this launch from my kitchen table, and yes, I was wearing my bathrobe when I pushed the Send button. Below is a photo my wife took just a few moments after we opened the shopping cart for the launch.

I was smiling in that photo, because it was AFTER we opened the cart. But I certainly had a tense few moments waiting for the clock to tick down to the opening. And I'll admit that my finger lingered over the button before I clicked—just like it does for every one of my launches. I wondered whether I had everything in place, and I wondered what that next click would bring.

It didn't take long to find out. After I hit the Send button, it took fewer than four minutes for the first order to come in. The

Opening the launch in my bathrobe at the kitchen table.

second order came in five seconds later, and we were off to the races. In the first hour we had more than $27,000 in orders, and when we closed down the launch a week later, we had more than $110,000 in sales.

We did it all without any affiliates, any distributors, any phone calls, any outside sales—just a simple website and an email list. Of course, there was a lot more involved in getting those sales than the Pre-Prelaunch. There was more going on than a simple 80-word email and a simple survey. And that's where we're going next—into the heart and soul of the Product Launch Formula. It's time to put together your Prelaunch Sequence.

CHAPTER 7

Sell Them What They Want: The Power of Prelaunch

Is it possible to improve your tennis game by watching training videos online? Can you replace (or supplement) tennis lessons with an online membership? And more to the point for Will Hamilton, will people pay for online tennis instruction?

That was Will Hamilton's premise when he started FuzzyYellowBalls.com with a friend. Will was just out of college, and he wasn't excited about the long-term prospects of being a tennis coach. So he set up shop in his parents' basement and started an online business. The initial plan was to publish videos on YouTube and make money through advertising. But it quickly became apparent that there was no future in that. In a niche market like tennis, there would never be enough video views to drive a serious advertising-based business.

The next strategy Will tried was creating a membership site with instructional videos. He and his buddy priced membership at $25 per month. But the site languished and sales were slow. After 10 months, they were getting close to writing off the whole idea as a failed experiment, closing up shop, and moving on. It seemed that the answer to the question of whether people would pay for online tennis instruction was no—at least not at the volume needed to support Will and his business partner.

That was when Will discovered my launch formula. Since it was desperate times, he leapt into action and put his first launch together in just a few weeks. As he describes it now, that first launch had some rough edges. Will threw his Prelaunch together quickly and used only the very basics of the formula.

Still, as you'll see in this chapter, even if you get only the core principles right, the results can be dramatic. That first launch did $35,000 in sales in a week's time, which was as much as the business had made since the partners opened the doors 10 months earlier. And since the product was delivered digitally, those sales were almost all profit.

All of a sudden, FuzzyYellowBalls.com was in business. The future was clear—and it definitely involved more product launches. For their second launch, Will buckled down and got serious about following the formula, and results nearly doubled to $65,000 in sales. The next launch did even better—it broke the six-figure mark, closing out at $105,000 in sales. Again, these were digital products, so the profit margin was very high.

With each launch, Will and his partner built their list and their positioning in the market, and their launch skills got better. The next launch was for their new Tennis Ninja product, and that one brought in $170,000 in sales. But it also did something else that was remarkable: It attracted the attention of the agent for tennis pros Bob and Mike Bryan. Twin brothers who are simply referred to as "the Bryan Brothers" in tennis circles, Bob and Mike are arguably the most successful pro men's doubles team in tennis history. And they were interested in working with Will on a product.

The result was *The Bryan Bros Doubles Playbook*, which Will produced and sold as a full-blown course with Bob and Mike. The launch blew away all Will's previous launches, doing a whopping $450,000 in sales. And a few months later, after the Bryan brothers won Wimbledon and then the Olympic gold medal, Will got a chance to have his photo taken with the pair posing with their medals. Here's the photo—Will is the guy in the middle wearing the medals.

Will Hamilton posing with the Bryan Brothers and their Olympic Gold Medals.

Of course, I definitely can't guarantee Product Launch Formula will get you a photo with a couple of Olympic gold medals. ☺ But Will's results show just how powerful a well-executed launch can be. One of the greatest strengths in his launches are his Prelaunch Sequences. That's what this chapter is all about. If you get your Prelaunch right, it makes everything else come together.

(You can see my case study with Will, along with an example of his Prelaunch video content, at http://thelaunchbook.com/will.)

BRINGING A GUN TO A KNIFE FIGHT

Okay, we've now laid the groundwork for my formula. By now you know about the power of story, conversation, and sequences in your launch. And you've gotten a solid introduction to the powerful influence of mental triggers. You've also learned about the Sideways Sales Letter. And along the way, I've introduced you to some regular people who have enjoyed tremendous success using these tools in all kinds of markets and with all kinds of products.

Now it's time to get down to the nitty-gritty: the Prelaunch Sequence. This is where it all starts to come together. This is where you leave behind Hope Marketing and start to actually engineer your results with a truly powerful launch. The thing to remember about your Prelaunch (and the entire Product Launch Formula) is that it's not a one-trick pony. It's the confluence of all these tools that create a conversion machine for your business. There's an old saying that goes something like this: "You don't want to bring a knife to a gunfight." I'm not a big fan of violent metaphors, but I like this one. It reminds me of that scene from the movie *Raiders of the Lost Ark*, where the hero, Indiana Jones, is suddenly confronted with a dangerous villain threatening him with a scary-looking sword. Indiana Jones watches the impressive display of swordsmanship, then pulls out a pistol and shoots the villain. Danger averted. Game over. It's a memorable scene.

Well, that's what the Product Launch Formula brings to your business. It changes the game and tilts the odds dramatically in your favor. And I'm not satisfied to bring just a pistol to that fight. I mean, if I'm going to have to fight, then I'd rather just go ahead and bring along a machine gun and rocket launcher as well!

Of course, this isn't about fighting, and your marketing isn't a war. It's about designing a great offer for a great product that's going to create great value for your clients. But you can't possibly deliver that value unless you can actually make the sale in the first place.

The bottom line is that this launch process is a coordinated, engineered formula that will transform your sales process. There isn't one specific thing that produces the outsize results we're getting. It's the overall confluence of the tools, tactics, and triggers. It started with your Pre-Prelaunch, and now we're going to really turn up the heat with your Prelaunch Sequence.

BUY MY STUFF, BUY MY STUFF, BUY MY STUFF!

One of the foundations of my launch formula is delivering value and building a relationship with your future customer before you ever ask for the sale. It sounds so simple, but it's crazy how few people actually do this in their business. Instead, people do the equivalent of standing on a street corner, shouting, "Buy my stuff, buy my stuff, BUY MY STUFF!"

The problem is that no matter what business or market you're in, there are tens, or hundreds, or thousands of other people out there shouting just as loudly as you are. They are all screaming at your very same prospect. It's hard to stand out with that strategy, and it continues to get more and more difficult. The deluge of media keeps getting bigger and louder every day, and there will always be people who can shout louder, or shout longer, or sell at a lower price. You don't want to be fighting that battle. That will wear you down, and in the end it's a losing battle for nearly everyone. Even worse, when you're launching a new product or a new business, then you're automatically going up against established businesses with lots of resources. You need to fight a different battle, a battle in which you've created a set of rules that work in your favor.

How do you do that? It's simple. Instead of *screaming* for attention, you *attract* attention by giving value before there is any hint of asking for the sale. My friend Joe Polish has a saying: "Life gives to the givers and takes from the takers." I think that's always been true, but it's never been more true in business than it is today. And the great news is that the Internet and digital marketing turn the economics of giving on its head. Giving is a lot easier and a whole lot cheaper than ever before, because you're going to be giving away content, and doing it digitally. That content could be written material or video or audio or any of a number of other media, but the bottom line is that it will cost you almost nothing to distribute that content.

Of course, randomly giving people stuff is not going to do you any good. If you're trying to sell coaching services to high-end corporate executives, then sending them a cookbook of vegan recipes is not going to generate much business for you. You need to structure your content into a sequence that naturally builds up to your sale. And that's the very essence of the Product Launch Formula.

YOUR PRELAUNCH SEQUENCE

Your Prelaunch Sequence will generally have three pieces of Prelaunch Content (which I abbreviate to PLC). Think of it as a three-act play with a beginning, middle, and end. Each piece of Prelaunch Content has a specific job. Each one needs to stand alone, but all three tie together into one big story arc. You want to avoid just throwing out three pieces of unrelated content, because you're just not going to get the results you want that way.

The framework for the overall story arc is that you start off teaching people about the opportunity for change or transformation. You follow that up with some solid teaching, and you show that transformation or change. Finally, you give the "ownership experience." This is where you start to pivot to talking about your product and the impact it will make on your prospective client.

Throughout this entire sequence you are layering in all the mental triggers we covered in Chapter 5. Since you're giving out great free content, you naturally will hit the **Reciprocity** trigger. And by showing your knowledge of the topic and your ability to give great content away for free, you hit the **Authority** trigger. As you move through the launch, you'll naturally start to build **Trust**, and as you gather comments and create a conversation about your Prelaunch Content, you'll start to build **Community**. Since you're taking your prospects through this entire sequence together, it becomes a shared experience that hits the **Events and Ritual** trigger. Then, as you get closer to your launch date, the **Anticipation** will start to build. In fact, you'll find that your Prelaunch Sequence will naturally trip trigger after trigger, because the process is designed to do that. When you do this right, you end up in a supremely influential position without having to resort to a bunch of sales tactics that feel like they belong on a used-car lot. Instead, you're building influence in the exact same way humans have always built influence. You're just doing it in a hyper-accelerated way.

It's important for you to understand that the magic is in the process. Success doesn't depend on your being a gifted copywriter or master salesperson. Of course, it doesn't hurt if you bring either of those talents to the table, but at the end of the day, the Product Launch Formula is something of an equalizer in the marketing world. It allows people who aren't ninja marketers to put together a super-effective sales process. At the end of your Prelaunch, if you do this correctly, you will have garnered a list of prospects who can't wait for the moment when they can finally buy your product.

A quick word about formats: You'll find that this is a very flexible process. Your PLC can be delivered via email or as blog posts or as PDF reports or podcasts. But most of my Product Launch Formula Owners have been using video or live broadcasts for the last few years. Video (whether it's live or recorded) has a number of advantages. Our society has clearly become one where most people spend more time watching video than they do reading. It's often easier to craft a compelling video than to sit down and write a meaty PDF report, and unless you're a truly gifted writer, it's a lot easier for your potential clients to get to know you and feel like they have a relationship with you via video. Finally, video content often has a higher perceived value than other types of content.

Without getting too technical, I need to mention that there are two primary types of video: screen-capture video and full-motion video. Screen capture is a video recording of a computer screen with a voice talking over it; with it you can record a PowerPoint-style presentation or a demonstration of a website or some software. Full-motion video is like the video you see on TV; it's shot with a camera. Neither of these types of video is better or worse than the other; each has its strengths and weaknesses. For instance, some people prefer screen-capture video because they don't feel comfortable appearing on camera. Others prefer full-motion because there's often less prep work involved—if you know your material and have a rough outline, you can just turn on the camera and start recording.

Since video has become the predominant format for Prelaunch Content, for the rest of this chapter I'm going to assume that you will be using video for yours. Please remember, however, that you don't need to use video. I've done plenty of great launches using nothing more sophisticated than email.

Okay, let's take a closer look at each step of your Prelaunch Sequence.

PLC #1: THE OPPORTUNITY (OR THE JOURNEY)

Your first piece of Prelaunch Content (PLC #1) is critical. It has to grab your prospects' attention and draw them in, so it has to be compelling. And it must answer the all-important question "Why?" Why should your prospect care? Why should they spend their precious time paying attention to you? Why should they listen to you? What can you do for them?

So how do you answer those questions? How do you get your prospects to sit up and listen? How do you get them to care?

Let me give you the short answer. At the heart of every product, every offer, there is some opportunity for transformation or change. If you're selling a training product that will help golfers take five strokes off their score, you're offering a transformation. If you're selling a product that will help people meet the love of their life, you're offering a transformation. If you're selling a machine that helps people open the mail coming into their office 380 percent more efficiently, you're offering transformation.

Some people have a hard time seeing transformation in their offer. That's fine—you can use the word *change* if you want, or even *impact*. The bottom line is you need to focus on the end benefit that your product will create for your prospect. At the most basic level, you are either taking away some pain from your client, or you're delivering some pleasure.

And that's not true just for your launches—it's true in any situation where you're selling anything. There's an old adage among direct marketing copywriters that if you have a hardware store and you're selling drills, you're not really selling drills; you're selling "holes in wood." People want to buy an end result. It doesn't matter what you're selling. People aren't so interested in the actual tool. The tool is just a means to get that result, and that's what you want to sell them.

Here's another way to think about it. If you want to travel to your favorite beach resort, you're interested in getting there quickly, efficiently, safely, comfortably—and for a lot of people, as inexpensively as possible. You probably don't really care exactly what means of transportation you're going to use. Whatever gets you there while fulfilling those requirements is fine. If all those factors were equal, it wouldn't matter if you flew on a plane or rode on a train or drove a car. You're buying the destination, not the means of transportation.

Now, if you look at why people don't buy from you, the first and most common reason is that they're not interested in what you're selling. For instance, you might have the greatest wheelchair in the world—the most comfortable, efficient, reliable, flexible design in existence. It might even be priced lower than any other wheelchairs in its class. However, if you're trying to sell that wheelchair to someone who doesn't need a wheelchair, then you're not going to make the sale.

The second reason people don't buy is that they don't have the money. They just simply do not have it, and they have no means to get it. That reason is a deal-breaker as well.

The third reason people don't buy is that they don't believe your claims about how great your product is. They either flat out don't think you're telling the truth or they think you're mistaken. In other words, they don't trust either your ethics or your competence.

A fourth reason is that although they believe you're right about the product and that it actually does work, they don't believe it will work for them. Let's say, for example, you're selling some way for people to quit smoking, and your prospect completely believes you and believes your method has worked for lots of other people. However, in the back of their mind they're thinking, "I've tried 15 other ways to quit smoking, and none of them worked for me."

Product Launch Formula isn't going to help you with either of the first two reasons why people don't buy (they don't want what you've got or they don't have the money), but if you do this right, then it will handle the third and fourth reasons. They're going to believe you and that your offer has value. And the first piece of Prelaunch Content is the critical first step.

Here's a general recipe that works well for PLC #1:

— **Show the opportunity.** Show/tell your prospect how their life is going to change with your product.

— **Position your authority.** Show/tell why they should listen to you.

— **Teach.** It's important not to just go on and on about the opportunity; you have to deliver value.

— **Raise objections and either answer them or promise to answer them in upcoming videos.** No matter what your offer is, there will be objections. You need to face them head on.

— **Foreshadow PLC #2.** Let them know there's another video coming, and spark their desire by revealing some of the really cool stuff they're going to learn in PLC #2.

— **Call to action.** Ask for a comment on your Prelaunch pages or in social media.

PLC #2: THE TRANSFORMATION

If PLC #1 is all about the "why," your second piece of Prelaunch Content is all about the "what"—what is this transformation or opportunity and how is it going to change or transform your prospects' lives? PLC #2 is more about teaching; you want to impart some type of tip or trick that is truly valuable.

What can you teach in 5 to 10 minutes that will make an impact on your prospect? How can you start to create that transformation in their life right now, or at least create a shift so they can start to believe that transformation is possible? It doesn't have to be a huge change or huge impact—just get them moving.

For instance, in one of my launches for the PLF Coaching Program, my PLC #2 was all about the Seed Launch; I actually taught my prospects how to do it. (You'll learn about the Seed Launch in Chapter 9—it's a way to do a super-quick launch even when you're starting without a list or a product.) Of course, since that Prelaunch video was only about 18 minutes long, I couldn't teach it as deeply as I do in the actual Product Launch Formula Coaching Program, but I went as deep as I could in that amount of time. And I've had people successfully do a Seed Launch based on that video alone.

Of course, most of my viewers didn't immediately go out and do a Seed Launch after they saw that video, but I wanted to give them enough training so that they could at least see themselves doing one. That's key: If PLC #2 can get your prospects to see themselves having the transformation that you promised in PLC #1, then you've done your job.

Here's the general recipe for a strong PLC #2:

— **Express thanks and recap.** Thank people for their comments and questions from PLC #1, then give a quick restatement of PLC #1.

— **Recap the opportunity.** You won't spend as much time as you did in PLC #1, but you need to quickly reiterate the opportunity. Don't ever assume that your prospect has seen or paid attention to or remembered PLC #1. They've got busy lives, and your launch isn't nearly as important to them as it is to you.

— **Recap your positioning.** You need to remind them who you are and why they should listen to you. But don't take too long with this—do it quickly.

— **Present a case study or do some real teaching.** Deliver some real value for your viewers. Teach them one cool thing (or several) that they can put to use quickly.

— **Crush objections.** Talk about the top two or three objections and answer them. You want to go after your prospects' big objections to the change or transformation that you're promising.

— **Foreshadow PLC #3.** You need to let your prospects know you have another video coming soon. Build some anticipation for it by telling them a little about what you're going to teach in that video.

— **Call to action.** Ask for a comment on your Prelaunch page or a share on social media.

PLC #3: THE OWNERSHIP EXPERIENCE

PLC #1 was the "why" and PLC #2 was the "what." Now, in PLC #3, you will start to answer the "how" question.

In other words, you've shown the potential transformation or change—whether it's being able to play the piano or being a great parent or learning to meditate. Usually, though, your prospects still don't see how they're really going to have that change in their lives. PLC #3 is about them taking ownership of that future change. It's about having them really feel and understand that they can have that transformation.

Of course, the ultimate answer is for them to buy your product or service, and by the end of PLC #3, you will have started to show them that answer. But first you need to continue to build value.

One of the important things you should do throughout your Prelaunch Sequence is to build excitement and tension. Think of it like a movie or a novel. As you move through the story you have the "rising action," to use a term from your high school creative writing class. That means that the story is clearly building and moving toward a climax. You want your product launch story to do the same thing. As you move through each piece of PLC, you want to keep building your level of pacing and excitement.

Here's the recipe for PLC #3:

— **Express thanks and excitement.** Thank your viewers for their comments and questions from PLC #2. Tell them how excited you are and how excited all your viewers are. (And if you did a good job in PLC #1 and #2, then your viewers WILL be getting excited.)

— **Quickly recap the opportunity and your positioning.** Don't assume your prospects remember (or even saw) your first two videos. Briefly describe the opportunity, and remind them who you are and why they should listen to you. Don't take too long with this—move through it quickly.

— **Possibly present a short case study**, if you've got one. If you don't have a case study yet, that's fine; you'll have one for your next launch.

— **Answer the top questions you've been getting.** In other words, you're going to answer the top objections. Do this even if you've already raised and answered those objections in your earlier PLC videos. People raise the same objections in different ways by asking different questions. Go ahead and answer those questions that keep popping up in the comments on your blog.

— **Explain the big view and how to make it happen.** This is where you step back and look at what's really possible. What's the ultimate transformation or change that your prospect can have in their life if they buy your product? Look at it from all angles, and project that transformation out into their future.

— **Pivot to your offer and create a soft landing.** Do this in the last 10 percent of your PLC #3. By now your prospects have fallen in love with you, because you've given them huge value. And it's time for you to start preparing them for the offer—that's the "soft landing." You don't want to go from being their best friend in one video to being a used-car salesman in the next. You have to tell them that in your next video you're going to have an offer for them, and they need to watch if they're ready to take their transformation to the next level.

— **Seed the scarcity of your launch offer.** You will want to have some type of scarcity in your launch offer, and near the end of PLC #3 you should make some mention of that scarcity. You're not looking to hit viewers over the head with it, because they still haven't seen your offer. But this is a good time to mention that they should be on the look-out for your next email, because this is going to be a lim-ited offer.

— **Call to action.** Ask for a comment on your launch blog or in social media.

So that's your three-part Prelaunch Sequence. When you do this right, you will build a warm relationship with your prospects, you'll demonstrate massive authority, and you'll create all kinds of reciprocity. Of course, you'll also deliver massive value in every step of the process.

You'll also create a Launch Conversation as your prospects leave comments on your launch pages. That Launch Conversation will create something of an instant community as people start to read one another's comments (and even start to converse back and forth). That Launch Conversation will also give you some strong insights into your prospects' big objections, and it will give you a way to gauge whether your Prelaunch Content is striking a nerve with your prospects.

CASE STUDY CAUTION

There is one thing I have to mention here about case studies and the law, but before we go any further, I have to clarify that I am most definitely not a lawyer. Nor do I play one on the Internet. What I'm about to say is a layperson's understanding, and you should definitely get an expert's opinion. In addition, as I type this, the latest rules, regulations, and laws are far from clear, and they're still being interpreted.

The bottom line is that a few years ago, the U.S. Federal Trade Commission published new guidelines about the use of testimonials—specifically, testimonials that make any results-based claims. In the past, a seller could include a disclaimer that "these results are not typical" when publishing any results from their products. That disclaimer is no longer enough. I don't want to go any further in my explanation here, because, well, I'm not a lawyer, and there's still plenty of murkiness around this topic.

I bring this up only because I've mentioned using case studies in your PLC. Where case studies fall with regard to results-based testimonials is still unclear as I write this. If you're in doubt about some part of your sales process or your PLC and you plan to sell in the United States, you should consult an attorney to see if you're in compliance with the FTC regulations and guidelines.

YOUR PRELAUNCH TIMING

Now comes the question on the timing of your Prelaunch Sequence: How long should it be, and how long should one wait between each piece of Prelaunch Content? The answer, unfortunately, is that it depends.

I've personally had Prelaunches that lasted anywhere from 3 days all the way up to 27 days. But I wouldn't recommend either of those extremes for your first few launches. I think a good starting point is 7 to 10 days. That time is measured from when you release your first piece of PLC up until you actually launch and start taking orders in the Open Cart period.

If you're selling a lower-priced product, say a $27 ebook, then I would tend toward the short end—7 days or possibly even 5. If you're selling a higher-priced product, say a $297 training course on getting a job on a cruise ship, then I would move toward the longer end and go with 10 days.

A typical 7-day sequence might look like this:

Day 1: Release PLC #1

Day 3: Release PLC #2

Day 5: Release PLC #3

Day 7: Open Cart

A 10-day sequence might look like this:

Day 1: Release PLC #1

Day 5: Release PLC #2

Day 8: Release PLC #3

Day 10: Open Cart

The important thing to remember is that the timing isn't nearly as important as the Prelaunch Content. Deliver real value, follow the formula I just gave you, and you'll be fine.

ONE CRITICAL THING THAT MAKES THIS WORK

Okay, by now you're probably deep into thinking about all the nitty-gritty details on how to make this work, but let's step back for a second and look at the big picture. Sometimes when people first look at this Product Launch Formula process, they think it's a bunch of marketing tricks, a big basket of psychological tactics that cast a magical spell on their prospects. Now, I won't deny that you can truly create amazing influence when you put it all together, but that's not what really makes PLF work. That's not what is going to grow your business over the long term.

The way you put together a great Prelaunch Sequence is by delivering massive value to your market. If you focus on only one thing, it should be creating value for all the prospects going through your Launch Sequence. That doesn't mean you're giving away the farm. That doesn't mean you're catering to a bunch of freebie seekers who will never buy anything. It doesn't mean going broke as you use all your resources to offer everything you've got for free.

What it means is giving real content that creates real value for people. Don't just tease them—give them some substance. Teach them about the opportunity in your first PLC, but go beyond the opportunity. Teach real content that people can actually use. Every time I do a launch, I get comments from people who are shocked at the amount of content I give out for free. With my Product Launch Formula Coaching Program, I have hundreds of people who have done successful launches just based on the free material that I've given out during my Prelaunch. And I think that's awesome—there's no way I'll ever sell to everyone, so I might as well create as much value as I can as I move through my life.

In the end, your success and the success of your business are going to be closely tied to the amount of value that you create in the world. Putting together a powerful Prelaunch Sequence is a great way to create a lot of value—and you won't have to wait long until the payoff. That comes on launch day, when you Open Cart.

CHAPTER 8

Open Cart: It's Time to Launch!

Amy Small loves yarn, and she loves knitting. In fact, she's so passionate about it that she started a business designing and selling hand-spun yarn as well as patterns to go with it. She started her business in 2010, but in the early years, she told me, it was entirely based on Hope Marketing. She was selling to retail yarn stores, and her margins were really low. She was struggling, and her business was in debt. Possibly the most frustrating thing was that her yarn was very unique and her end users loved it, but she had no real contact with them—Amy's customers were the retail stores that stocked her yarn.

Then a friend told her about the first edition of this book. Amy says that when she picked it up she figured it was just another book about business. She wasn't prepared for the impact it would have on her business and her life. Her first launch did $12,000 in sales, and Amy says "it was completely life changing."

Just as important as the dollars was the fact that Amy was now working directly with her clients. In addition to selling yarn, she was also offering knitting patterns and a "knitalong" to her new clients. Her first product wasn't perfect, but she kept working to make it better. She also kept building her connection to her new clients as well as the people on her growing email list.

Amy's next launch did almost 50 percent better—her results grew to $17,000. The launch after that more than doubled, to $40,000. Each step of the way she kept improving the entire experience, both in her launch and in her product. She was working hard, but the results were so spectacular that it was almost difficult for Amy to believe.

Amy Small

This part is critical: Amy was selling a physical product—yarn—but she was also transforming people's lives. First was the knitting itself—which can take on an almost meditative quality. Then there were her knitalongs, which built a very strong sense of community among her clients—and community is something people are incredibly hungry for. Simply being part of that community was transformative—her clients felt like they were part of something bigger than themselves. The community also helped people complete their knitting projects, and completing hard tasks is one of the most transformative things a person can do.

In her interactions with her clients, Amy could feel the transformation in their lives, so for her next launch, she decided to add that transformation into her messaging. If Amy thought her early results with the formula were hard to believe, well, she just wasn't prepared for what happened next.

In a word, it was spectacular—she did more than $100,000 in sales in just the first hour! When you get that kind of result, then you know that you got your Prelaunch messaging right. Amy's focus on the future transformation in her clients' lives made all the difference. She also leaned strongly into the scarcity trigger (see Chapter 5) because she had a limited amount of yarn, and there were certain color combinations that were even more limited. That launch went on to do a total of $264,000 (as Amy says, "It was completely bananas!"), and because her clients were so hungry for a continued connection, she launched a membership site off the back of that launch. She had 250 people join at $22 per month—another $5,500 in monthly recurring revenue.

One critical piece of Amy's story is how she shifted who her customer was; before she read this book, her clients were the yarn stores. Now she has direct contact with her enthusiastic clients—the people using her yarn. And she gets to see her yarn being knit into beautiful sweaters and scarves. Amy's level of satisfaction and joy in her business have grown just as much as her financial results.

Amy isn't done launching, either. She now launches twice a year; her most recent one had 1,400 people join her knitalong, and she did \$322,000 in sales. These launches all add up, and this year her business grossed well over \$1 million. It's an amazing story that all happened in a little over two years, and Amy started this entire journey with the book that you're holding in your hands right now.

Of course, there's a lot more to Amy's story than I can fit here, but you can see the entire case study at http://thelaunch book.com/amy.

IT'S ALL ABOUT ENROLLMENT

You'll remember that the Prelaunch was all about opportunity, transformation, and ownership. As you move into your actual launch phase (Open Cart), the message is all about enrollment. This is what the entire sequence looks like:

PLC #1: Opportunity

PLC #2: Transformation

PLC #3: Ownership

PLC #4 (or Open Cart): Enrollment

By enrollment, I mean getting your prospects to enroll in your offer—to buy your product or service (or to give to your non-profit, if that's your goal). But this isn't the only enrollment that's going on. You're asking your prospect to enroll in their future. Remember that whatever you're selling, you're offering some type of transformation in their life. Your product will either give them more pleasure or reduce pain in some way. Before they can get that transformation, however, they have to say yes to it. They have to enroll themselves in that change, in their future self.

Now, this might sound mystical, but it's a simple fact. If some-one is going to sign up for your program to quit smoking, they first need to understand that it can work for them, that they can follow through and get that result. They have to say, "Yes, I can stop smoking. I can be an ex-smoker." They need to enroll in that future change. Or, in Amy's case, her prospective clients have to say to themselves, "Yes, I can complete that sweater."

Bottom line, your future clients have to enroll in their new and enhanced future selves. And your messaging during Open Cart has to be about that enrollment.

AN ASTRONAUT'S PERSPECTIVE

It's hard to describe the exhilaration of launch day. This is Open Cart day, and you've been building toward it for weeks or even months. You've focused a lot of energy on this day. In fact, that's the entire point of the launch: to get the attention of the people on your list and in your market and have them anticipating this day. If you've followed my formula, you've raised their interest level to a peak state, and naturally, your emotions and energy are going to be in a peak state as well.

You are never going to forget that first time you push the Send button and open your cart. I have a friend who is an astronaut and has traveled to the International Space Station three times. He's described to me those first few minutes of liftoff in a space launch—that incredible rush of power and acceleration. As silly as it might sound, his account reminded me of the feeling that comes with a well-executed product launch, where you can get a crazy sensation of almost unbelievable power and acceleration.

LAUNCH DAY NITTY-GRITTY

First off, the reason I call launch day Open Cart day is because that's the day you open your shopping cart and start taking orders. As you might guess, the day your launch closes is called Cart Close day. Although you're often not technically closing your shopping cart on this day, you still need a clear end to your launch. But I'm getting ahead of myself. I'll get to that in a little bit.

If you've followed my formula so far, you've had a strong Prelaunch Sequence leading into your Open Cart. Your PLC has connected with the people on your list. You've hit the mental triggers to create a lot of authority, social proof, and community. And in the last few days of Prelaunch you've started to hit the scarcity trigger. Your list knows that you have an offer coming. Your final piece of PLC had a strong pivot where you started to foreshadow your offer. In other words, your Prelaunch has already completed most of the heavy lifting for you in terms of making the sale.

Now, the actual mechanics of opening your launch are pretty simple. You need to have a strong sales page, which is typically done through a sales video or a sales letter. Even though the people who have been through your Launch Sequence have already been presold, it's important not to skimp on your sales message. You have to start with the opportunity, then tell the entire story of your offer—and remember to focus on the transformation.

Once you have your sales page ready, whether you're using a sales video or a sales letter, the next step is simply a matter of sending an email to your list to let them know you're now live and open for business. This is a short, simple email with a link to your sales page. By now you've spent enough time and energy priming the pump, so you want this email to get right to the point.

Here's an example of an Open Cart email that I've used when I opened up my Product Launch Formula Coaching Program:

Okay, I just opened up registration for Product Launch Formula. We're now live:

CLICK HERE for Product Launch Formula

http://www.productlaunchformula.com

(I opened it up a bit early to avoid any bottlenecks and spread the load on the server.)

Best regards,

Jeff

P.S. Remember . . . you don't need to panic. I don't expect to sell out immediately. However, if you want one of those spots at my PLF Live Workshop, then please don't delay. They're going to go fast.

Here's the link:

CLICK HERE for Product Launch Formula

http://www.productlaunchformula.com

As you can see, the email was short and simple. The open of the email had just one sentence before I gave the link to the sales letter. And, of course, when I sent this email, the link was clickable.

NOTE: The "P.S." is often the single most-read part of an email, and I used it to hit the scarcity trigger, warning my readers that they shouldn't delay or they would risk missing out on part of the offer.

BEFORE YOU HIT SEND

At the risk of stating the obvious, before you send that Open Cart email, make sure you've gone through and tested—even retested—every step. Is your sales page live? Are all the links on the page working? Is your order form set up and proofread? Have you gone through the entire order process thoroughly? Do you know firsthand what happens after an order is placed? What about the thank-you page after someone buys? The confirmation email? The fulfillment process?

If everything is tested and ready to go, then get someone else to test it—it's good to get fresh eyes to look through the entire process.

After that, it's time to send that email. I have to tell you, no matter how many times I've done this, I get nervous every single time. I still hesitate before I hit that button to send the Open Cart email. It's a big moment, so expect to have some butterflies and feel some strong emotions. But once you've done your final checks, it's time. You are ready to launch.

WATCHING THE EARLY RESULTS

Once your launch is live, the first hour or two often end up being something of a spectator sport. It's really, really hard not to obsess over the early results. You can breathe a sigh of relief when the first order comes in, because it means everything is working properly.

After that, I usually spend the next hour or two watching statistics. I watch the traffic on the site, the traffic to the actual order form, the opens and clicks on the launch email, the number of orders, and the details behind the orders (which option people are choosing, where they're from, who they are).

There's plenty of data, and you can make it a nearly full-time job to watch all of it. But after an hour or so, it's important to pull yourself away from the stats and get back to work, because your Open Cart has just begun.

(On my Resource Page I've got links to my favorite statistics and data tools. You can access that page at http://thelaunchbook .com/resources.)

YOUR OPEN CART STRATEGY

Your open is certainly a big high point, but it's just a part of your entire Open Cart Sequence. Typically, you will want to keep your cart open somewhere between four and seven days. Sometimes my personal launches are shorter. There have been times I've completely sold out all of my product in as few as 24 or 36 hours.

But you should probably avoid doing a hyper-compressed launch like that until you've gone through a few launches and you have some experience. With a short-fuse launch, you have little time to recover if you make any mistakes. For your first launch, just plan on keeping your cart open for five days.

Your results will vary dramatically based on your market, your offer, and your entire launch strategy. However, a typical result is that you'll get about 25 percent of your orders in the first day and about 50 percent on the final day. The first day is big because you've built so much anticipation. The spike at the end of the launch is the scarcity trigger kicking in. Obviously, the rest of the orders will come in between your open and close.

THE BIG CLOSE

One absolute, cardinal rule for creating a successful launch is setting a definitive close for your launch. And there must be some negative consequence if people don't buy during that limited Open Cart window. Make it clear that your prospects will miss out on something if they don't buy before your launch ends.

That negative consequence is what puts real teeth into your Cart Close, and it will generate a big spike of sales in the last 24 hours of your launch.

IMPORTANT: Lots of people avoid creating real scarcity at the end of their launch. Don't make that mistake or you will cripple your results. In fact, you will likely cut your sales in half. Put some real teeth into the end of your launch and you will double your results.

There are three primary ways to create scarcity in your offer:

1. **The price goes up.** You have a special price during your launch, and people need to jump onboard during your launch to get that price. This is an easy one to understand. A "Grand Opening Sale" and Black Friday, the mega-shopping day after Thanksgiving in the United States, are two familiar examples. While this is a good incentive to get people to jump during your launch and it's an easy one to use, it's not the most powerful form of scarcity during a launch.

2. **Bonuses are removed.** Let's say you're selling a product that teaches people to play blues guitar. During your launch you offer a special bonus of a personal Skype guitar lesson from you. If prospects don't sign up during your launch, then they don't get the bonus lesson. This can be a very powerful form of scarcity. If you have a strong enough bonus, this can actually be a more effective incentive than a price increase.

3. **The offer goes away.** If your prospects don't buy during the launch, then they get shut out of the opportunity—meaning that they can't take advantage of the offer at all, or at least for a long time. In most cases, with most offers, this is the strongest form of scarcity—it's usually a much more robust incentive than the price going up. The only problem is that this type of scarcity doesn't fit well

for a lot of offers. If you're opening a restaurant, you don't want to close down after a week. I've personally used this form of scarcity quite a bit, especially with my online programs. It makes a lot of sense for my offers because I teach the program to groups of students in a fashion similar to a college class. That means registration is available only for a limited time when I'm starting a new class. If someone misses the registration period, then they can't get in. This type of scarcity is an extremely strong incentive for people to jump onboard, if it fits with your offer.

One key point: You can combine these three forms of scarcity and layer them on top of each other. If you can have the price go up and bonuses go away at the end of your launch, then you've just created more scarcity and a more powerful launch.

Finally, remember that using these types of scarcity is not about manipulation. The scarcity has to be real.

The reason this hard close works so well is that your prospects would much rather put off making a decision, and that goes double if the decision involves them opening their wallet and giving you money. If you have a great product that's going to make a big impact on their lives, then you owe it to your prospects to make the best offer possible to get them to overcome their procrastination. Ending your launch with an exclamation mark—some form of scarcity that instills a sense of urgency—is the way you do that.

IT'S NOT JUST THE OPEN AND CLOSE

It's critical that you don't let up on your messaging during your Open Cart period. I've seen some of my students make this mistake, and they end up leaving a lot of money on the table. You need to continue your promotion each day during your Open Cart. You've put in a lot of work to get to this point, and you want to keep your launch in front of your prospects.

Early in your Open Cart, your messaging will mostly be about social proof. As you get further in, your messaging will start to shift to scarcity. You'll want to use every means of communication at your disposal—email will be your primary tool, but you should also be using social media and any other channels you have.

Here's the bare minimum Open Cart sequence:

Day 1 (Launch Day): Two emails + social media. The first email is the one that opens the cart (see the email above), and the second one, about four hours later, lets your list know that everything is up and running and you're open for business.

Day 2: One email + social media. This is the day after Launch Day. The message will typically be a social proof email, where you talk about the great response to your launch. Your email will have a link that goes to your sales page.

Day 3: One email + social media. Send a longer email that answers many of the top questions about the product. Be sure to include a link to your sales page (do this with every email during Open Cart).

Day 4: One or two emails + social media. The message starts to shift to scarcity. You are basically giving a 24-hour warning ahead of your close. You should be absolutely clear about when you'll close (give the date and exact time) and what your prospects stand to lose if they don't act before the launch offer closes down.

Day 5: Three emails + social media. The first email is sent early in the morning reiterating that you're going to be closing that day (give the exact time). The second email goes out about six to eight hours before the cart closes. The third is a final courtesy reminder, and you should send it about two or three hours before you close.

Remember, if you've followed the formula, then closing day will be filled with fireworks and a massive rush of orders. Unfortunately, I've seen lots of people make the mistake of letting up on the last day. Either they don't mail their list at all or they mail just once. This typically happens when they start to worry that they've already sent too many emails during the launch and wonder what good one more email could do.

That's bad thinking. Don't make that mistake. You need to send those final emails on closing day. Trust me, doing so makes a big difference. Many of your prospects have a natural procrastination streak, and they'll wait until the last minute. In fact, after you do your first launch and watch the final rush, I think you'll agree with me that MOST people are serious procrastinators. It doesn't matter what time you close your launch; you will see people placing orders right up until the very last minute. So do yourself a favor—send three emails on your closing day.

That's a basic Open Cart Sequence. Now let's look at some advanced approaches.

ADVANCED OPEN CART STRATEGIES

One of the bigger innovations in the PLF world in the last few years is the evolution of the Open Cart Sequence. In my launches, this sequence now gets just as much care and attention as my Prelaunch Sequence. A more robust Open Cart gives you plenty of opportunity to stay in front of your prospects, and it keeps their attention going right through your Cart Close.

Now, if you're just starting out, you're already going to be busy building out your launch, and the core formula is all you need to have a great launch; just follow the basic flow that I outlined up above. But when you're ready to take it to the next level, here are some things you can add in.

All-Access Page—This is a page where I'll put all of my Prelaunch Content. It makes everything super-accessible. If I'm doing a JV Launch (see Chapter 10), then I'll let my JV partners send their people direct to this page with no opt-in required.

Additional PLC Video—I'll sometimes add a fourth PLC video that teaches a small, bite-size piece of content.

This content is designed to be stand-alone (so it doesn't bring up a lot of questions about the earlier PLC), and it's designed to give a soft landing for sending people to the offer.

Additional Live Training—This is similar to releasing an additional PLC video, but I do it as a live broadcast (see Chapter 11). Again, the content is designed to be stand-alone and relatively short, and it should lead into the offer.

Case Studies—I love to feature case studies during Open Cart. Showing your prospects how other people have already had success using your product or service is powerful. You can do this in a number of formats, including video, live broadcasts, and written case studies.

FAQ Page—This is a web page (or a social post or video or email) that simply answers all the top questions your prospect might have. In one of my recent launches, my team and I created a page that answered more than 50 questions. It's important to note that most of this Q&A should be about moving your prospect forward toward your offer. In other words, you're answering all the top objections that your prospects have.

Live Question and Answer—This is similar to the FAQ page, but in this case the format changes to a live broadcast. If you're comfortable being on camera live, this can be easier and more powerful than creating a written FAQ document. (There's no reason you can't do both—a live broadcast AND a published FAQ page.)

Student Panel—I love this one, because I love to show off my students and their success. I've done this as a live broadcast with six to eight of my students talking about what they've done with the formula and how it's changed their lives.

Celebrity Panel—This is similar to the student panel, but in this case you feature some of the celebrities in your market or niche. It can be especially powerful if you can persuade those celebrities to offer a bonus to the people who buy your offer during the broadcast. (Personally, I'm not a big fan of this approach—it can be very effective, but I would rather focus on my students than the celebrities in the market.)

AN ADVANCED OPEN CART SEQUENCE

If you wanted to use some of the ideas above to build out a more robust Open Cart Sequence, your five-day sequence might look something like this:

Day 1 (Launch Day): This will be unchanged from Day 1 of the basic Open Cart outlined above. You should send two emails + social media. The first email is the one that opens the cart, and the second, about four hours later, lets your list know that everything is up and running and you're open for business.

Day 2: Share an additional PLC video or additional live PLC broadcast. If you're doing it as a video, your email will go to the video instead of your sales page. If you're doing it as a live broadcast, you will email early in the morning to announce the broadcast and then follow up just before you go live.

Day 3: Post an FAQ page or do a live question-and-answer broadcast. If you're posting an FAQ page, your email will go to that page instead of your sales page. If you're doing the Q&A as a live broadcast, you will email early in the morning to announce the broadcast and then follow up just before you go live.

Day 4: Add case studies, a student panel, or a celebrity panel. Remember that this is the day your messaging starts to shift to scarcity, so even though you're sharing videos or a broadcast here, you should be starting to warn that this is the last full day of the launch and your special offer is about to end. You need to be absolutely clear about when you'll close and what your prospects stand to lose if they don't act before the launch offer closes down.

Day 5: This day is all about the impending close. You can do a live broadcast to answer any last-minute questions. Definitely send three emails + social media.

That's what a more advanced sequence could look like. Remember that in Open Cart you really shift from teaching to guiding people to a decision about your offer. This is the time to answer your future customers' objections, demonstrate the path to making real change in their lives, and gently move them to a purchase decision.

WHEN STUFF GOES WRONG

As much as I wish that everything always went perfectly and that every launch was a huge success, sometimes there are problems. Occasionally a launch can underperform, and sometimes they just plain fail. I want to walk through some of the most common problems and give you a few pointers on what to do when your launch doesn't go well.

The first class of problems is technical. It's possible to crash your web server if you send too much traffic. The good news is that this is not a problem you're likely to have with your first launch. It takes a huge launch with lots of traffic to cripple a server, and unless you've already got a significant business with a large list, you're probably not going to be putting a strain on your server in your first launches.

However, if you do have a serious business with a large list, then this is definitely something to pay attention to. I crashed a server in one of my biggest launches, and it cost me a lot of heartache, plenty of orders, and ultimately a lot of money. It also cost a lot of customer goodwill, and my reputation took a big hit. Make no mistake, server crashes are not fun. You can see my current list of recommended web hosts and servers on the Resource Page at http://thelaunchbook.com/resources.

Another problem that a lot of people don't think about is collecting the money—in other words, getting paid. If you're taking orders online, you're going to be using some type of payment gateway or merchant account, and no matter what service you're using, if you have a sudden, huge influx of orders, it can make your provider nervous. Most likely they will look at that huge increase in orders as a credit risk and be worried that you might take all that money, not bother delivering your product, and then skip out to sit on a beach in Tahiti. If you did something like that, they would be liable for all the refund requests that would come pouring in.

Bottom line, a huge increase in orders over your normal rate will scare your merchant account provider. I've personally run into this several times, both with my merchant accounts and with PayPal. The best way to avoid these troubles is through a lot of communication with them before your launch. You should also do business with a "launch friendly" merchant account provider. There are those who will understand when you tell them you're doing a "Jeff Walker–style" or "PLF-style" launch. For a current list of providers I recommend, check out the Resource Page at http://thelaunchbook.com/resources.

WHAT IF NO ONE BUYS?

What if your launch just doesn't convert? You open the cart and you have very few sales. As much as I would like to tell you that this doesn't ever happen, sometimes it does. When it does happen, it's time to go into diagnosis mode.

First off, if you have no sales at all, you need to start testing your process. Start with your launch email. Open up the email broadcast in your email program and try clicking the link to make sure it works. Then go through the sales process at your site. Does the sales page or sales letter load? Can you get to the order form? Try to place an order to make sure it goes through. Does everything work?

The next step is to determine whether you're getting any traffic to your site. Check the stats on your email broadcast. Did the email go out? Did anyone click through to your site? What are the traffic stats on your website telling you? How much traffic do you have to your sales page? To your order page?

If everything is working and you're getting traffic to the site but you're still not getting any sales, then you've got a conversion problem, and it's likely to stem from either your offer or your sales message. It can be tough to tease out which of these is causing your low conversion, and it could possibly be a combination of both.

First let's look at the offer. Is your offer compelling? Does it present a solution or solve a problem that your market cares about? Are you selling something that the market desperately wants as opposed to something you think they need or something you just wanted to create? Does the offer speak to your prospects' hopes and dreams? Does it address the fears and aspirations in the market? Is it on point in terms of what the market wants?

Now let's consider the message in your sales video or sales letter. Does your sales message articulate the transformation or the change your product offers to your prospects? Does it make the benefits in your product come alive? Does it make those benefits feel tangible and concrete? Is your buying process simple and understandable, or is it confusing in any way? Do you clearly tell your prospects exactly what they're going to get? What they can expect with every step of the process? How much the product costs? What your guarantee is?

If you determine that you have an offer problem or a sales messsage problem, then it's time to get to work. It's not too late to pull a rabbit out of the hat. I've seen remarkable turnarounds right in the middle of a launch due to a tweaked offer and/or a reworked sales page.

WHAT TO DO AFTER YOUR LAUNCH

One of the most powerful and surprising results of a launch is the amount of goodwill that you will create. When you deliver real value in your Prelaunch Content, your market will fall in love with you—both the people who buy from you AND those who just watch your Prelaunch Content but don't buy. Not everyone will love you, of course, but a big chunk of the market will. Those people are your tribe, and your Prelaunch creates a great self-selection process for identifying that tribe.

Once you've gone through your launch and closed your cart, you will want to strengthen your relationship with those who bought from you. This is the Post-Launch, and it's critical to the long-term growth of your business that you use this time to extend your momentum and positioning from your launch. I make a huge effort to overdeliver to my new clients, and I suggest you do the same. I always have a few extra bonuses that I never mentioned during my launch, and I start sending out those bonuses shortly after the cart closes. In these days when we are so often underwhelmed by our experience after we buy a product, adding something extra makes you stand out in the market. It's amazing what a few extra, unannounced bonuses will do. You don't have to go crazy; just give more than you promised.

One of the biggest—and easiest—wins you will have in your market comes from putting together a solid follow-up process for new clients. Much of this can be done through automated follow-up emails.

Another thing you shouldn't skimp on is customer service. I didn't offer much when I first started my business, but I learned my lesson in the early years. I now provide world-class customer service—and it's worth every penny I spend on it. I don't look at customer service as a cost center, but as a big part of my overall strategic business building.

Finally, don't forget about following up with the prospects who did NOT buy. You just spent considerable energy romancing them in your Prelaunch, and even if they didn't buy this time, they are still great prospects for future offers. Don't let that romance go cold. Send them some more content in the days after you close your launch. Then they'll be primed for a follow-up offer or for your next launch.

Now that we've gone through the launch, I've got something special in store for you—the secrets of the Seed Launch, which is all about how to do a launch even if you don't have a list or a product. I'll show you how I built up a business from a simple Seed Launch right into a multimillion-dollar empire.

CHAPTER 9

How to Start from Scratch: The Seed Launch

Tara and Dave Marino's lives were turned upside down by the loss of their young child. It's a nightmare that no parent wants to even think about. I can't imagine that pain, but I do know the pain of losing someone who is very close and who passes away before their time. It's not easy to move beyond that type of loss.

Dave had a great, secure job that paid him more than six figures, year in and year out, but he felt like he was drifting in corporate cubicle land. And after the tragic loss of his child, he found it difficult to get excited about anything in his life. Tara sold a little real estate on the side, but she was mostly a stay-at-home mom with two young kids.

Tara, however, had a passion: helping her friends, mostly other moms and wives like herself, live a more sensual life. When she first heard about the Product Launch Formula, she knew it was exactly the right tool to bring her message to a bigger audience and build a business. She thought it might even give Dave something that would spark a new outlook on life.

But Tara faced a huge challenge—she was starting from scratch. After helping her friends, she knew she had the raw material for a program about leading a more sensual life, but she didn't have a book or a seminar or even a speech. And she certainly didn't have a product.

Another problem: she didn't have any type of an email list or any platform whatsoever. She had a few followers on Twitter and some Facebook friends, but that was about it.

Given a situation like Tara's, how do you get started?

GETTING PAID BEFORE YOU CREATE YOUR PRODUCT

With the magic of the Seed Launch, you can create a business from literally almost nothing, which is exactly what Tara did.

She pulled together a list of about 200 people from her personal inbox and social media, and she started her Prelaunch. The product would be a course called "You're Perfect." To hear Tara and Dave talk about it now, the whole venture was a rag-tag process they made up on the fly. But when you're launching your first product to a tiny list like they had, you can often overcome any mistakes due to your close connection with the people on your list. And in her Seed Launch, Tara was able to sell five spots in her program and make almost $3,000 in sales!

Tara had promised a series of six weekly teleseminars along with worksheets and templates—and now that she had sold them, she would have to create them. Each week she created the material for the call, then got on the phone and delivered a class. Since the entire process was extremely interactive, she was able to use the feedback from her clients to fine-tune the next call to exactly what they needed. Of course, Tara recorded each call, and those recordings became the basis for her product after the initial program was finished. The Seed Launch delivered a payday and a finished product.

Now, making almost $3,000 from scratch is exciting, but it's what happened next that makes this an amazing story: As Tara delivered that first training class, all the interaction gave her the idea for two more products: "The Power of Sensuality" and "The Beauty Formula." And with the momentum from that first launch, Dave and Tara were able to build up a list of 1,000 email subscribers. Their next launch did almost $12,000 in sales—a huge increase from their first launch. But again, that was just the beginning. The next promotion brought in $90,000, and then another did $190,000. Each launch built their list and their reputation in the market. They have now done over a half million dollars in sales of Tara's products, trainings, and coaching.

Along the way, Dave quit his job. Suddenly the "security" of cubicle land didn't look all that great. And while no business success can ever take away the pain of losing their child, they've built an entirely new life for their family. That new life took a dramatic turn when Tara and Dave and their two young sons took a summer trip to France and decided to stay. Tara had always dreamed of living there, and her new business and lifestyle suddenly made it possible . . . so they flew home, put most of their stuff in storage, and moved to the south of France.

(To read the full case study of Tara and Dave, go to http://the launchbook.com/tara.)

WHEN YOU'RE JUST STARTING OUT

At this point I'm sure you can see the power of a well-orchestrated product launch. And you've seen how Product Launch Formula is a proven system that has worked over and over for businesses of every size.

However, I've been at this long enough to know there are some folks who just don't see how it can work for them, especially if they're just starting out. You might be one of those people. Perhaps you're thinking that while this all makes sense, you don't know how to get started. Maybe you're thinking you would love to launch something, but you have neither a product nor a list of prospects. Or maybe you've got a business right now, but you would like to start a different one. You're ready to move on, but you don't know where to start. Well, this is the chapter for you, because the Seed Launch provides the answers to all your questions.

I call it the Seed Launch because it's a little launch that can grow a product, a list, and even a business into a great big success.

Think of a tiny seed that can one day become a towering oak tree that stands 100 feet tall. To look at that seed and think it can grow to such an incredible size seems improbable at best, yet we know that's exactly what happens. It's no different with a Seed Launch. It starts with an idea and a handful of sales, but it can grow into a serious business.

DISASTER STRIKES ONE SUNNY FRIDAY AFTERNOON

Before I get into the exact mechanics of a Seed Launch, let me give you another example that shows just how it can work and how far-reaching the impact can be. This Seed Launch took place in 2005, and like many launches it was driven by a serious need. In fact, this was my launch, and I was starting over from scratch.

After a number of years in business with a variety of products and services, I had a partnership break apart very abruptly. I've had many partnerships over the years, and the one thing you learn about partnerships is that, by their very definition, none of them can last forever. In this case, my partnership ended without warning. One Friday afternoon my partner called me to say not only that was he leaving, but that he would be taking almost all of our paying clients with him.

Most businesspeople have been through something similar to this. A sudden loss of your business (and the majority of your income) sure has a way of focusing your attention, so the first thing I did was sit down and think about what type of business I wanted to create next. I spent a lot of time listing what I liked and what I didn't like about the business that had just disappeared. Then I created a list of criteria for my new business and spent a lot of time selecting the niche I wanted to target. Most important, I focused on what value I could bring to the market.

For years, I had focused on the stock market investing and trading niche. All my products had been about teaching people how to invest in the stock market. Although I loved that business, I was burned out. I had been publishing my stock market newsletters an average of more than 500 times per year. And since I did it all without any staff, the whole process had become a real grind. I was ready to move on to a different market that had a lot fewer deadlines.

There was another driving factor to consider as well: I had discovered a passion for entrepreneurship and marketing. I had known nothing of marketing when I started out, but over the years I had developed a real knack for it. I had created my first business out of nothing, built a huge list of subscribers, and invented this crazy system for launching my products. In fact, I had been sharing my product launch techniques with some other entrepreneur friends, and they had been getting outstanding results, so I knew my method would work for others just as well as they worked for me.

So I had an area of expertise (marketing and product launches) that could create a lot of value for people, and I loved the entire niche of entrepreneurship and marketing. But I had two problems: I had neither a list nor a product in that market. The big email lists from my previous business were made up of people who were interested in the stock market; those lists wouldn't do me any good in this new venture. But I did have one thing going for me—I had been invited to speak at a marketing conference that would take place in just a few weeks. I decided I would use my talk at that conference to begin building my new business.

I put together a great presentation that walked through my entire launch process—or at least as much as I could fit into a 90-minute presentation. Then, at the end of the presentation, I made an offer: If anyone in the audience wanted to go deeper and learn exactly how to implement my strategies, I would coach a small group of clients through every step of the process. I called it the Product Launch Workshop. The coaching would take place via a series of teleclasses that I would be conducting after the event.

There is an art to "selling from the stage," and let me just say I was neither skilled nor experienced at that art. So my offer at the end of the talk did not get an overwhelming response. There were nearly 300 people in attendance, and I sold only six spots in my workshop. As a point of reference, that's NOT a very strong performance. I now know that a 10 percent response rate is at the lower end of what you should expect after you make an offer from the stage, and I had gotten less than 3 percent.

Nevertheless, I realized that while I might not be a great pitchman, I definitely knew how to do product launches—and I now had real, live clients. I was confident that I could give them a skill that would forever change their lives.

A COUPLE OF PROBLEMS . . . SOLVED!

At that point I had a couple of other problems. First, I knew how to do launches, but I didn't necessarily know how to teach them. Second, to get a strong level of interaction, I wanted more than six people in the class. So I invited several of my entrepreneurial friends, other business owners I had met over the years, to join. Since I understood that it was far more important to get a "critical mass" in the class than to extract every last dollar out of it, I extended the invitation on a complimentary basis. Many of these people knew of my successful launches and were interested to learn my formula, so this was a win-win for them and for me: I got my critical mass, and they got to learn my secrets. And that brought the total class size up to just over 30 people.

That solved my critical mass problem, but I still had the problem of figuring out the best way to teach the material. I knew from experience that when you're an expert on a topic, you often suffer from "the curse of knowledge." You forget what it's like to be a beginner, and you end up teaching at too high a level. So I went back to one of my favorite tools—the one I taught you when we covered the Pre-Prelaunch. I asked my audience what they wanted to know. As part of my offer, I promised five teleclasses. But before I did even the first one, I surveyed my 30 students to learn their most burning questions about launching their products and services. I took the responses and split them into five broad categories to correspond with the five calls I would make. For the first call, I wanted to give a broad overview of the product launch process, so I took all the questions pertaining to that and put them in a logical sequence. Then I simply went through and answered each question on the call.

Before the next call, I ran another survey. I asked my students if they had any questions about the material I'd covered in the first call, and then I asked them for their top questions about the second topic: creating the Prelaunch Sequence. Once again, I arranged those questions in a compelling sequence and went through all of them in the teleclass.

I continued that process for each call—wash, rinse, repeat. After I had completed all five teleclasses, I added a bonus call in which I answered additional questions that my students had. Then, because I've always been obsessed with overdelivering on my promises, I added a few extra case study calls in which I walked through examples from some additional launches.

In the end, I think I ended up doing nine or ten calls instead of the five I had promised. We went deep, and I taught everything I knew. And that led to some terrific testimonials and several successful case studies from my students. I received those testimonials partly because I had overdelivered and partly because my material (which later became Product Launch Formula) was truly revolutionary. But there was also a third, very important reason my students loved the course so much, and it's critical that you understand this third reason.

You see, even though I had never taught the material before, I did a great job teaching it—but it wasn't because I'm a natural-born teacher about launches. It was because I let my students guide the process. I continually asked them, both on the calls and in the surveys before each call, what they needed to know. What wasn't clear in the material I'd delivered? What did I need to go back to and cover more thoroughly? What unanswered questions did they have? In effect, I used that first group of students from my Seed Launch to learn how to teach the material.

In my current position in the industry, I get to see a lot of products come to market, and some of them are not very good. But if you use the Seed Launch, you're almost guaranteed to create a great product. It gives you an interactive process to build your product, and when you involve your clients by asking for their input, you end up with something really good. Simply put, you naturally become attuned to your market's need. There is no guesswork. You avoid the curse of knowledge, and you deliver true value to your clients.

YOUR SEED LAUNCH

Now let's get to the nitty-gritty of the Seed Launch. This is the ideal launch if you're just starting out and you don't have a list or a product. It's also great if you have an idea for a new product but aren't sure of the demand for it, or if you would like to get paid for the product before you create it. You're going to find that the Seed Launch is enormously flexible. The one real limitation is that this style of launch doesn't work for physical widgets. But if you have a knowledge- or learning-based product, then this is a perfect fit. If you want to teach how to lose weight, build a better relationship, find a better job, run your first marathon, train your dog, bring in more chiropractic patients, get more followers on social media, or anything like that, then you're going to love the Seed Launch.

The good news is that by now you've already learned nearly all the tools and concepts that you need in your Seed Launch. The even better news is that the Seed Launch is the simplest launch of all. The best news is that you're going to end up with your own product by the time you wrap it up, and it's going to be a great product that's perfectly tuned to your prospects' needs and desires.

The Seed Launch takes advantage of two phenomena that very few people are aware of unless they've done some list-based direct marketing. The first is that, on a percentage basis, smaller lists are more responsive than bigger lists. And I'm not talking a LITTLE more responsive—I mean they're a LOT more responsive. For instance, I once did a launch to a list of 299 people. I was trying to make one of the most difficult sales ever by taking an online service that had originally been free and charging for that exact same service. And the new price was not inexpensive; it was $100 per year.

On the face of it, I was looking at an extremely difficult sale, but the list was very warm (in other words, I had a very strong relationship with the people on the list). In the end, I had 297 out of the 299 sign up for the product, which gave me a conversion rate of 99.3 percent. That's one conversion stat that I'm pretty sure I'll never be able to top! My results were certainly not typical; I only had this result because of the strength of the community and my super-warm relationship with it. But more to the point, if the list had contained 3,000 people, then I wouldn't have had anywhere near that conversion rate.

The second little-known leverage point the Seed Launch capitalizes on is that in almost every list there's a percentage of people known as "hyper-responsives." These are your raving fans. They open up every email or letter you send them. They'll eagerly buy whatever you offer. These people are the first you hear from every time you send an email, the first to comment on your blog or other social media, the first to give you a share on social. As I said, these hyper-responsives exist on nearly every list, and they're usually overrepresented on the smallest ones. When you combine the fact that small lists are more responsive with the fact that there are hyper-responsives on that small list, you have the seeds of . . . well . . . a Seed Launch.

Of course, you might be wondering why I'm telling you all about small lists when I said you could do a Seed Launch with no list. Well, the first step in your Seed Launch is to build some type of micro-list. That list might have only 30 people on it. It would be better if it contained more like 100 people, and 300 would be even better.

The good news is that pulling together a micro-list like this has never been easier, and your most effective tool is social media. The process of getting those first subscribers is as simple as starting to post good content about your topic on social media sites like Facebook, Twitter, Instagram, and whatever new social media darling emerges next (and be sure to revisit Chapter 3 for more on list building).

Since social media moves faster than books can be published, and since the Seed Launch will still be working decades after I write these words, I'm not going to give you exact tactics on how to build a micro-list via social media. But at the end of the day, you attract followers by publishing relevant, interesting content about your topic. It can be either content you create or content you curate (i.e., material from others that you find and repost). Either way, it doesn't take long to attract a small following. Again, aim for 100 to 300—and get to work. Tens of thousands of people have successfully built lists of that size before you, and you can do the same. (One thing to remember—ideally you will drive people from your social media following to your email list.)

The goal of the Seed Launch is not to make a million dollars but to get you in the game, help you learn about your market and automatically create a great product, and set you up for a bigger launch just a bit further down the road. Remember, Tara Marino started with a $3,000 Seed Launch, and it quickly grew into something much bigger.

Just like I did with my Seed Launch of the Product Launch Workshop, your offer is going to be a series of online classes. You'll do them for the entire group of people who buy from you in your Seed Launch. You'll do them via webinars or live broadcasts. The actual tools you'll use to deliver them are very simple to learn. They're either free or very inexpensive, and new (and better) ones come out every year. The bottom line is that you'll essentially be giving a class or lecture over the Internet to your new students. You'll have the ability to interact with them if you want—and taking questions and comments will always make the classes more interesting for both you and your students. You can get more details on the various tools to use for webinars and live broadcasts on the Resource Page at http://thelaunchbook.com/resources.

One quick note: you can actually do this entire process as a live, in-person training if your audience is local—but you'll want to figure out a way to record it, hopefully on video.

Let's just say you're going to do a series of five classes about your topic. (You could do any number that makes sense, but most of the time five is about right.) Plan on doing one per week. Also plan on doing a surprise, bonus question-and-answer call just to make sure that you overdeliver to your new clients.

About the actual launch: Since you're going to be selling to a small, warm list that almost certainly has a number of hyper-responsives, your launch doesn't need to be elaborate. Just use what I taught you in Chapters 6 and 7.

You do need to have a good offer, though, and you need to do a good job of explaining the benefits people will receive from your class. That means you focus on the transformation or change people will experience by going through your training. You must show your clients how you're going to help them reach their dreams and aspirations and/or avoid their fears and frustrations. For example, if you're going to teach someone how to play guitar, don't focus on how quickly they will learn all the primary open chords; instead, focus on the transformation they will go through. What will the final outcome be? Will they finally be able to play songs for themselves and their friends? Will they gain the confidence to start playing with other people? Will they finally feel like a real musician? Will they get more dates?

Now let's get to your launch. With the Seed Launch you want to keep things simple, beginning with the Pre-Prelaunch. In fact, your Pre-Pre will do a lot of the heavy lifting for your launch. Go back and review the Pre-Prelaunch chapter, then run a classic Pre-Pre "ask" campaign where you ask your micro-list to tell you their most burning questions. You can do this either by putting together an actual survey or by using email or social media. That survey will tell you a lot about the hopes/dreams/fears/frustrations of your market, and it will be invaluable as you put together your offer. Remember that your Pre-Pre is a shot across the bow—it sets the stage for your offer and starts to build awareness and even anticipation.

After the initial survey in your Pre-Prelaunch, your next step is an email follow-up in which you talk about some of the findings and conclusions from your survey. You can share part of your own journey of transformation, such as a few of your early challenges and how you overcame them. At the end of your email, you can talk a little bit about your upcoming class. If you like, this follow-up can be done as a video.

After that, your next email is the one in which you make your offer. Generally, you will want to direct people to a sales letter or sales video. But remember, you don't need to oversell. The people on your micro-list will feel as if they have a personal relationship with you (and for many of them, that will likely be true), so you want your sales message to reflect that. Of course, you still have to work hard to explain the benefits, and you still need to focus on the ultimate transformation or change that your new clients will experience. But you don't want to come across as a used-car salesman, because that won't resonate with your micro-list.

Your goal in all of this is to get 30 people (60 would be even better) to say yes and buy your product. You'll want that many people in order to have a lot of interaction in your classes. Attrition is a sad fact of human nature; you'll almost always have some people who just don't show up or participate in any way. So if you start with 30 people, then you'll still have some sticking around to the end. If you come up short of 30, that's okay. Tara started with five, and I started with six. In that case, do what I did with my Product Launch Workshop and discreetly invite a few people to participate on a complimentary basis.

A quick note on prices and sales: I've seen Seed Launches for products priced between $50 and $3,000, depending on the market and offer; financial results are going to vary dramatically from person to person and from offer to offer. But remember, this is more about building a great product and getting you in the game than it is about the money you make from this first launch.

DELIVERING ON YOUR SEED LAUNCH

Now it's time to deliver . . . and create your first (or next) product at the same time!

As you deliver your product, remember that feedback and surveys are your friends. I survey people before each call. I ask them what their top questions about the next topic are. So, returning to that "learn guitar" example, if the first call is about how to strum, I would briefly explain the topic in one sentence, then ask, "What are your top two questions about strumming the guitar?"

Your job isn't to get on the phone and answer every question. You want to go through the responses to the survey, group them into themes, and rewrite them into good questions that you can expand into teaching points. Then put them in a logical and compelling order. Once you've done that, you're ready to get on the phone and give a great presentation.

After that first call, you send out another survey. First you ask if there are any additional questions about the topic of the first call, and then you ask for the top questions about your next topic. Repeat this process before and after every call. The happy result is that you're building a product to perfectly match what your market wants. Along the way, you're getting deep insight into your market and how to talk to it, and that's going to pay off in a big way when it comes time for you to do your first big launch. It might sound crazy, but you're getting paid to gather all this market research.

WILL YOUR MOM BE PROUD?

This brings up a big question some people have about Seed Launches. Many times, when people first learn about them, they wonder how they can actually sell something that hasn't been created. Will people pay for something like that? For that matter, is it actually ethical to charge money for something that doesn't exist yet? I get it—this might sound impossible, and even a bit shady. But I know that when I went to college, I paid a lot of money in tuition before the classes were delivered. When I go to a play, I pay for my ticket before the play is performed, and when I subscribe to newspapers and magazines, I pay for my subscription before anything is created and delivered. In reality, if you start to look around, there are many things you pay for before they're created or delivered, and your Seed Launch is no different. Your new clients are paying for the experience and training that you'll be giving them. It's actually a benefit to them that you'll be teaching them live—that way, they get the opportunity to ask you questions and help guide the entire experience. Bottom line, what you're really getting paid for is creating value for your new clients, and the fact that you're creating a product and getting paid to do market research are all happy by-products.

NEXT STEPS AND A FINISHED PRODUCT

Of course, you're going to be recording these classes—and whether you're doing webinars or live broadcasts, the recording is something that will be built in (and usually happen automatically). If you do five calls and then add a bonus Q&A call, you've now created six recordings. And you can get those audio recordings transcribed. Each hour of content will equal about 15 to 20 printed pages, so you'll have the makings of a book (or PDF or ebook) that's 90 to 120 pages long. Now you've got audio (and probably video) and 90 pages of written content. This is the core of your online course or membership site. Congratulations—you just got paid to create a product!

You will also want to focus on getting your new clients some strong results, because they're going to be great candidates for case studies as you move forward and get ready to launch your product in a bigger way. Creating those case studies is as simple as getting on a video conference and interviewing them about their results. Any case studies you add will further build out your product.

So that's the essence of the Seed Launch—simple, fast, flexible. And it sets the stage for much bigger launches to come in your business. It's the perfect way to dip your toe in the water; learn how to teach your topic; get to know more about the hopes, dreams, and fears of your target market; and create a great product without much effort.

FROM SEED LAUNCH TO EMPIRE

Just to show you where a Seed Launch can go, there's a postscript to the story of my Product Launch Workshop Seed Launch. Even though I was able to persuade only six people to buy that workshop, I felt like I had a winner on my hands. The people who went through the training loved it. And once they started to put my teachings to work in their businesses, the results started to roll in. It was the beginning of a huge tide of Product Launch

Formula success stories from nearly every market and niche you can imagine.

Unfortunately I'm a bit of a perfectionist, so I took all the material I delivered in that first workshop, and I re-created it in a more polished version. I used all the lessons I had learned about teaching the material, and I added in some of my students' case studies. A few months later I finished the creation of the first-ever Product Launch Formula course.

Of course, I had to put together a product launch for it. That was in October 2005. In the one-week launch that followed, I did more than $600,000 in sales. Since that time I've done tens of millions of dollars in sales of my PLF Coaching Program, and I now have thousands of PLF Owners. You're part of this story as well, because you would not be holding this book in your hand if it weren't for that first very oh-so-modest Seed Launch that I did. (The original edition of this book became a *New York Times* #1 bestseller only two weeks after it was released—all due to the platform I built with my launches, all started by that first Seed Launch.) That just shows what can happen when you start with a Seed Launch and continue to leverage up your launches.

One thing to remember about those numbers: Even though I had previously run a successful business, I was starting over again. I had entered into a completely new market with a completely new product. The big list I had from my prior business was of no use to me. I was starting from scratch again, and the Seed Launch is how I started out.

However, I had one more secret weapon in my arsenal to help build my new business, and that weapon let me come out of the gate with that $600,000 launch—the biggest launch I had ever done. How did I do it in a brand-new market, a market where I had no presence and almost no list?

My secret was the enormous power of the JV Launch, and that's what the next chapter is all about.

CHAPTER 10

The JV Launch (and How I Made a Million Dollars in a Single Hour)

Exactly where is the line between fear and panic?

The minutes were counting down toward the open much too quickly, and I was far too stressed and sleep deprived. It had been more than 48 hours since I had gotten any sleep more substantial than a catnap. I was getting bombarded with emails and instant messages with questions, comments, suggestions. The traffic to my site was like nothing I had ever experienced. This wasn't my first rodeo—I had already done dozens of launches. But the stakes were a lot higher this time, and I was playing on a much bigger stage.

The clock was ticking down, and I still had lots to do. I needed a headline for my sales letter. I needed to test the order process. I needed to mail my list. I needed to communicate with my partners. Arrrrrgggghhhh . . . The minutes kept ticking away toward the open at 10 A.M. mountain standard time.

It had been a little more than six months since my prior business had imploded due to a partnership breakup, and it was time for a "revenue event"—meaning time to make some money. I was ready to be back in business. This time I wanted a business where I had complete control, where I didn't have a partner to consult every time I had a new idea or plan.

I was also ready to leave the stock market niche behind. I had loved the stock market when I started that business, but I had come to realize that I loved marketing even more, and I was really good at it. Still, I knew I didn't want to be a marketing consultant. After years of being an information entrepreneur, I was in love with publishing and teaching. I was in love with the inherently leveraged nature of the business; my income wasn't tied to the number of hours I worked but to how well I could sell my products and help my clients. I was also in love with the impact I could make. Instead of helping a few dozen people as a consultant, I could impact thousands as a publisher. And I was clearly legit—I'd been making a living with a marketing-driven business on the Internet for longer than most people had had access to the Internet.

I had only one issue. It was a crowded market. There were thousands of people trying to make a living as an "Internet marketing" expert. Some of them were wildly successful, but a lot of them could barely afford to get their business cards printed (not that there's anything wrong with not having much money—that's certainly where I started—but if you don't have any money or success yet, you probably shouldn't be teaching others how to start a business). It was also a market in which I had no positioning or traction. Even though I had long been doing business online, even though I had a completely revolutionary new way to sell online, even though I had been making more money online than most of the so-called online marketing gurus . . . well, none of that mattered because I didn't have a presence in the niche. All my email lists and websites were about the stock market. My tens of thousands of email subscribers in the stock market niche wouldn't do me any good starting a business in the online marketing niche.

However, I did have an ace in the hole. It was only one card, but it was a powerful one, and I was going to play that card with everything I had.

A couple of years earlier, in February 2003, I had attended an online marketing seminar. When I walked into that seminar, I felt like I had found my tribe. You see, doing business online back in those days could be lonely. I fought the good fight every day out of my home office, but almost no one understood what I was doing. The idea of an online business was completely foreign to almost everyone.

But at that seminar, I was suddenly among a couple of hundred other people who did the same thing I did—they all had the same hopes, dreams, challenges, and frustrations. At the back of that conference room a small group of us forged a bond that would last for years and change an entire industry, but that was all in the distant future.

In the short term, I learned one important fact—that the product launches I had quietly been doing in my stock market business were truly unique. No one else was doing anything like them. Before that seminar, I didn't realize how unusual my product launches were. I had recently done the launch that brought in $106,000 in seven days and helped me buy my house, but I didn't realize just how unusual that result was, and I didn't realize how unique my strategies were. I had assumed that I couldn't be the only person doing this type of launch. I had figured it out on my own, and I thought others must have done the same. But I was wrong. Each time I mentioned one of the launches I had done in my business, everyone listening would go silent and their ears would perk up. My launches seemed to defy the normal laws of marketing and business as they were understood at that time.

I left that seminar with lots of new friendships—some of them with people who were leaders in the online marketing industry. These were people with lists and connections. At that time I was still publishing about the stock market and years away from thinking about publishing in the online marketing niche, but I loved talking to my new friends because of our shared passion for marketing and business building. At some point, I started helping a few of them put together product launches, and they enjoyed some spectacular successes with those launches. Word slowly spread among many of the major players in the nascent online marketing industry that this guy Jeff Walker had a brand-new technique that could bring in crazy profits in a very short period. I didn't know it at the time, but I was sowing the seeds for my next business.

MY FIRST JV LAUNCH

One of the critical components of any launch is your list of prospects. I've been hammering away at that fact for the entire book and went deep on it in Chapter 3. As I showed you in the Seed Launch chapter, it's entirely possible to do a smaller-scale launch when you're first starting out without a list (or with just a tiny one). Still, if you're going to make a big impression in the market, you need a list. Now, there are lots of ways to build a list, but the single fastest way to do it is by using the lists that other people have already built and curated. That's the essence of a Joint Venture Launch (or JV Launch).

In a JV Launch you have partners mail their lists and tell their people about your launch. If you make a sale to one of the people your partner sends your way, you pay your partner a commission. The way this generally works is that your JV partners will encourage their readers to visit your Prelaunch Content. Your JV partners actually send their lists to your squeeze page, so that the visitors have to join your list before they get to see your PLC. Throughout your launch, you follow up with your new prospects. You use special affiliate tracking software on your website to track which JV partner referred each prospect (see the Resource Page at http://the launchbook.com/resources). Then, when you Open Cart and start making sales, your software automatically tracks who referred each new client to you so you can pay commissions to the right partner.

One of the most powerful by-products of doing a JV Launch like this is that you end up building a significant Launch List out of all those leads. And after you do the launch, you get to keep that list. This is the single fastest way to grow a list. Of course, list size is completely dependent on your niche, who your partners are, and the size of their lists . . . but it's possible to add thousands of people to your list in just a few days during a JV Launch.

That's exactly what happened to me. Because I had built relationships with the leaders in the online marketing industry—and often gave them lots of help with their launches—these experts were ready and willing to help me out. So when I came out with my first piece of Prelaunch Content, I had many of the major players on board and mailing their lists about my PLC. Within a couple of days, I had 8,000 people join my list, and it didn't stop there. My JV partners kept mailing throughout my Prelaunch, and I built a list of more than 15,000 email subscribers during the launch. That was a breathtaking number. In my old stock market business, where I was operating in a much bigger niche, it took me years to build a list that size. And now I had done it in a matter of days in my new business—all through the power of my JV partners.

So there I was on October 21, 2005, just a few minutes before it was time to Open Cart on my launch. Yes, I was scared, and there was an important reason for that fear. You see, I knew my capabilities. I knew I could put together a great launch, and I knew I had a great product. The feedback I had gotten during the Prelaunch told me that everything about my offer was resonating with my prospects. It was clear that my launch was hitting on all cylinders, but since it was a JV Launch, I felt an extra layer of responsibility. My partners had trusted me with their support, and it was my job to make that trust pay off. I'll cover this in more detail a little later, but you have to treat your JV relationships like gold. That's why I was extra nervous as the minutes ticked away before my open.

Of course, if my partners had any doubt about the result, they were blown away in the opening minutes of the launch. Within the first hour, I had already done more than $70,000 in sales. By the end of the first day, after only 14 hours, the sales were over $200,000. When I closed down the launch a week later, the final sales total was just over $600,000. Not a bad way to start a new business—especially since it was in a brand-new market, with a brand-new product, and I had spent zero dollars on advertising. I did all this from my home office out in the mountains of

Colorado, and my only staff was my wife, Mary, helping me with customer service. It was a great start for my new business.

Of course, the devil is always in the details, and as is true with any business venture, I certainly had costs. All those sales didn't flow directly into my wallet. One of the biggest costs in a JV Launch is your affiliate commissions. Your JV partners are not going to mail their lists about your launch out of the goodness of their hearts. The core part of the JV Launch, which makes it work for everyone, is that you track who the leads and sales came from, and you pay commissions on the sales you make to those leads. In this case, I was paying a commission of 50 percent for each sale that came from a referring partner. Back with that very first launch of Product Launch Formula, the price was $997, so I paid a commission of $498.50 for every sale that a partner referred to me.

Students often ask me what's a typical commission to pay JV partners. My answer is always the same: There is no "typical." A commission varies by launch, by market, by niche, and even by partner. What you pay, and exactly how you structure your JV compensation, is a business decision. I was able to pay a 50 percent commission because the margin on my product was relatively large. In my business, a large part of our expenses go toward generating the lead and making the sale. But other businesses will be different. If you're selling physical goods (computers, barbecue grills, humidors, etc.), then the commissions you pay are going to be a lot lower. There are also some markets where the initial commissions are a lot higher than 50 percent. Such can be the case where there is a lot more revenue in the "back end" sales—that is, the follow-up sales after the original one.

No matter how you structure your JV compensation, one big advantage of this type of promotion is that you pay your commission AFTER the sale is made. Compare that to standard advertising, where you spend a bunch of money before you even know if the advertising is going to work. No matter if it's Facebook, Instagram, TV, radio, newspaper, direct mail, or some other medium, your money is spent and you're left hoping to get a return on that up-front investment. With JV or affiliate relationships, what you pay is based only on the results, and you pay after the sale is made.

AFFILIATE OR JV PARTNER: WHAT'S THE DIFFERENCE?

Exactly what is the difference between a Joint Venture (JV) partner and an affiliate? They're actually pretty much the same. In each case, it's someone who is going to promote your product and get paid a commission if one of the prospects they refer to you buys something. So if Affiliate John sends Prospect Alice to your website to look at your product, and Prospect Alice buys your product, then you'll pay Affiliate John a commission. You set the level of the commission (either a percentage of the sale or a fixed dollar amount per sale), and that commission level is part of your agreement with Affiliate John.

The mechanics of this arrangement are the same whether we're talking about JV partners or affiliates, and you can really use the terms interchangeably. However, "JV partner" generally implies a closer relationship. I know almost all of my top JV partners personally, and during a launch I'm communicating with them closely—always via email and often on the phone or via text. Many of them are close friends of mine.

WHY JV LAUNCHES WORK

When you look at all the advantages of a JV Launch (far bigger sales, crazy-fast list building, huge expert positioning in your market), this might sound like the answer to everyone's problems. However, there are some core elements you need to have in place before you even think about a JV Launch, and there are many mistakes to be avoided. Let's walk through this one step at a time.

The first thing you have to remember is that, just like you, your potential JV partners are in business to make a profit. If they've built up a substantial, responsive list, that is a considerable asset they've put a lot of time and investment into. The odds are very high that they understand just how powerful an asset their list is, and they're not going to be interested in mailing their list about any old offer that comes wandering down the lane. In other words, just because you put together a PLF-style launch and an offer, don't expect them to be falling all over themselves to promote your launch. The fact is, if they have a strong list they probably have more opportunities to promote offers than they can possibly accommodate. That's reality. (And if they don't have a strong list, they're not going to be very good partners, so you shouldn't be bothering with them.) A list can be mailed to only so many times, and anyone with a substantial list most likely gets requests every day to promote someone else's product. To have a good list is to possess a scarce resource.

This is where a well-constructed PLF-style launch shines. Since a PLF launch is such an incredible conversion machine, you're going to be generating some outsize results, and that generally means outsize commissions for your JV partners. One of the ways this is measured online is in EPC—or earnings per click—which is the amount of commissions someone gets for everyone who clicks through to a promotion. If someone sends 100 clicks, and those clicks generate commissions of $450 for the partner, then that's an EPC of 450/100, or a $4.50 EPC.

I'm often asked, "What's a good EPC?" There is no single answer to that question because an EPC will vary depending on the market and offer. What's important is that if your launch can generate a strong EPC relative to the other offers in your market, then it's going to be a lot easier to persuade partners to mail for you. And again, a solid PLF-style launch is an EPC-generating monster.

DON'T TEST WITH YOUR PARTNERS' LISTS

If you're going to have any success in the JV game, you need to build long-term relationships with your partners. I see plenty of people approaching this like a "one and done" type of relationship, but that makes it really tough to have any type of longevity in your business.

The reality is that when your partners promote your offer, they're going to be watching their numbers, meaning they're going to be watching their EPC. They're also going to be watching what type of experience you provide for the people they referred to you, because that experience will reflect on them. If they tell the people on their lists to go watch your videos, and your videos are boring and content free, it will negatively impact what those visitors think about your partners. Your partners have real skin in the game. Mailing for your launch has real costs and substantial risks to them, and if the results from their promotion aren't good, then they probably won't be promoting for you again. Before you ask someone to mail for you, you need to be sure you have an offer that converts.

Fortunately, there's an easy way to make sure your launch will perform for your partner, and that's to do an Internal Launch first. In other words, you first run the launch for just your list (even if you have a very small list). That way, you get to test your Launch Sequences and your offer. That's how you can be sure you have a winner before you ask your JV partners to take a chance on promoting your offer to their lists.

When I tell my students to do an Internal Launch first, many of them want to skip over that little bit of coaching. They want to jump directly to the excitement and glory (and big dollars) of the JV Launch. There are several reasons to avoid doing that. When you do an Internal Launch, it gives you the opportunity to test out all your systems and get some experience under your belt. That's really important, but what's truly critical is that you have the opportunity to test your offer and your Prelaunch Sequence to make sure you've got a winner. This is the deal: You never want to test an offer with a partner's list. You don't want your partners being your guinea pigs. If you have an offer that isn't going to convert, you want to be the one taking that bullet.

Remember, your relationships with your JV partners should be treated like gold. You need to nurture and cherish them so they turn into long-term bonds. I said this above, but it's so critical that it bears repeating: If you ask JV partners to mail an offer and it doesn't convert, then there's a good chance they're not going to mail for your next offer. On the other hand, if you've got a tested and proven offer (i.e., one that you ran an Internal Launch for) and you can show them your results, then they're going to be a lot more interested in mailing. They're going to be a lot more likely to get some great results, too, and the better their results, the more likely they'll mail for you in the future.

GETTING JV PARTNERS

It's obvious that the JV Launch has some really huge benefits, so how do you go about getting great JV partners? This is a big topic, and I've spent entire days teaching about finding and nurturing JV relationships. But I'm going to do my best to break it down for you in a few pages.

First of all, you have to realize that you don't need thousands, or hundreds, or even tens of JV partners. You've undoubtedly heard of the 80/20 rule, which says that 80 percent of your results come from 20 percent of your effort. Well, when it comes to affiliates and JV partners, it's generally more like the 99/1 rule, where 99 percent of your results come from 1 percent of your partners. In my business, we're extremely selective about who we take on as partners—and even so, the vast majority of our sales in any given launch will be generated by our top 10 partners. It gets even more selective at the very top, where the top three affiliates might generate a quarter of our sales. The way these numbers split out in any given launch will vary widely, but my point is that your top affiliates will generate the majority of your sales. That means you don't need a lot of affiliate partners; you need only a few good ones. I often have students ask me how they can get 100 or 1,000 affiliates. I always tell them to not worry about getting a lot of affiliates but to get three to five high-quality partners that will really support them.

Finding potential partners is easy. They are the other people who are publishing in your market. Just type the top keyword search for your market into Google. For example, if your site is about teaching people to play guitar, just do a search for "learn guitar." Go to each of the top 50 listings and look around the site for a way to opt in. If they have an opt-in box, then they're building an email list, and they are a potential JV partner. At this point you should go ahead and join the list. Of course, if you join 50 lists (and you should), you're going to be getting a lot of email. You might want to set up a special email address for this so that your regular inbox won't be flooded.

After you're on those lists, watch what they send to their subscribers. Track who and what they're promoting. Watch to see if they promote only their products or if they promote products from other businesses. Evaluate the quality of their marketing as well as the quality of the relationship they're building with their list. Follow them on social media. See if you can reverse-engineer their marketing and their offers.

What you're trying to do is create a target list of potential partners. Remember, you need only three to five high-quality partners, although you may need to approach 50 potential partners to find those few who are really going to rock for you.

As you go through this process, remember that good JV partners always have more people who are trying to get them to promote than they could possibly support. That's a reality of business. Their JV support is truly a scarce resource. So when you ask them to promote, you're just another hungry mouth looking for a meal. That means you need to create some value for them if you want to stand out.

One of the best ways to build value for potential partners is to have a great Launch Sequence that generates a lot of commissions for them. But even before you get there, you need to find other ways to create value just to get on their radar. One of the very best ways to build value for them is to promote their product first—if you generate a bunch of sales for them, they will definitely take notice. Another easy thing you can do is buy their product, put it to use, and then give some constructive feedback and/or a positive testimonial. You can also engage with them and give them regular feedback on their social media. The bottom line is that there are 100 ways to create value for a potential partner—and the more value you create, the more you'll get back.

A MILLION DOLLARS IN 53 MINUTES

There are few things that can make as big an impact on your business (and your financial life) in as short a period of time as a successful JV Launch. And the impact goes far beyond the sales you generate in the launch. The long-term effect of the increased positioning in the market and the rapid list growth will reverberate in your business for years to come.

Still, if you're going to have success with JV Launches and JV relationships, then you absolutely must remember the two things I've hammered on throughout this chapter. First, you need to build long-term relationships with your JV partners. And second, you need to create real, long-term value for those partners. That doesn't mean it's going to take you years to build those relationships or that you are years away from doing a JV Launch. It can all happen surprisingly quickly, but it takes effort, and you should be thinking long term.

When I did my first JV Launch, it literally created a business for me. That was the launch I mentioned at the start of this chapter, when I first rolled out Product Launch Formula in 2005 and the launch generated just over $600,000. I was instantly in business with sales, and I had a bunch of happy partners to whom I paid some big commissions. It also generated a list of more than 15,000 people. And it gave me huge positioning in the market. After that launch I was seen as one of the leaders in the industry, and Product Launch Formula was a recognized brand in the market. Sales continued to come in, and in my first year I did over a million dollars in sales. Those results all traced back to that initial JV Launch.

However, that was just setting the scene for what was to come next. In early 2008 I started working on an all-new version: Product Launch Formula 2.0 Coaching Program. I remade the product from the ground up, based on everything I had learned since I first released PLF. This entirely new offer would have greatly expanded content, over-the-top bonuses, and live coaching calls with me and my coaches. With this new offer, I increased the price to $1,997, and naturally it was time for another big JV Launch.

After two-plus years of building and nurturing my JV relationships, I had a lot of support to call on. During Prelaunch we generated more than 34,000 opt-ins—a truly amazing number to get over a matter of days. As I reviewed all the data coming in during the Prelaunch, it sure looked like it was going to be a great launch. But you just never know exactly what's going to happen, and as usual I had plenty of nerves going into launch day. It seemed like every possible JV in the known world was promoting my launch, and PLF had been a proven seller for years. Still, this was a new offer and a new price point, so I was plenty anxious.

Launch day was March 27, 2008. As usual, the days leading into launch day had been a blur. There's always a lot to be done, especially during a JV Launch. And the morning of launch day found me with my usual set of nerves, but I didn't have much chance to dwell on them; there were too many last-minute details to attend to. I remember that the minutes leading into the launch were complete chaos as we touched up the sales letter and the order form. And then it was time. All systems were go, and I hit the Send button on the email.

I didn't have long to wait. The orders started coming in within seconds. They were piling in as fast as I could refresh the stats on my page. Later on, when I went back and analyzed the data, I found one single second in which we had more than $12,000 in sales. $12K in one second! We hit a million dollars in 53 minutes. And the sales didn't stop there. By the time I closed down the launch, after being open for only 34 hours, we were at $3.73 million in sales.

Of course, that wasn't all profit. By that time I had a small team of three contractors to pay (although I was still working out of my home office and my team was all virtual). I also had affiliate commissions to pay, and there were other costs. Since I've always offered a generous money-back guarantee, I knew we would have some returns. But the numbers were still completely staggering. I clearly remembered how, just a few short years earlier, my ultimate dream for my business had been to make an extra $10,000 a year to help support my family. Or even more recently, when I had to start over again after my first business imploded following that fateful call from my business partner. And now here I was sitting with a launch that did nearly $4 million in just 34 hours. Unreal.

That's the power of the JV Launch. It's just about the most powerful weapon in the whole PLF arsenal. And your JV launches can be even more powerful when you add in elements of the "Live Launch," which I'll cover in the next chapter . . .

CHAPTER 11

Going Live: How Live Launches Are Changing the Game

One of the most powerful evolutions in launches in the last few years is the Live Launch. This is where you deliver your Prelaunch Content and/or your Open Cart content as live broadcasts. The ability to do a live video broadcast is something I couldn't have imagined when I first started out.

My first launches were delivered purely via email. All the Prelaunch Content was sent as simple, plain-text emails. The innovation from those early launches started almost immediately—soon we added blogs and PDF reports, then audio, then very simple video, which gave way to more polished and professional video. And now we're using live broadcasts, streaming our launches live in real time around the world. Amazing.

It's important to note that every launch innovation is a new tool—but the core formula remains essentially unchanged. Also, having new tools doesn't make the old tools obsolete, and you're not required to use every new thing. In other words, live broadcasts can be an incredibly powerful tool in your launch, but if it's not the right tool for you or for your launch, then you don't need to use it.

That being said, as I type this I've personally leaned very heavily into Live Launches in my business, and they have been working very well for me and many of my students. In this chapter I'm going to share everything I've learned after doing some of the most successful Live Launches in the industry.

SHOULD YOU DO A LIVE LAUNCH?

One of the core premises of the Product Launch Formula is that you need to turn your marketing into an event. In a world that is continually filled with more noise, more advertising, more offers, this is the only way you can hope to stand out. If you follow the formula in this book, any launch you do will tap into the power of being an event, but a Live Launch takes it to the next level.

By it's very nature, anything that's "live" is an event—it's ephemeral. If you want to experience a concert or a play, then you have to be there. It happens at a certain point in time, and in a certain place—and if you want to experience it then you need to be present at that place and time. This might feel like a simple point, but it's very real, and it's very powerful. Of course, concerts and plays can be recorded, and so can a Live Launch. But the recording is a different thing, with a different feel and a different urgency. Live is live, and that has real power.

Now, as I already mentioned, the Live Launch isn't the be-all and end-all. It's not the answer to every situation. So why and when would you want to use a Live Launch?

The first potential reason is speed to market. One thing a Live Launch doesn't allow is endless editing and retakes. If you commit to a live broadcast and you get people to register for it, you're going to show up and do the broadcast. Once it goes live, you're going to deliver your material. It won't be perfect, but you're going to get it done and delivered, instead of endlessly spinning your wheels on creating PLC. (And there are always opportunities to recover from any mistakes!)

Another reason to consider a Live Launch is that it allows you to change your messaging in the midst of your launch if you're in a very dynamic situation that might require it. For instance, in the COVID-19 pandemic of 2020, every public message by every company shifted throughout the crisis. I personally did a major launch in the midst of the early days of the crisis. News of the pandemic dominated the public discourse, and the world seemed to turn upside down on a weekly (or even daily) basis. I used a Live Launch during this time, and it allowed me to lean into the news and tune my message to the conversation that was happening in the moment. If I had tried to launch with video that was recorded even just a few weeks earlier, it would have come off as tone deaf. It just wouldn't have matched the conversation that was going on in the minds of my audience.

One more reason to consider a Live Launch is if "being live" is something that you're good at and something that energizes you. This is the biggest reason that I've personally leaned into Live Launches. I had been using fancy video in my launches for years, and it had been working really well. But I knew from the large live events I did (which typically had 800–1,200 attendees from around the world) that I was really good in a live, in-the-moment setting. Reacting to what was happening "in the room" was a sweet spot for me—and I suspected I could create a similar experience with a live broadcast. As it turned out, the experience did translate; my Live Launches were really successful, in every sense of the word. I delivered a huge amount of content to my viewers, I generated crazy-good word-of-mouth, and my conversions on a per-viewer basis increased significantly.

Now, I don't want to be the Pied Piper leading everyone into a Live Launch. It's a very powerful tool that fits into some situations, but it's not for everyone nor for every situation. When you're live, you are playing without a net. Things can (and probably will) go wrong. If you forget to say something, you'll have to deal with it. If you forget what you're supposed to say, you'll have to work your way through it.

However, if the appeal to you of a Live Launch is that there seems to be so much less work—you just turn on the camera and talk—don't be fooled. There's still plenty of preparation needed, and the material that you deliver has to be just as carefully crafted as it would be if you were creating Prelaunch videos. In other words, everything you say or do or write in your launch is "copy." It's either going to move people forward toward the sale or move people away from the sale. When you're performing live, you're delivering your copy live. That means you're essentially creating and editing yourself on the fly. This shouldn't be your first rodeo.

GOING LIVE

The primary differentiating factor of a Live Launch is that you are delivering some parts of your launch via a live broadcast. Typically this means your Prelaunch Content and possibly your Open Cart material.

Technology is always changing, and this book and the PLF process will outlive any platform that I mention here, but right now the two primary platforms we're using for Live Launches are YouTube and Facebook. Both platforms allow anyone to do a live broadcast—it's as simple as logging into your account and clicking a button to begin.

Of course, there's more to a Live Launch than starting a live broadcast. The first thing you need to do is use all the material you've learned in this book—in other words, follow the formula. Your Prelaunch should follow the Opportunity/Transformation/ Ownership flow that you learned in Chapter 7, and then your Open Cart Sequence should follow the formula in Chapter 8.

Remember that your live broadcasts are just part of your launch—they need to be supported via email and social media. In other words, you need to be using email and social to drive people to your broadcasts. And you can't be shy about this—the people who show up live for your broadcasts are going to be the ones who have the highest conversion for your offer. So you need to get people to register for the live broadcast ahead of time, and then you need to follow up with reminders to get them to attend.

For a broadcast on a Thursday, you'll typically start pushing people to register for the broadcast on Monday, and keep pushing each day right up until the broadcast. You'll do that via every channel and tool you've got—email, social media, paid traffic. Meanwhile, you'll need to send reminders of the upcoming live broadcast to the people who have already registered (this is your Launch List). Send a reminder the day before the broadcast (in this case, on Wednesday), and two reminders on the day of the broadcast (in this case, Thursday), with the second reminder going out 30 minutes before the broadcast.

TURNING IT INTO A SHOW

Because of my position in the market, I always want to be leading—and I want to stand out from what others are doing.

So when we did our first Live Launch, we wanted to do something that hadn't been seen. We wanted to turn our broadcasts into a "show." For instance, in a time when most live online broadcasts had a slow and sloppy start, we decided ours would be more like a TV program. It would start on time, to the second. We had a countdown timer, and the moment the timer clicked to 0:00, the broadcast began.

We broke our show into segments, used multiple sets and multiple cameras, and had a behind-the-scenes segment. We also added case studies, prerecorded video clips, and even a "Super Secret Segment." And as we continued to evolve our Live Launches, we added even more elements.

OR YOU COULD KEEP IT SIMPLE

While we get fancier with each launch, the reality is that you can keep your Live Launches very simple. When I started teaching Live Launches, I assumed it would be a strategy only for my most advanced students. It turns out I was wrong. Many of my less experienced students started using Live Launches right from the start.

For instance, Anne LaFollette is a 60-something woman who was downsized out of the corporate world. After she was laid off, Anne started to lean more into her lifelong interest in creating visual art, particularly surface pattern design, and she rapidly developed her skills in her new hobby. Eventually she decided to create an online course and start teaching others how to do surface pattern design, and that's when she found her way into my world.

Anne started out with no online business experience, no entrepreneurial experience, no list or following, no social media presence—she was starting from absolute zero. Anne began by doing live broadcasts in which she practiced teaching her material.

Anne LaFollette

Her first live broadcast had literally zero viewers, but she was very clear that the size of the audience didn't matter—she was learning the process. She kept doing a live broadcast on Facebook every week. Her broadcasts weren't part of a launch—she was using them to build her skills and build her audience. In the early days, her broadcasts only had one viewer, her cousin Katie.

This is an important point: Anne had no experience with being on camera, no video experience, no live broadcasting experience. But starting out simply meant starting a Facebook Live broadcast with her MacBook computer. She likes to say that she was just "talking to the green dot"—the small green light next to the camera on her computer that indicated the camera was on.

Anne started with no list, but gradually started to grow a small following. She also started spending $5 per day on paid traffic (see Chapter 13). Eventually, she had more people showing up for her weekly live broadcast.

When Anne's email list reached approximately 1,000 people, she did a small test launch. Since she had gotten comfortable with live broadcasts, and since it seemed easier than putting together polished videos, she did a Live Launch. Her first one did $500 in sales. That was a proof of concept for Anne: it showed that she could sell her training course.

In the next year she did four more launches that totaled just under $100,000. That's an amazing result for someone who started from scratch with no list, no following, no entrepreneurial experience . . . and who had been downsized out of the corporate world in her late fifties.

But Anne was just getting started. In the next 12 months (her second full year in business), she brought in nearly $400,000 in revenue. That's a truly remarkable result.

As I said earlier, when I started teaching Live Launches, I thought it would be a strategy for my most advanced students, but Anne (and others) have proved me wrong. While they're not for everyone, in some ways Live Launches take down some of the initial obstacles to getting launched. The tech can be a lot simpler, and your audience a lot more forgiving.

I'll come back to Anne's example later in this chapter to share some of her timelines. And you can see the full case study with Anne at http://www.thelaunchbook.com/anne. Be sure to check it out because there's lots of extra details that I couldn't fit into this chapter.

SOME LIVE LAUNCH GOTCHAS

Like every tool, there are some disadvantages to Live Launches. The first is pretty obvious—since you're broadcasting live, things will happen that are out of your control. Just when it feels like everything is humming along and going well, something will break. No matter how much redundancy you build in, there are always unanticipated problems.

My launches, of course, are not immune to this. In our most recent launch, with thousands of people watching our second broadcast, we entirely lost our Internet connection. That sent us scrambling for 10 stressful minutes. We've also lost power during a broadcast, and on another occasion we lost our audio feed right as I was making my offer.

Those miscues all fall under "technology" troubles. But you could face other challenges. In my most recent Live Launch, we had a census taker walk up to the house we were using for the broadcast and knock on the door. Because the door had a large window, she could see me on set doing my broadcast, and she wondered why I wouldn't come and answer the door.

That same door and large window played into what would become a memorable moment in our first Live Launch. The window looks out on a deck that's surrounded by woods. In the middle of my first live broadcast a squirrel showed up on the deck and proceeded to scurry back and forth for an extended time. This was in my direct field of view—the main camera was set up just in front of the window—and as I tried to focus on the camera it was impossible not to see the squirrel playing on the deck.

My reaction in the moment was to lean into the distraction: I stopped in the middle of my presentation and mentioned the squirrel playing directly behind the camera. Since I was talking to entrepreneurs who can easily be distracted by bright, shiny objects as well as cute animals like squirrels, it became a great teaching moment. We quickly set up an extra camera that we could switch to whenever the squirrel showed up. The "Squirrel Cam" became a viewer favorite, to the extent that each time we do a launch we'll have people asking for the Squirrel Cam.

Here's the thing to remember with all these "gotchas"— you're in a live broadcast environment, and your viewers understand that. They get that you're playing without a net, and they're going to be more forgiving. In a world where authenticity and transparency are ever more highly valued, these are the moments that show you're a real (and relatable) human. I had no idea that we would have a squirrel show up for our Live Launch, but I think the way I handled it probably helped our results more than it hurt.

OTHER STUFF TO CONSIDER IN YOUR LIVE LAUNCH

In addition to tech problems and small woodland creatures showing up for your broadcasts, there are a few other things to think about with Live Launches.

The first is the timing—when you're delivering your Prelaunch Content live, your delivery will never be as tight as in a carefully shot (and edited) video. In my recent video-based launches, my first PLC will be somewhere around 20 minutes long—that's a tightly scripted, tightly edited video. If I deliver the same material live, it will take me twice as long. Part of that increase in time is that I always find myself teaching more deeply when I'm live. But another big part of it is that I'm just less "edited"—I'm less efficient with my words.

Now, with that being said, viewers will understand that you're live, and they'll generally be more forgiving of a "less edited" version of you. Especially when being less edited means you can react to questions and comments in the moment.

Another consideration with Live Launches is that you probably won't be reusing your material as you can in a video launch. The "shelf life" of a recorded video might be years—I've reused my videos over a span of a year or two—but in general a Live Launch is a one-time performance. You could attempt to reuse the recordings from a Live Launch, but in that case, either you'll have to go to great lengths to pretend it's live (and I'm REALLY not a fan of this—it's inherently dishonest), or you'll have to be clear that it's a recording—in which case you lose much of the power of "live."

HOW TO DO A LIVE LAUNCH

First things first, you're still doing a PLF-style launch. You'll want to follow the formula that I've given you in this book. Your Prelaunch will have three broadcasts, and they'll focus on opportunity, transformation, and the ownership experience. Your fourth broadcast will be all about enrollment.

In my broadcasts, I'll often use a flip chart to teach from. You can use whatever teaching aids make you comfortable. I personally find that the flip chart keeps me focused and on topic—I'll typically create some notes on the pages of the flip chart that act as an agenda for the broadcast.

Remember that people will understand that you're live, and they're not expecting perfection. I'll generally have additional notes on a desk or computer nearby, and I'll be quite open about consulting them. If you don't pretend to be perfect, then you don't have to be perfect.

Your setup can vary widely—plenty of people have done Live Launches using their phone camera or the webcam on their laptop, and sometimes those phones and laptops are balanced on top of a stack of books to get to the right height! Because my business has grown up over the years, we build out a pretty sophisticated live set with multiple cameras and lots of gear.

But either way, one of the things that work really well in a Live Launch is delivering a huge amount of value in your Prelaunch Content. As I mentioned earlier, your audience will generally stick around longer in a live broadcast then they would if they were watching a video, so you have a bigger palette to work with in terms of delivering your content. This doesn't mean you should be cavalier in how you spend that time, but in general it gives you a little more space to deliver value.

Remember that the longer your broadcast is, the harder it is to keep your viewers' attention. Most of my students are doing live broadcasts that are about an hour in length.

THE TIMING OF YOUR LIVE LAUNCH

One of the major innovations we've made in just the last few months is to compress the timing of our Live Launches. The first couple of times I did a Live Launch, the timing was similar to that of a video-based launch. The Prelaunch phase might take place over seven to ten days. A typical schedule for a JV Launch might look like this:

Day 1: Prelaunch Content #1 (Opportunity)

Day 4: Prelaunch Content #2 (Transformation)

Day 7: Prelaunch Content #3 (Ownership)

Day 9: Open Cart (Enrollment)

There's a lot of flexibility built into PLF, but that's a tested schedule that's worked for years. However, our Live Launches have evolved to have more of the feel of a live, in-person seminar or workshop, and I've started to follow a much more compressed schedule where I deliver the live sessions over consecutive days:

Day 1: Prelaunch Content #1 (Opportunity)

Day 2: Prelaunch Content #2 (Transformation)

Day 3: Prelaunch Content #3 (Ownership)

Day 4: Open Cart (Enrollment)

This schedule has been working very well for me. Remember that the essence of PLF is turning your marketing into an event, and this schedule truly does give the feeling of taking part in an event.

However, it's important to note that you do NOT have to follow a compressed schedule like this. In fact, if you're just starting out, it would be quite stressful to pull something like that off. A tightened schedule like this means you have little rest or preparation time between broadcasts. Also remember that there are other things that will be going on during your launch—you'll be sending emails, responding to comments, and attending to a myriad of other details. Unless you have deep experience and support, it's better to have some time to collect yourself and course-correct between broadcasts.

THE ART OF THE OPEN CART

Another recent innovation in our Live Launches is a greatly expanded Open Cart sequence. As I covered in Chapter 8, your Open Cart is when you actually launch—when you open your shopping cart and start taking orders.

For most launches, your Open Cart should be five to seven days long. You could go shorter, but that's a move only for the most experienced, because if you go shorter it gives less time to correct for things that don't go as planned. And you don't want to go longer, because you want urgency in your launch. If you go longer, your Open Cart can turn into a beg-a-thon (you don't want to keep sending emails that say "please buy my stuff").

In a Live Launch, that five- to seven-day window still works, but I've greatly expanded the amount of follow-up and content during Open Cart. However, and this is a key point, it's important to remember that this is still the enrollment phase. I'm still teaching during Open Cart, but the teaching is more directed toward getting your prospects to enroll in their future and ultimately in your offer.

Think of it this way. At the start of the launch you showed your prospect an opportunity to change their life. It's an opportunity (PLC #1) to have either more pleasure or less pain—to be a better parent, to quit smoking, to learn to meditate, to recover from an abusive relationship, to lower their golf score. Then as you moved through your Prelaunch, you showed them how their life would be transformed (PLC #2) if they got that result, and then what it would be like to truly own (PLC #3) that change.

That's your Prelaunch. Now in Open Cart you're asking your prospect to enroll in that future: to take the next step, to take the action that will give them that future. At the end of the day, for someone to buy from you means they are enrolling in the future change that they will get if they buy your product.

What does this actually mean in terms of your Open Cart and your Live Launch? It will generally take the form of an additional broadcast (or broadcasts) where you are answering questions, delivering some coaching that highlights how you or your offer can deliver the transformation. You might also highlight the successes of your clients.

This is what it might look like:

Open Cart Day 1: PLC #4 Live Broadcast (Enrollment)

Open Cart Day 2: Sales Video

Open Cart Day 3: FAQ Live Broadcast

Open Cart Day 4: Case Study Live Broadcast

Open Cart Day 5: Final, Closing Broadcast (Celebration and Final Q&A)

That's just an example schedule, but let's go ahead and break that down:

The PLC #4 Live Broadcast is where you actually make your offer—this is your official Open Cart, and you start taking orders. The content of this broadcast is the same as your PLC #4 would be in a standard launch.

For the second day of Open Cart, I've been releasing a sales video. This is an enrollment video designed to make the sale. It builds on all the Prelaunch material you've given up to this point, and in it you make your offer. You might ask why I would drop a video into a Live Launch, and that would be a great question. Not everyone who is following your launch will attend all your live broadcasts, and I like to have a succinct sales message to send people to. A sales video will always be shorter and tighter than the replay of your live PLC #4 broadcast, so I put in the extra effort to create that video. Note that you do NOT have to do this—it's extra work and extra complexity. If it's your first launch, this is probably not something you should worry about.

The third day is another live broadcast, and in it you could simply focus on answering the top questions that your viewers have. A very important point about the questions you answer: you want to focus on the top objections people have to buying your product or service. This isn't about adding in new concepts or additional teaching—you did the bulk of your teaching during the Prelaunch phase. These questions and answers should be about moving the sale forward.

Day four of your Open Cart could be dedicated to case studies. You can share examples of your customers or clients and the results they've gotten. This could be done in a live broadcast where you also play prerecorded videos that you've made with your successful clients. In this case you're acting like an MC playing the case study videos. Alternatively, you could host your clients live on the broadcast, where they are sharing their stories live. Personally, I absolutely love sharing my students' success stories, so I go really big with case studies. I introduce them all throughout my Prelaunch, and then during my Open Cart week I'll host a live broadcast where I bring a group of students on live with me and turn them into the stars of the show.

On my final day, I'll do one more live broadcast to close down the entire launch. This is Cart Close day, so you have the element of scarcity going on (see Chapter 5), and it's always an exciting day. In this final broadcast where you bring it all to an end, you can answer questions, welcome your new clients, and celebrate the experience you've all had. Now, it might seem strange to have a celebration at the end of a marketing campaign, but if you've done this right then you've delivered a true experience for all the people following along (whether they've decided to buy or not).

ANNE'S TIMING

Earlier in this chapter I told you about Anne LaFollette, who has a great business teaching people how to do surface pattern design (and possibly make money from it). Starting from scratch—with no list, no product, no social media presence, and no entrepreneurial experience—Anne launched a business that did $400,000 in sales in its second full year. Along the way Anne's done more than a half dozen launches, most of them live.

One of the things Anne has done in her Live Launches is to tighten the timing (similar to what I've done with my launches). Currently, her preferred timing is:

Monday: PLC #1—Live Broadcast

Wednesday: PLC #2—Live Broadcast

Friday: PLC #3—Live Broadcast

Monday: PLC #4—Open Cart—Live Broadcast

Tuesday: Open Cart—Sneak Peek—Live Broadcast

Wednesday: Open Cart—Livestream with Former Students

Thursday: Open Cart—Closing Day with Questions
and Answers

You'll note that Anne's timing is a little different from the examples I gave up above. This just shows that there is no one perfect launch sequence. The things to focus on are the core fundamentals of PLF and the narrative story arc of your Prelaunch Content.

Again, there's a lot more detail in the full case study with Anne at this link: http://www.thelaunchbook.com/anne.

CAN YOU BE PART LIVE?

So far I've talked about using live broadcasts in a Live Launch, where most (if not all) of your launch content is delivered live. But you don't have to go totally or mostly live. You can instead use live broadcasts as a supplement to a traditional launch. For instance, you could release your Prelaunch Content as a series of videos and then add live broadcasts as supplemental content.

Here's an example of what a hybrid sequence could look like for your Prelaunch:

Day 1: Video—PLC #1 (Opportunity)

Day 2: Live Broadcast—Questions and Answers

Day 3: Video—PLC #2 (Transformation)

Day 4: Live Broadcast—Questions and Answers

Day 5: PLC #3 (Ownership)

Day 6: Live Broadcast—Questions and Answers

Day 7: Video—Open Cart (Enrollment)

In that example, you do a simple question-and-answer session the day after you release each Prelaunch video.

Another hybrid approach is to use live broadcasts during your Open Cart week. Here's an example of what that might look like:

Day 1: Video—PLC #1 (Opportunity)

Day 3: Video—PLC #2 (Transformation)

Day 5: Video—PLC #3 (Ownership)

Day 7: Video—Open Cart (Enrollment)

Day 8: Live Broadcast—New Content

Day 9: Live Broadcast—Case Studies

Day 10: Live Broadcast—Questions and Answers

Day 11: Live Broadcast—Final, Closing Broadcast

I want to be clear that none of this is set in stone; you can improvise. In fact, that's one of the most powerful aspects of adding live broadcasts into your launches. It allows you to react in the middle of your launch to what's happening in the world and what's top of mind for your prospects.

DON'T FORGET ABOUT THE REPLAY EXPERIENCE

When you do a Live Launch, there is one thing you can count on: not everyone will be able to attend the live broadcasts. This is especially true if you have an international audience, when time zones will become an issue for many. (This is always top of mind for me during my launches—I'll typically have people register to attend my Launch Masterclass from 150 or more countries.)

Since many people will NOT attend live, you want to put some real thought into creating a great experience for the people who are watching the replay. I see a lot of people make this mistake—they spend all their time and energy thinking through their live broadcasts and how to make them great, but they completely neglect the experience of the people watching the replays. The reality is that you will likely have as many people watching the replays as watching you live (or more).

How do you improve the replay experience? First, think about editing the beginning of the session. Many live broadcasts have a rather slow start as the host warms up the crowd and does a bit of a tech check. For the people watching live, that's part of the live experience, and it's expected, but it's painful to sit through if you're watching the replay. Fortunately, removing that part is an easy edit to make in the replay recording. You could also edit other parts of the replay so that it moves faster.

You could also consider giving the viewer more control over the replay experience—things like full video controls (the ability to pause, fast-forward, and rewind the video) and the ability to increase the playback speed. I'm not advocating for automatically including those things, just raising it as a possibility. Those types of controls can change the replay experience, and you may have valid reasons to NOT give that control (e.g., you may want your content watched in a strictly chronological manner, or you may have music or audio that wouldn't present well at a higher speed).

My point is this: many people will watch your replays instead of watching you live. Think about what their experience will be like, and make conscious choices about the experience you're going to deliver. Your effort here will pay off in higher conversions.

A GREAT TOOL (WHEN IT'S THE RIGHT TOOL)

Live broadcasts are a great tool to consider adding to your launches, whether you do a full-blown Live Launch or just use a few live elements. They allow you to react quickly to the Launch Conversation and to changing market conditions. Live broadcasts also allow you to respond to anything that goes awry in your launch.

It's important to remember that live broadcasts are an option—you don't need to use them. If you're not comfortable being live on camera, then don't do it. We all have different strengths and capabilities, and if live broadcasts aren't calling to you then you shouldn't use them.

Above all, remember that you're still following the same Product Launch Formula. You'll still be using all the sequences, stories, and triggers that you would use in an email-based or a video-based launch.

CHAPTER 12

Using Social Media in Your Launch

When I published the first edition of this book in 2014, social media was already a big deal. Since then, it's become a much bigger deal. This isn't news to you—everywhere you look people are focused on their phones. And I mean literally focused; that's what they're staring at whether they're in a coffee shop, on a train, or walking down the street. If you look over their shoulder to see what they're looking at, the majority of the time it's some form of social media.

The one constant in the social media world is change. There are plenty of social media platforms, but the landscape continues to evolve, as new platforms appear and old ones disappear. Still, at any given time, certain social platforms will be a better fit than others for particular niches and demographics. There will be some businesses that should focus on Facebook and others that should focus on LinkedIn, while Instagram or Pinterest will be right for still others, and so on.

The bottom line is that social media isn't going anywhere, and it's a fantastic tool for building your business. But it can also be a minefield, and you can waste a lot of time and money if you don't approach it correctly. Think of this chapter as a road map helping you not just to survive that minefield but to come out thriving as you strategically use social media in your launch and in your business.

In this chapter I'll start with a very big-picture overview of some of the strengths and advantages of social media (and there's some really powerful stuff here). Then I'll walk through the ways to use social media in each phase of your launch, from the Pre-Prelaunch through the Prelaunch and your Open Cart period. Toward the end of the chapter I'll give you the bad news: the potential pitfalls of social (and they're significant).

One thing I won't do in this chapter (or the following chapter on paid advertising) is give you guidance on which specific social media platforms to focus on. The reason is simple: the platforms will change (and some will come and go), so anything I tell you here will be at least partially out of date by the time this book is published.

The only way I've been able to survive and thrive in the digital business world for 25 years is by playing the long game. That means starting with big-picture, enduring strategies . . . and then having those strategies drive the shorter-term tactics. I suggest you do the same.

THE BEST THINGS ABOUT SOCIAL MEDIA

The most significant benefit for your business is that you can find your people on social and then attract them into your world. In other words, your prospects are already gathering on social, actively creating communities and having conversations with people who are just like them. That means you can find them, learn about them, draw them into your universe, and turn them into clients. Along the way, you can build your presence within your niche so you're seen as an expert or leader.

People have always been connecting to each other and to businesses (just like yours). Ever since the online world started to grow in the 1990s, like-minded people have gathered in various places and in various ways. All the way back in the early days—even before the modern Internet, people connected through BBS systems and online services. Then in the early days of the Internet, that evolved into Usenet groups and forums. The bottom line is that the online world is all about connections and conversations, and it always has been. Right from the beginning, people naturally started gathering around common interests, concerns, and passions.

Of course, social media and all our connected devices have taken that to an entirely new level. Now anyone with a phone can nearly instantly find the people in their target market and do market research—all while sitting in their favorite coffee shop.

That means you can quickly research your market and get to know your avatar (i.e., the typical prospect in your target market). Remember that the key to putting together a great offer (and a great launch) is to know the hopes, dreams, fears, and frustrations of your avatar. And when you find your prospects on social media, it's just a matter of starting the right conversations with them, asking the right questions, and then listening. The conversations that are already happening in those places will identify those hot buttons. The questions that people keep posting over and over—those are the sticking points that people have. Read between the lines and you'll see their hopes, dreams, fears, and frustrations. You'll see the things that are holding people back and the aspirations that people are really striving for.

Those last few sentences make it sound really simple—and that's because it is. When Amy Small started to really tap into the transformation that her yarn and knitting patterns made in her clients' lives, it was because she could see and read about that transformation in their social posts. Understanding your ideal client and what keeps them awake at night is the key to creating a great offer that they'll want to buy. Using social media correctly will help you find what your people most want. Find your audience, then listen, and you can do it just like Amy did.

After coaching literally thousands of entrepreneurs, one of the biggest mistakes I've seen people make is creating products and services that they want to sell (or that they think people should have) instead of creating offers that people want to buy. Now, make no mistake; many times what people want isn't what they need. In other words, if someone just bought their first guitar, they're likely looking for the shortcut that's going to get them playing songs (and impressing girls or guys around the campfire) by sometime next week.

That's what they want. What they need is entirely different, and it's going to involve learning the basics like how to hold the guitar, how to practice, how to use a metronome, and so on. This is where you have to "sell them what they want, and give them what they need," and do it in an ethical manner.

That's a bit of a sidebar, but the reality is that if you want to have a great launch and build a successful business, you need to be able to crawl inside the head of your avatar. You have to get to the point where if I woke you up at 3 A.M. and asked you what the top three hopes, dreams, and fears of your avatar are, you could recite them without thinking twice.

Social media is where you can truly get to know your avatar. It's where you'll find your avatar talking about all those things and telling you what they really want to buy.

BUILDING POSITIONING AND AUTHORITY

Here's an eternal truth of the online, connected world: if you're building your business online, then you're in the publishing business, and publishing will build your authority (being seen as a leader or expert in your space) and your positioning (how you're seen relative to others in your market). Connecting with people on social media helps you build both positioning and authority in a big way. Here's why that's important:

When you're selling online, you're in what's called the direct marketing business. You are marketing and selling your product directly to your consumer. Back in the old days, there was a big demarcation between direct marketing and brand marketing— branding was what the big companies like Coca-Cola and Apple did, and direct marketing was what the scrappy, bootstrapped, upstart businesses did.

But today those lines have blurred, and as you build your business online, you're going to be building your brand. I don't consider myself to be any type of expert at branding in the old-school sense—I'm not the one to teach you about logos and colors and typefaces. But I learned early on that your reputation and positioning online are key to building a brand. You need them both in order to grow your business.

In fact, my Product Launch Formula Coaching Program was arguably the first brand in the online entrepreneurial education market. When I released the program in 2005, it definitely wasn't the first training product on the market—there were thousands that came before it. But it was the first one that became an enduring brand in the marketplace. Before PLF, training products would come and go, but they would rarely stay on the market for longer than a few months, and they would never create a lasting reputation or mindshare.

Of course, I didn't start off with a master plan to create the first brand and build a new business model. I just knew I had a really great launch process, and I could see my clients having amazing success with it. So I kept improving the process, and my clients kept having that success, and all these years later, all of a sudden Product Launch Formula is now a brand.

In any case, let's get back to publishing, because that's the primary way you build positioning in your market. Whether you're an unknown who's just getting started or someone who wants to build a business into a brand like I did—either way, the key is publishing. And by that I mean regularly releasing content, whether it's written, video, audio, or whatever the next iteration of technology brings us. You create the content and then publish it on the social media platform of your choice.

Social media is a fantastic publishing platform. They've already built the platform for you, they've already got your audience there, and you just need to start publishing content for your future customers. What's more, on social media you can get instant feedback on whatever you publish. That enables you to fine-tune your publishing so that it hits the mark.

Another huge advantage of social is that as you begin to build a following, it will inherently build social proof and authority. On nearly every social channel, users can see the size of your following and the level of interaction that's happening.

Of course, it's never quite that simple. You have to figure out how to be discovered on the platform (i.e., how to get distribution of your content), and the ways to do that vary on each platform. If it is Instagram you might focus on reels or stories, on Facebook it might be lives or interactions in groups, on Pinterest it might be adding some short video content. The tactics change like the weather, but the bottom line is that publishing on social is a great way to grow your following and your positioning as a leader in your market. Just follow the same PLC framework for your content wherever you are interacting with your future customers.

CORSETS, WEIRD KIDS, AND SIX-FIGURE LAUNCHES

Cathy Hay sews replica corsets and dresses from the Victorian era. This has been a nearly lifelong passion of hers. Though she makes her pieces to be worn, what she creates is exquisite art, and she has an online membership site where she teaches others to do the same.

Cathy has had her membership site for 13 years. Initially it was a very modest site that generated a very modest income. But about five years ago, when she had an unforeseen financial need, Cathy decided to get serious about her business. That was when she found her way into my PLF community, and her business has grown up in a big way. Her first launches did tens of thousands of dollars, and they've continued to grow. About 18 months ago she did a launch that came in just under $100,000. Then, just as I was finishing this chapter, she wrote to tell me that she had just done a launch that topped $750,000. Incredible!

Note that all of her sales are for a monthly membership site, so she's projecting that revenue based on the normal "stick rate" of her members. But she has a long history to base her projections on, so that $750,000 is a pretty solid number—and it's not going to be her last launch. ☺

Now, there's always hard work involved in that type of growth, and it didn't happen overnight. Cathy has now built up a team of

15, so her business has real overhead to pay. But it's still a remarkable result, and in my opinion, she's not done growing.

How do you do a launch of $750k in a niche as small as sewing Victorian corsets and dresses? Especially when it's difficult to advertise something like corset making, because the major advertising platforms keep labeling it as "adult"?

Cathy Hay

These days, Cathy does her list building purely via social media. But even before social, she built her initial following by interacting on forum sites and places like "Live Journal," which was an early type of online community site.

Here's the key lesson: going online makes it possible for people to gather around areas of shared interests. This was a radical change in the way the world operated, and it happened in the 1990s and early 2000s. The rise of the digital world allowed people with passions in rather obscure niches to find one another, even if they were distributed around the world. This is something we take for granted now, but 30 years ago if you were interested in sewing exquisite Victorian-era corsets, it was hard to find people who shared your passion. You were unlikely to run into people in your neighborhood with a similar interest, and it would be difficult to find information on the topic, much less converse with others about it.

As Cathy says, "In school I was one of the weird kids. When I went online I was able to find all the other weird ones; we had a place to connect and talk to each other and learn from each other." Interacting and building relationships and connections for her readers both to her business and to one another (which is what social media does) made it possible for Cathy to have this success, and it will work for you too.

When Cathy started developing an online presence, she did it on forum sites dedicated to sewing costumes and period clothing. She answered questions and generally became a valued member of the community. Eventually, when she rolled out her membership site, it was from that early online presence she built by delivering value in those forums.

Those communities and discussions eventually migrated to social media. These days Cathy's people hang out mostly on Instagram and YouTube, so that's where she puts her focus. She posts a weekly video on YouTube, where she has more than 110,000 followers. That's a big following for such a narrow niche. She also regularly posts her work and her students' work on Instagram.

Over time, Cathy gradually pulls her followers on social over to her email list. From there she'll generally do two launches per year for her membership site, using a straight-up PLF launch. Her results are amazing, but as I said, they didn't happen overnight. And they're all driven by organic list growth from social media.

Of course, there's more to the story, and if you want to dig deeper into it, I've got a full case study with Cathy at http://the launchbook.com/cathy.

USING SOCIAL TO BUILD YOUR EMAIL LIST

My cardinal rule for social media is that it shouldn't be your list, but you should use it to build your list. In the same way you wouldn't build your dream home on rented land, you don't host your most valuable business on a platform you don't own (and your list is your most valuable asset).

In other words, don't depend on social to be your list hosting platform. Once you start to gain traction on any social media platform, you should do your best to drive your followers over to your email list. This is critical, because any given platform could shut down or change its rules, and if you haven't moved people over to your email list, then your following is gone.

The way you do this is simple. I'm not saying it's easy, but it's quite straightforward. This goes back to basic email list building, which I covered in Chapter 3. You create a lead magnet (something of value for your followers), and then you create an opt-in page where people can get that thing of value if they join your email list. Then you tell your social media followers about that really cool lead magnet and give them the link to your opt-in page so they can get it.

Again, this is simple but it's not necessarily easy. When people are on a social platform, they like to stay there. And it's in the best interest of the owners of that platform to keep people on it, so they often make it harder to get people to click away to another site. They've got all kinds of subtle ways of doing that. It's sort of like the Las Vegas casinos: they like to keep people on the premises, so they make it difficult to find exits.

However difficult it might be to drive people over to your email list, it's absolutely paramount that you do this. And it's 100 percent doable. You can feature your list builder in posts to social media, you can build a hashtag around it, you can feature your lead magnet in a video tutorial; the methods are endless with a little creativity. Create conversations and posts that lead to: "Join my list for _____" or "Want to see _____? We have a newsletter created just for you" or "I've got a complete list of _____ at my site."

The good news is that the people you can move over from your social media following to your email list will be incredibly valuable to you and your business. Not everyone on your email list is created equal—some leads are more valuable than others. When you can get people to leave one medium and move to a different one (i.e., from social media to your email list), that makes for a very valuable lead.

ONE BIG, HAPPY LIST

One big evolution in social media is that you can now directly target the people who are on your email list on many social platforms. In other words, if someone is on your email list, you can also reach them on social. Take the list of email addresses and upload them into Facebook, Instagram, YouTube, even Pinterest and LinkedIn and other platforms. You can use that list to retarget your future customers. The combined impact of being able to reach them in their email inbox and also on their favorite social platform is very powerful.

While I still think email is king, it's all about the overall reach—and social is another place where you can reach your people and get them to click over to your launch. I'll cover this more in the chapter on paid traffic (Chapter 13).

SOCIAL MEDIA IN YOUR LAUNCH

Now let's talk about social media and your launch, because there are a lot of cool things you can do with social to drive your results. You can use your social following in every part of your launch, from Pre-Prelaunch all the way through your Open Cart.

The key here is to do your best to be "omnipresent." When people pick up their phones or turn on their computers, they're looking at a lot of different things—including their email and all their favorite social media sites. Ideally, you're reaching them in as many places as possible—on social media as well as in their email inbox—and you want that reach to extend throughout your launch. Ask yourself what platforms your future customers are using and be there, whether it's Facebook, Instagram, YouTube, LinkedIn, Pinterest, TikTok, or Clubhouse. Remember, the list of places is endless, but it doesn't mean you have to be in all of them. Talk to your audience, find out which platforms they prefer, and be there.

Let's start with your Pre-Prelaunch. Remember that your Pre-Pre is all about creating an initial buzz in the market and using it to identify possible objections and test the interest for your offer. If you've got a following on social media, it can be a perfect place to do a lot of the heavy lifting in your Pre-Prelaunch.

One core piece of the Pre-Pre is the "shot across the bow," and often I like to have several of those shots. This is where you start to talk about your upcoming offer without actually making an offer or any type of ask, aside from simply asking for feedback or suggestions.

In its most basic form, the Pre-Prelaunch is a simple email or two to your list that talks about the upcoming project in a very general sense and asks for some level of feedback. (See Chapter 6, "The Shot across the Bow"). I would suggest that you follow that formula and send that email. But since publishing to social media is so quick and simple, consider expanding your Pre-Prelaunch campaign a bit. Give yourself some more runway and start the Pre-Prelaunch earlier with some very simple mentions on social media about the thing you're working on.

These are not sales messages; you simply find ways to mention your new project on your social platforms. You could talk about the challenges, the trials and tribulations, and the excitement of producing something new. People love to support things they feel they had a hand in creating, even if they've just followed along as it's taken shape. This is really just about sharing your journey of creating your product or offer (which is the type of thing that tends to play well on social media).

One way I did that with the first edition of this book was by asking my followers to vote on the cover design. I posted several possible designs and then put up a survey on social asking for feedback. This started to build interest and anticipation months before the book came out. This was just one of the little Pre-Prelaunch strategies I used that drove the book to the top of the bestseller lists. Another thing I did was create a series of behind-the-scenes videos where I teased what was coming and asked my audience for their preferences. Pre-pre is about building interest and connection with your followers, and having them do the same with you and your content.

WHAT ABOUT PAID TRAFFIC AND SOCIAL?

One of the best things about social media platforms is that almost all of them allow you to advertise. This is called paid traffic, and it's hard to talk about social media without talking about paid traffic. It's a big topic, so I've split it out into its own chapter . . . and it's coming up next.

SOCIAL MEDIA IN YOUR PRELAUNCH AND OPEN CART

One of the places where social media will shine in your launch is during your Prelaunch. The entire point of your Prelaunch is to get your prospects to consume your Prelaunch Content. The primary tool we've used for years has been email—every time you release a new piece of Prelaunch Content, you email your list and tell them about it. Now, with social media, you have another place to tell your followers about your PLC.

The point here isn't to think of your email list and your social media following as two different things. You should consider your entire following as part of one big platform. Every time you release a new element in your launch, you tell everyone who's following—whether they're on your email list or following you on social. You can do this with links on photos on Facebook and Pinterest or with bio links on Instagram, Clubhouse, and TikTok. This is the time to be creative, so here are some ideas for social posts:

Behind the scenes of success

Countdown to launch (or Cart Close)

Benefit breakdown: what does the transformation do?

Sneak peek at the product (or a bonus)

Myth busters to slay objections

Bonus announcement and why they're needed

Future casting: what life will look like in 5 years

Obstacle that stops "the other people"

FAQ—all the nitty-gritty details of your program

Selfie of you with a mentor in your niche

Rant: something your audience does not need . . . and why not

Motivational memes to show them they can

Testimonials and case studies of possibilities

Doable tactic demonstration

The story of your journey to success

Tip to get followers a fast win

Poll to tease what's coming (and get feedback)

Quote from an influencer in your niche

Rant: why _____ is important

A story of someone who didn't _____

A screenshot of proof of success

A series of quick tips

In an ideal world, there will be 100 percent overlap between your email list and your social media following. Everyone who's following you on social will be on your email list, and everyone who's on your email list will be following you on all your social media platforms. So when you release a piece of Prelaunch Content, your followers will see you in multiple places. The reality never matches up to this, but it's better to have two or three chances of reaching your followers than to depend on a single message on any one platform.

The same applies once you get into your Open Cart—you'll want to be posting to social every step of the way, from your initial open all the way through your closing. And if you release any additional content during your Cart Week, then be sure to tell your social followers. Here's a potential publishing schedule for an 11-day launch:

Day 1: Release PLC #1, email your list, post to all your social platforms

Day 2: Post to all social platforms about PLC #1

Day 3: Release PLC #2, email + social

Day 4: Post to all social platforms about PLC #2

Day 5: Release PLC #3, email + social

Day 6: Post to all social platforms about PLC #3

Day 7: Open Cart, email + social

Day 8: Open Cart—new content, email + social

Day 9: Open Cart—FAQ, email + social

Day 10: Open Cart—case studies, email + social

Day 11: Cart Close, email + social

Note that you're publishing to your social media platforms every day. In reality, depending on the platform, you might actually publish more than once a day. That's a significant difference between social and email: you will fatigue your email list if you mail multiple times each day, but on most social platforms, where your content quickly gets buried in the feed, it's perfectly okay to publish more often, especially as your audience grows.

LEVERAGING FACEBOOK GROUPS

As much as I want to avoid talking about any specific platforms (because things change so fast, and I want this book to be useful for decades, not months), one social media tool that's really proved useful is Facebook Groups. These are places within Facebook where people with a specific interest can gather, post material, and have discussions. Anyone can create a group in a matter of moments. As the group owner, you can define the purpose of the group and set the ground rules.

A great way to leverage Facebook Groups is to create a group just for the people who are following your launch. This gives you another way to provide Prelaunch Content to your followers. It's also another place for the Launch Conversation to develop. I've used this to great effect in my launches—and we've had thousands of comments and interactions in our groups. Your prospects can comment on your Prelaunch Content and ask questions, and you can give answers and further engage with them.

If it's your first launch, you'll have enough other stuff to worry about—and you can wait until later to add a Facebook Group to your launch. Once you're experienced, though, doing so can give a nice boost to your launch.

Even if a group is not something you want to create on Facebook, the principles remain the same. Connect with your audience; give them a chance to learn from you, see your face, or hear your voice on social media. Whether it's Amy Small on Instagram, or Cathy Hay on YouTube, or Anne LaFollette on Facebook Live, they connected with their future customers, and that led to sales. It will lead to sales for you too.

Note: at some point in the future, when Facebook Groups are long gone (or the format and rules have been completely changed by Facebook), this broad concept of an "enclosed garden" within a social media platform will surely still exist somewhere on social media.

USING SOCIAL MEDIA AS YOUR LAUNCH PLATFORM

PLF is always evolving, and I'm always testing new things. One of my recent tests was to use one social media platform (in this case, Facebook) to host an entire launch.

Now, this was a fairly radical test, because I like to control as many variables as I can in our launches, and using Facebook in this way meant giving up a lot of control. But I tested it as a way to deliver a launch very quickly and with minimal technology.

We used Facebook to host our launch content—both the Prelaunch Content and the Open Cart content. In fact, we did it as a Live Launch (see Chapter 11), and we did all the live broadcasts directly on Facebook. The only things that we did NOT host on Facebook were our opt-in page, sales page, and order page.

We used a Facebook Group as the home for the launch, the place for people to view and comment on all of the launch content. It was also where they could watch the live broadcasts. We did our best to drive people from our email list (and from our paid advertising) into that group.

The results were strong—we had a great launch with excellent sales, and because we were able to keep the technology super simple, we were able to create the launch in a much quicker timeframe than normal.

I did that launch as a test and as a way to create speed to market. But this approach would be a great fit for a first launch, because it drastically cuts down on the tech that you need to figure out.

SOCIAL MEDIA: THE BAD NEWS

It's not all good news with social, and it's important that you understand some of the dangers before you pour yourself into building your social media strategy. These dangers will cost you time and money if you're not careful.

First off, when you build a following on social, you have to understand that you're fundamentally building on a bed of sand. The social media world is not a stable one. It's constantly evolving, and no one knows exactly where it's going. Social platforms come and go—even big, dominant ones.

Anyone remember Myspace? It's where social media really started, and it was completely dominant. As I write this, Myspace actually still exists . . . but it's a ghost town. No one goes there anymore. How about Vine? It's gone. And what about Google Plus—the platform that Google was so determined to make successful that it announced that all of its employees' bonuses would be tied directly to how well it did? It no longer exists. As I type this, even the almighty Facebook seems to be losing its firepower for many demographics (my kids tell me it's for "old people") as Instagram, TikTok, and Clubhouse increase in popularity among younger generations.

The one constant in the social media world is change. Your platform of choice could lose traction with your target market— they could just stop going there—or it could literally fold. When that happens, all the time, money, and effort you put into building your following there will have been in vain.

An even more common problem is that you don't own your following on social media. You might think that since you put in the effort to attract and nurture an audience, they're your people, and you might be right in a relationship sense. But the reality is that you're building on someone else's property. You don't own the platform, and the owners of the platform can change the rules at any time. Or they can just decide that they really don't like you or your presence, and they could close down your account.

If you're relatively new to the online world, that might sound far-fetched. If you're a good social media citizen and you follow the rules, they're not going to shut down your account, right? And they wouldn't change the rules in the middle of the game, would they?

The answers are yes and yes.

I've seen people have their accounts shut down for all kinds of reasons, many of them as arbitrary as the market they're serving (your favorite social platform might decide that your market is no longer politically correct). Sometimes accounts are shut down purely by mistake. It might sound crazy, but it happens. In fact, I'm going through that myself as I type this; one of my social accounts is essentially frozen due to a case of mistaken identity. Even given my positioning in the industry, it can be nearly impossible to get a response from an actual human at one of the big social media companies. Usually this type of error can be corrected, but it can take days or weeks—or longer.

Ultimately you need to stay aware of the terms of service and the algorithm whims of the various platforms. If you break the rules or stop creating the content that the algorithm wants, your accounts could be shadow banned (where you post but no one sees the content), or worse, you could lose access to your accounts entirely.

TWO MORE SOCIAL MEDIA DANGERS

To continue on with the doom and gloom, there are two more danger points about social media to consider.

The first is that it's easy to look at social media as a source of "free" eyeballs for your business or offer. If you find where your prospects are hanging out on social, then you just have to start engaging with them there, and you'll start to attract them into your world.

Everything about that is true—except the "free" part. Because even if you're not spending money, you'll be spending something even more valuable: your time. Any audience building that you do on social will come at a cost of time or money, or both. People usually do a relatively good job tracking the money they spend on paid traffic, but they often overlook the time spent on organic social media. The reality is that publishing content on social takes time. Attracting and engaging with followers takes time as well, and once you build that following, you will need to continue to feed your social media machine.

Ultimately, while there are tactics that you can use to make it easier to create content, it is not something you do once and never again. Social media is ultimately a relationship between you and your people, and all relationships fizzle and die if they don't get attention. Make no mistake—building, cultivating, and nurturing a relationship with your social following will add up to a lot of time. And as an entrepreneur (or a soon-to-be entrepreneur), your time will be in short supply.

Bottom line, know that the following you build on social is not truly free—there's a real cost in time and effort. I'm not saying it can't be a great investment of time, but it's one that you need to be aware of. There's no such thing as free when it comes to building your following.

The final big gotcha is that the social media companies are spending millions (and maybe billions) of dollars to make their sites as addictive as they possibly can. They have some of the smartest social engineers and behavioral scientists in the world, along with nearly unlimited testing and data, and they're using it to make their platforms incredibly addictive. And you're not immune to that addiction.

Now, you might be thinking, "I'm only here for business" and "I'm a professional; I'm just here to generate leads"—and then you look up from that funny cat video and it's three hours later. Seriously, when you're working on a social media platform to build your business, you're in a very high-risk environment. The thing you're risking is your time and focus, and the people who created that platform are your opponents. They're the best in the world at what they do. The game is rigged against you, and it's really hard to win. Even if you win one day, you have to show up and win the next day, and the day after.

If you're going to win in the long run as an entrepreneur, your time, energy, and focus are all you've got. When you step into the social media arena, you're putting all of them at risk, and you have to protect them at all costs.

FINAL THOUGHTS ON SOCIAL MEDIA AND YOUR LAUNCH

Despite my ending this chapter with a bunch of warnings about social media, it's a great tool for digital entrepreneurs. You should definitely use it in your launch. Social media is a place where you can find your people and connect with them. It's a place to learn about their hopes, fears, dreams, and desires. It's a place where you can build your list, and it's a place where you can reinforce and broaden the reach of every step of your launch, from Pre-Prelaunch all the way through Open Cart.

Increasingly, it's also a place where you can actually deliver significant parts of your launch content—from doing live broadcasts to hosting PLC videos to answering questions and comments. When you combine the power of social media with paid advertising on the social platforms (which is coming up in the next chapter), it can create a large, positive impact on your launch.

CHAPTER 13

Paid Traffic: The Shortcut to a Bigger Audience

One of the most significant developments since I wrote the first edition of this book is the growth of what is called paid traffic. We now have the ability to advertise and send traffic to a business or product. In other words, we can pay for people to see our launches and our offers.

When I first started my online business in the Internet Dark Ages (way back in the mid-90s), this just wasn't possible. Back then, driving traffic to your website was all about word of mouth and getting listed on the right search engines (there were dozens, and Google wasn't one of them). There was *definitely* no good way to advertise your site or your offer.

The first clumsy attempts at this were banner ads: not only were they ugly, but they could only reach a broad, nontargeted market. After banner ads came the first pay-per-click advertising (anyone remember GoTo.com?), and the ability to target your audience started to improve. It still had a long way to go, however, and it still only worked for search traffic. In other words, you could only reach people who were on search engines and actively looking for a specific thing (like how to find a locksmith). But there are lots of markets and niches where search traffic doesn't work very well (for example, any market or niche where people don't know exactly what they're looking for).

It's hard to overstate just how much this environment has changed, even in just the last few years. The ability to micro-target your prospects based on their interests and actions has reached levels never seen before in any type of advertising.

Paid traffic is incredibly powerful, because in addition to micro-targeting, you have the ability to take your prospects on a defined and controlled journey—AND you're able to track all the elements within that journey so you can further optimize your conversion rates.

Finally, over time, the big advertising platforms have created incredibly sophisticated algorithms for reaching your avatar. They've removed a lot of the complexity of using their platforms to target your market, and the algorithm does much of the heavy lifting for you. As you "feed" the algorithm more data, it gets more accurate in its targeting, and your acquisition costs can often drop.

A QUICK DRINK FROM THE FIRE HOSE

Paid traffic, like social media, is an area where the landscape changes almost daily. I'm not going to give specific tactics here, because they'll be out of date by the time you read this book. Instead, I'll focus on the paid traffic strategies that will continue working in your launch—and make no mistake, the upside for paid traffic is *huge* . . . especially for people who are just starting out (more on that in just a bit).

Before we go any further, I need to make one important distinction: the difference between "cold" traffic and "warm" traffic. When we talk about cold traffic, we're referring to people who don't know you and aren't part of your world. They're not on your list or following you on social media. Sometimes when we're talking about advertising to cold traffic, we'll just say "cold." On the other hand, warm traffic refers to people who are already on your email list, have visited your website, or are following you on social media. These people know you at some level. We'll use "warm" as shorthand for warm traffic.

Your approaches with warm and cold traffic will vary dramatically—both in how you do it and in the messaging that you use. (The actual messaging—what's expressed in your ad—is referred to as "creative.")

THE HOLY GRAIL OF COLD TRAFFIC

Sometimes cold traffic can feel like the Holy Grail of online business. Think about it: if you could spend $1 to drive someone to your launch, and that $1 in advertising could turn into $2 in sales . . . how often would you do that? In fact, even if that $1 could turn into $1.10—well, that would still be a pretty amazing deal, wouldn't it?

That's the promise of advertising to cold traffic. Sometimes that promise works, and when it does, it's amazing. At that point you're just trying to figure out how to spend as much money as you can on your paid traffic, because the more you spend, the more you make.

However, the reality of advertising to cold traffic is never quite that simple. Your return on ad spend (ROAS) will not be a static number. It will change with the competition, the season, and a host of other factors. Most important, it will likely change with the scale of your ad spend.

In any market, if you've honed your avatar from a demographic, psychographic, and targeting perspective, then your first leads will most likely be your best leads. It might sound obvious, but the first people with the most intense interest in your product or service, the ones your message really resonates with, will probably be the most responsive to your ads. They will also be the ones who are most likely to turn into buyers. That means your initial ad costs will probably be lower and your sales conversion rate will be higher.

Generally, after you reach the most responsive people in your market, your ad costs will start to increase and your sales per visitor will start to drop. This all means that your early days with any offer in any market will typically be the easy days. It also means your advertising costs relative to your sales will probably go up as you scale your traffic.

Now, none of this is meant to discourage you from advertising to cold traffic. Remember, it's still the Holy Grail. It just means that your ability to grow with paid traffic will typically get more challenging as you start to scale up. That being said, on some of the larger platforms, there are times when the inverse is true. Your costs actually decrease as you continue to feed the algorithm with more data. That allows the algorithm to get smarter and more effective at homing in on your avatar.

The key point is that if you're just starting out, then you'll generally be able to get good early results with your ads and drive some list growth for a relatively small ad spend (if you have a solid offer and good copy). Lots of caveats apply, but I'm seeing a lot more of my beginner-level students have success with paid traffic early on in their business.

USING COLD TRAFFIC IN YOUR LAUNCH

Using paid advertising to attract cold traffic in your launch is actually pretty straightforward. You start by building out the best opt-in page that you can and creating a lead magnet that will be your Prelaunch Content. For my own launches for my Product Launch Formula Coaching Program, I've referred to my Prelaunch Content as a "Launch Workshop" or a "Launch Masterclass." I'll create an opt-in page offering the workshop or masterclass, and then I'll run paid traffic to that opt-in page. The goal is to get people to enter their email address to get access to the Prelaunch Content. From that point, the prospect is on your email list, and you'll follow up with them throughout your launch in the same way you would with anyone else on your email list.

Note that you're most often paying for that lead on a per-click basis, meaning you pay when someone clicks on your ad, which is linked to your opt-in page. That action on the prospect's part occurs *before* they decide to actually opt in, *before* they go through your Prelaunch, and *before* they decide if they're going to buy. What that means is you've already paid for the click, but you're not sure how much revenue that click is going to drive for you. So if a given prospect clicks on your ad right at the beginning of your 11-day launch, it will take up to 11 days to find out whether that prospect will buy. You've already paid for the ad, and you've got to wait to see if the investment is a profitable one.

To put that in perspective, with most forms of offline advertising it will take weeks or months to get your results. I remember in the early days of my business, when I placed an ad in a magazine, I paid for that ad *three months* before it actually ran. Nevertheless, even if you have to wait only 11 days to be able to calculate the return on your ad, it's still a risk.

You can see how this becomes a game of math. Whether any specific lead does or does not buy isn't important—it's your overall conversion for all the paid traffic you've sent. Before you try to scale your paid traffic, it's a good idea to have solid data on what type of conversions you can realistically expect, and you need to be prepared for your numbers to not meet that expectation precisely. In other words, this is a Holy Grail that you need to be careful with.

Remember, not all traffic will convert the same. Usually the traffic you send into your launch from your list will have a very high conversion (this makes sense, since these people already know and trust you at some level). Next in line in terms of conversion rate will typically be JV traffic (because your JV partner will give you some type of endorsement). Then comes the cold traffic, which will commonly convert at a lower rate than most other types of traffic. This doesn't mean it's "bad" traffic or that you shouldn't use it. It's just something you should be aware of when you're projecting the conversion rate you'll have.

Whatever your projection, if and when you use cold traffic in your launch, you'll want to start advertising a few days before the start of your Prelaunch. Then you'll run your campaign through the end of your Prelaunch. As a rule, you don't want to spend a lot of money sending cold traffic into your Open Cart, because going from a cold ad directly to the sale is difficult for launches.

By now you may be thinking that cold traffic is something you should be wary of until you build up some experience and get some good metrics about your launch. And it is . . . except for those times when it works for people who are just starting out.

$3 PER DAY TO $120,000 A MONTH

When I taught you about Live Launches in Chapter 11, I shared the story of Anne LaFollette and her business teaching surface pattern design. She started with no list or following but gradually built up a list using cold traffic. She set her initial ad budget at $5 per day. Her results didn't come overnight and there was lots of work involved, but in her second year in business she did $400,000 in sales.

That all started with $5 a day in ad spend. It's an example of a newbie using paid traffic to get a toehold in the market, and Anne's not the only one in my community who started that way.

Michael Walker (no relation) was a professional musician in a touring band. His band was quite successful—they toured with some top acts, had millions of streams online, and eventually had the number two album on iTunes. But then he got married and his wife became pregnant with their first child, and Michael realized that the life of a touring musician was not compatible with the life he wanted with his family.

That's when Michael learned about PLF, and he set to work creating a business. He decided to start teaching about something he had experience with—how to be a successful musician. His band had millions of views on YouTube, but that audience really wasn't a fit for his new business, which meant he was essentially starting from zero with no list. So Michael turned to advertising and cold traffic.

Michael was even more conservative than Anne. He set his budget at the bare minimum, just $3 per day. Because of the precise targeting on Facebook, he could select people who identified as a "musician" or "vocalist" or "guitarist." He could also target people who were fans of cdbaby.com, a site that indie musicians use to sell their music. By targeting his ads that way, he was able to get in front of the right people, and he gradually built his list.

Michael launched a coaching package where he taught aspiring musicians how to grow their audience. And once he launched, he could see how those leads from paid traffic were converting. For every dollar he spent, he was making a profit. In fact, Michael told

Michael Walker

me that as his business grew he "couldn't afford not to advertise," and he continued to increase his ad budget over time.

Now, three years later, his business has grown in a huge way. In addition to paid traffic, he's used some JV partnerships (see Chapter 10 on JV launches). All along, though, paid advertising to cold traffic has been a cornerstone in his business, and he's used it to add approximately 40,000 people to his email list. There have been a thousand other steps and lots of hard work over the last three years, but his business at Modern-Musician.com now has a team of 18 people and revenue of $120,000 per month.

(I've got a full case study with Michael at http://www.the launchbook.com/michael. Check it out, because there's a lot to his story that I don't have room for here.)

WHEN YOU'RE JUST STARTING OUT

Both Anne and Michael used advertising to cold traffic when they were just starting out. They had no list or following and had to make do with small budgets to begin to build their list. In other words, they used ads before they were ready to launch. If you're in a similar place, this is something you might want to do as well.

When you're running cold traffic into a launch, your lead magnet will likely be the Prelaunch Content for the launch. Whether you call it a workshop or a video series or a mini-course or a training or anything else, you're going to be delivering several pieces of Prelaunch Content. That content is the inducement to get people to opt in to your list.

What about when you're starting out, and your launch isn't ready, and you don't have Prelaunch Content to send people to? In this case, you do what Anne did (see Chapter 11): she put together an opt-in page with a lead magnet that she created. The lead magnet was a simple PDF report with some tips for the people in her niche. Then she set a small ad budget of $5 a day, ran some ads that sent people to her opt-in page, and some of the people landing on that page joined her list. That's straight, basic List Building 101.

This strategy meant she was investing money (her ad spend) without getting an immediate return. But it also meant she was building her list, which meant she could publish to the people on it, interact with them, and build her relationship with them. That gave her fantastic market intelligence as well as practice at speaking to the people in her niche. It also gave her the time and space to find her voice in the marketplace.

It's true that spending money on ads when you don't have something to sell immediately is a riskier strategy. However, if you keep your ad spend modest and within your budget, it can be a great way to give your business a jump-start before your launch. And with the increased power of the algorithms along with the simplified ad platform interfaces, it's actually gotten easier to use paid traffic—even if you're just starting out.

THE TIMING OF COLD TRAFFIC

Normally you don't want to start sending cold traffic into your launch until just before your Prelaunch starts. The reason is simple: if prospects opt in to see your launch content two weeks before your Prelaunch starts, they'll have completely forgotten about you by the time you release your PLC. So you should start running cold traffic approximately three or four days before your Prelaunch starts, then continue advertising to cold all the way through your Prelaunch, pushing to get people to opt in and join your Launch List.

That's the core of a cold traffic strategy for a launch.

There is an advanced strategy in which you can start advertising to cold traffic much longer before your launch. In this strategy, you run ads that deliver nothing but pure content in the weeks leading up to the launch. This is generally done with a video ad, and the ad has no call to action. You don't ask for a click or anything else in the video. You deliver your content and the ad is done; there is no push to get people to join your list.

This means you're running ads, but you're NOT building your list or getting any other type of immediate benefit. However, you're building awareness, and you're also building an audience, a group of people who have seen and consumed your ad content in the weeks leading up to your launch. Note that on most ad platforms at most times, these ads are usually cheaper to run than an ad with a call to action.

The second half of this strategy kicks in two or three days before the launch—when you run ads just to the audience you've built up. These ads will have a call to action, and that call will be pushing people into your launch (and onto your Launch List). So in the first half of the strategy there is no call to action; you are just delivering content. In the second part of the strategy, you run ads to the people who watched that content, and it pushes them to click through and opt in.

This is an advanced strategy, and the specific technique may not continue to work as effectively as it does now, when it can actually be cheaper than a single-step ad direct to your launch. But at its core, it's not unlike my overall PLF strategy: you're delivering content and building a relationship over time before you ask for anything. It's like you're doing a Pre-Prelaunch to cold traffic. Your Pre-Prelaunch is your content-filled ads, and then you eventually ask for an action, which is to click through to your site to get the full-blown Prelaunch Content.

USING WARM TRAFFIC IN YOUR LAUNCH

If getting cold traffic to work is something of a Holy Grail, using warm traffic is one of those things that routinely "just work." You use cold traffic to try to generate new leads and new business, and you use warm traffic to engage your current leads and increase their conversions.

When you use cold traffic in your launch, it's mostly a one-trick pony, driving people to your opt-in page. But there's a lot more to be done with warm traffic. The first thing is that it reengages your list and your social followers. You can put content in front of them with your ads. You might do this in the days and weeks leading into your launch, and you can think of it as a form of Pre-Prelaunch.

As you get closer to the start of your Prelaunch, your strategy will look a lot like what you do with cold traffic: you'll be driving people to your opt-in page for your Prelaunch. You might wonder why you would drive someone who is already on your list to opt in to your list again. The reason is simple—you're reactivating your list by building a Launch List, a sub-list of people who have specifically raised their hands to show they're interested in your launch. This approach (which I often use myself when heading into a launch) just plain works, for a couple of important reasons:

1. As you grow your list over time, people will join it for all sorts of reasons, and they might or might not be specifically interested in what you're launching.

2. Simply having prospects go through the action of "raising their hand" by opting in to your Launch List will actually create a more responsive list.

Using paid advertising to the people who are already on your main list to encourage them to join your Launch List is where you'll start the warm traffic strategy for your launch. When people click on your ad, they'll go to an opt-in page to join your Launch List. Your lead magnet on that page will be your Prelaunch Content—you're inviting them to opt in so they can participate in your launch. I usually start running these ads a few days before the Prelaunch starts, and I keep running them through the entire Prelaunch.

GETTING THEM TO WATCH

Once you get into your Prelaunch, you'll also want to use warm paid traffic to build the engagement with your content. You'll run ads to the people who are already on your Launch List to drive them to watch your Prelaunch videos or broadcasts or replays (depending on the format and timing of your Prelaunch). Remember that as people watch your Prelaunch Content, they become more engaged and they're more likely to eventually buy when you get to Open Cart.

So once you release PLC #1, you'll run ads telling people to go watch it. Or if you're doing a Live Launch, you'll push people to attend live, and then after the broadcast you'll push them to the replay. You repeat the same process with PLC #2 and then again with PLC #3.

What these ads look like will vary based on where you're advertising and what the current rules are. They could be video ads, or they could be static images and/or text. You could be pulling highlights from your videos, or you could be featuring some of the feedback you've received about the content.

Remember, the people you're advertising to have already joined your Launch List. That means they have some level of connection with you, so in this phase your ads should be all about why they should consume the content in your launch—in other words, what's in it for them. It's not about how cool your launch is, it's about how their lives will be better if they see the content.

GETTING THEM TO BUY

Once you get to the Open Cart, your warm traffic strategy will shift. When you first open up and start taking orders, you'll be sending your warm traffic to your sales page or sales video. As I've said, these are people who have already joined your Launch List . . . and hopefully they've seen your Prelaunch Content (or at least some of it). Now that you're in Open Cart, it's all about getting them to see your sales message.

In addition to sending people to your sales message, after opening day you'll want to run your warm traffic into any additional pieces of content you have for your cart period. This additional content during your Open Cart can really pay off, because it gives you multiple things to push your warm paid traffic to. This is also when paid traffic can be *really* powerful. If you crafted your Open Cart strategy carefully, then there's a lot going on during that week. And you have only so many emails you can send to your list before you start to fatigue your audience. On the other hand, you can run a lot more ads without the same concern of fatiguing your prospects, especially if you vary the creative of your ads.

As you get into the last two days of your launch and you enter the scarcity phase, your ads should change messaging. They should be focused on the fact that your offer is closing down. This is a prime example of how warm traffic is so different from cold traffic. Advertising (and all marketing) is about context. If you ran an ad to cold traffic that said, "The launch is closing down tonight; you have to act now," it would make absolutely no sense. The people seeing the ad would have no idea who you are and what you're talking about. There would be no context. But with warm traffic, you're advertising to people who have seen your Prelaunch. You don't have to spend a lot of time setting the context and explaining yourself.

Finally, the warmest of the warm traffic—and some of the highest returns you'll see on your paid advertising—is to your "Cart Abandon" ads. In these ads you specifically target the people who have been on your sales page and your checkout page. You probably know the consumer side of that; some ad platforms have the capability to follow you very closely. This can feel pretty creepy at some level, but I will tell you from experience that advertising to people who have already been on your sales page but haven't bought yet is generally a very good investment.

WARM TRAFFIC—BEHIND THE SCENES

At this point you might be wondering, how do you target the people who are already on your list? I mean, you have your Launch List . . . but how do you specifically reach the people on your list with your ads?

This is one of those areas that are constantly changing due to technology, and increasingly due to legalities too. No matter what I write here, it will soon be out of date. However, while the specific methods and tactics will change, the broad strategies will almost surely remain.

The first technique is to upload your list to your advertising platform. If you're using Facebook, you'll actually upload your list of email addresses. (Alternatively, you can use phone numbers instead.)

IMPORTANT: You need to make sure that your terms of service on your site specifically give you permission to upload subscribers' emails to a third-party service. And again, I need to make clear that this is NOT so any other service can email or spam your people.

KEY POINT: The reason you upload your list is so Facebook can match up the people on your list with the people who have registered on their platform. You will be the *only* person emailing your list. The only reason you upload your list of subscribers is so that you can reach them with your paid advertising on the Facebook platform. Obviously, not everyone on your list will have a Facebook account, and not everyone will have used the same email address for your list and for their Facebook account. But a lot of those email addresses will match up inside Facebook, and you'll be able to run ads specifically to that group of people. (Note that I use Facebook only as an example. Other platforms will have similar methods.)

The other technique of reaching warm traffic is by using pixels. This is basically a small bit of code that you will get from your advertising platform (i.e., Facebook or Google) to put on your web page. When someone visits your pages, the ad platforms will be able to determine if that visitor is active on the platform . . . and if so, the platform will track that this visitor has been on your page. The platform will then allow you to advertise specifically to the users who have been to that page. That's how you can run ads based on your prospects' actions, such as those super-effective Cart Abandon ads to the people who have been on your checkout page.

WARM + COLD = A POWERFUL COMBINATION

As you can see, cold traffic and warm traffic are very different approaches. Cold is all about getting new people into your universe, creating awareness of your launch, and getting them to opt in to your list. Warm is about getting your prospects to consume your launch content and then moving them toward the sale.

After you build up some experience with paid traffic, you'll likely be running ads to both cold traffic and warm traffic at the same time. This means you'll have different ad creative for each, and your ads will be sending them to different destinations. Your cold traffic will be going to an opt-in page for your Launch List, and your warm traffic will be going to your Prelaunch Content or your Open Cart pages. Here's one way it might play out:

Pre-Prelaunch:
Warm: getting excited about upcoming Prelaunch Content
Cold: building awareness about upcoming Prelaunch Content

Start Prelaunch (release PLC #1):
Warm: consume PLC #1
Cold: opt-in for PLC #1

Prelaunch day 3 (release PLC #2):
Warm: consume PLC #2
Cold: opt-in for PLC #1

Prelaunch day 5 (release PLC #3):
Warm: consume PLC #3
Cold: opt-in for PLC #1

Open Cart day:
Warm: go to sales page
Cold: opt-in for PLC #1

Open Cart day 2:
Warm: go to Open Cart content
Cold: opt-in for PLC #1

Open Cart day 3:
Warm: go to Open Cart FAQ
Warm: Cart Abandons
Cold: opt-in for PLC #1

Open Cart day 4:
Warm: 24-hour scarcity warning
Warm: Cart Abandons
Cold: generally not used during last two days

Open Cart day 5 (closing day):
Warm: last-minute scarcity warning
Warm: Cart Abandons
Cold: generally not used during last two days

Note that in this example, all the cold traffic is sent into PLC #1, so that the new leads coming into the launch get to experience the full launch journey. That's typical for how we're currently running cold traffic into our launches. However, there is no one answer to using paid traffic in launches, and there could be times where the data suggests sending traffic into PLC #2 or PLC #3.

THE BOTTOM LINE ON PAID TRAFFIC

The ability to run targeted traffic into your launch is one of the biggest developments since I first created this launch formula. The ability to use cold traffic to drive leads is hugely powerful. You no longer have to sit around and wait for search traffic or organic word-of-mouth traffic to find you. Now you can go out and target your ideal clients and turn up the traffic flow when you want. You'll need to watch your metrics and be careful about ramping up your spending, but this is still one of the most potent tools you have.

The ability to use warm traffic to engage those leads and increase conversions is just as valuable. Using paid advertising to warm leads has become a go-to strategy for increasing conversions in launches.

As I've mentioned several times, this is a constantly changing landscape, and it's also a complex one. However, the combination of paid traffic and the Product Launch Formula is incredibly effective, and it's well worth exploring for your launch.

CHAPTER 14

Creating a Business from the Ether

How do you reinvent a business when world events throw you a great big curveball? When someone flies a plane into a building and it jeopardizes your entire business model?

Ruth Buczynski is a licensed psychologist who runs the National Institute for the Clinical Application of Behavioral Medicine (NICABM.com). NICABM is a pioneer and leader in the field of mind-body-spirit medicine and has been an accredited provider of continuing education for health and mental health care professionals for more than 20 years.

Since starting the company, Ruth has helped tens of thousands of psychologists, counselors, social workers, doctors, and nurses build their skills and better help their patients. Initially she did this primarily through live, in-person conferences. Her conferences had up to 1,000 attendees from around the world, and she brought in top experts to provide cutting-edge training.

Ruth's business was doing great until September 11, 2001. The terror attacks in the United States that day turned a lot of people's lives upside down, bringing about all kinds of unforeseen consequences. One of the impacts was that a lot of people started cutting back on their business travel. That hurt many businesses, including Ruth's. Her primary source of sales and revenue was her

Ruth Buczynski

nicabm
www.nicabm.com

conferences—and it was becoming more and more difficult to persuade people to get on a plane and travel to her live events. While her business was still profitable, Ruth didn't like the direction in which her sales and profits were trending.

And life had another huge challenge in store for Ruth. Around that same time she lost her long-term partner after a lengthy battle with a terminal illness.

As Ruth emerged from a period of intense grieving, she looked at her business with fresh eyes, and she knew something had to change. Profits were down, and it was getting harder to fill her events. That's when Ruth looked to the Internet and digital marketing as a possible new path for her business. She decided to start creating "virtual" events instead of in-person conferences.

Ruth sells primarily to licensed practitioners. A small percentage of her clients are nonprofessionals, but most are accredited health care providers. Her marketing needed to have a very professional look and feel but still make the sale. It was a perfect fit for the Product Launch Formula.

SURGEON GENERAL'S WARNING: YOU DON'T KNOW WHO IS WATCHING YOUR PRELAUNCH

Ruth's online conference was successful right from the start. In many ways she runs a classic PLF launch for each of her summits. She'll publish three pieces of Prelaunch Content—generally videos, but occasionally a PDF report. For instance, in her recent "Brain Science" training, her first piece of PLC was a video, *The Two Things You Can Do Today for Your Brain*. That video generated more than 1,000 comments.

After Ruth runs a standard PLF-style Prelaunch, she opens registration for her virtual event. The event is a series of webinars, and people can sign up and attend the webinars for free. Where Ruth makes her sales is at the "Gold" level, which includes the recordings of the webinars as well as transcripts and other bonuses.

It's worth noting that while Ruth is a licensed psychologist, she is not the "expert" in her trainings. She brings in world-class experts such as Tara Brach, Jack Kornfield, and Daniel Goleman. It's also worth noting that Ruth actually gives away the bulk of her content; if you're willing to be on each webinar live, then you can listen to all of them without spending a single dollar. But lots of people pay for the extra benefits and bonuses that come with the Gold level.

Because of the success of this model, Ruth has expanded. She now holds three or four different virtual events a year, including one on mindfulness, a second on brain science, and another on the treatment of trauma.

To put this all in perspective, Ruth generates enormous numbers. In one of her recent trainings, she had 9,000 people (from 70 countries) logged in to listen to a webinar. Those numbers take on an even larger significance when you consider that the vast majority of listeners are licensed practitioners. Ruth is not really marketing to the general public, so she has a much smaller target group of people to sell to.

Ruth recently saw another measure of her impact when she was invited to a meeting (along with other leaders in her field) to discuss ways to help the U.S. Army with mental health services for their troops. While Ruth was there she met the Army's surgeon general (a three-star general), who told Ruth, "I read your emails." In other words, the surgeon general of the U.S. Army was watching Ruth's Prelaunch Content!

Of course, the biggest news is that Ruth's business not only survived her transition from live, in-person seminars to webinar-based training, but thrived. In the last three years her business has grown by 160 percent, and she directly helps tens of thousands of people every year. And those health care professionals use Ruth's training to help hundreds of thousands of their patients.

Ruth's story is one of a complete reinvention of her business. The delivery of her product changed from a live conference to a virtual one. Her marketing shifted from direct mail to an online-based launch. Along the way, she increased her profitability, expanded her reach, and lowered the risk in her business.

THE PROVEN FORMULA . . . EXPANDED

Okay, so by now I hope we've established that PLF is a fantastic tool for launching your products and services. Now I want to talk about how to take it to the next level with what I call the Business Launch Formula. This is how you take the core Product Launch Formula concepts and use them to build (or grow) an entire business.

I've shared most of my personal story in the previous chapters—the journey from Mr. Mom staying home taking care of a couple of babies to building a multimillion-dollar business that's impacted hundreds of thousands of people. If I had sat down and written a novel telling this story, no one would believe it. But the story is far bigger than me, because PLF is not just about launching products. It's about launching businesses . . . and even helping people create an amazing life and lifestyle.

You've learned about John Gallagher, whose family was on food stamps when he borrowed the money to get Product Launch Formula. He's now built a serious business that sells a whole line of products, employs six people, and does more than a million dollars in sales per year.

And Michael Walker, who was a successful touring musician but, with a new baby on the way, needed to find a way to stay home with (and support) his new family. He's created an amazing business helping musicians build their followings. Now Michael gets to stay home with his young family and have a great lifestyle—all while remaining connected to the industry he loves and helping musicians reach their dreams.

And Will Hamilton, who went from being a just-out-of-college tennis instructor with a struggling website to working with some of the top tennis pros in the world, helping them bring their knowledge and wisdom to others.

Out of respect for my clients' privacy, I'm not going to disclose the financial results they are seeing in their businesses, but most people would find the size of their sales and profits downright shocking.

So how have they done it?

THE BUSINESS LAUNCH FORMULA

With my Product Launch Formula Coaching Program, I'm in the business of teaching people how to start and grow their businesses, specifically their online businesses. I teach them how to do that in the context of a product launch. But the reality is that the training goes much deeper. In fact, I like to think of it as helping them reprogram their business DNA. Once they learn the strategies and tactics behind PLF, they usually start to apply those tools in every area of their business.

When someone comes into my PLF program, my personal goal for them is to do a year's worth of sales in a single week with their launches. That's a pretty lofty goal, and not everyone hits it. In fact, it almost never happens with a first launch. But the thing is, your first launch is not going to be your last one.

That's why there's a group of PLF students—like John Gallagher, Michael Walker, Will Hamilton, and Ruth Buczynski—who take the launch to an entirely different level by using the Business Launch Formula. This is the way it works:

FOOD STAMPS TO SEVEN FIGURES

Let's start with John Gallagher. As we saw in Chapter 2, his first launch was for a board game that taught kids about edible and medicinal plants and herbs. That launch generated a huge amount of goodwill, and it also added a lot of new leads to his list. He took the momentum from that launch and used it to sell another physical product, an herbal kit containing the necessary components to create home remedies from herbs.

All of this helped raise his stature and positioning in the market, which in turn helped him build his list even more. And with each launch, the interaction with his list (i.e., the Launch Conversation) helped him pinpoint what his next product should be. Why guess about your next product when your prospects and clients are telling you what they want?

At that point John put together a major new product: the membership site LearningHerbs.com. Naturally he did a launch for the site, using all the knowledge and skills he had picked up from his earlier launches, and had his best launch to date, acquiring hundreds of paying members. Subsequent launches have raised the number of subscribers into the thousands. They each pay about $12 a month for access to the membership site. If you do the math, just 1,000 subscribers at $12 each is $12,000 per month in sales—and John has many thousands of subscribers. But that's just the start of what he's got going on in his business.

That membership site gave him a very significant and automatic monthly recurring income, a revenue stream he could count on. That regular revenue meant he could begin to hire people, and he slowly started to build his team.

His membership site launch not only grew his business but also expanded his positioning in the market. John is now a major player in the herbal education field. Now, he has never positioned himself as the expert; he's more the person who brings the experts to his followers. Nevertheless, on the business side of things, John is clearly a leader in his market.

This has allowed him to create video courses with some of the top authorities in his niche, launching an entirely new product a couple of times per year. In addition, he will typically relaunch his membership site once per year. This means that two or three or maybe four times per year, John does a launch. Since he always delivers huge value in his Prelaunches, each one grows his list and his positioning in the market to an even greater degree.

It didn't happen overnight, but that's how John Gallagher went from a failed launch for a board game to a business with a small (but mighty) team and a global impact. And that's how he's gone from having his family on food assistance to running a million-dollar enterprise.

When you're constantly delivering value to the market, you're constantly building a relationship with your clients and prospects. You're also stimulating the conversation with your clients and prospects, and that means you're always getting ideas for new products and promotions. That's a winning formula for a continually expanding business. That's the Business Launch Formula.

A DOG'S LIFE . . . MADE HAPPIER

Susan Garrett is passionate about helping dogs and their owners lead better lives. She's one of the best dog trainers in the world, especially in the hypercompetitive sport of dog agility. In fact, Susan has won more than 25 U.S. and Canadian national championships and multiple world championships.

Her success and her skills helped her build a successful international business as a dog trainer, one that sent her to Europe, Australia, and New Zealand to work with her students. For someone who had a huge desire to help dogs and their owners, this was exciting and fulfilling work.

However, it also meant that Susan had a grueling travel schedule, and that she couldn't help her clients on an ongoing basis; when she gave a workshop anywhere overseas, it was a one-shot deal. So Susan was already looking for a way to cut back on her travel schedule. And she wanted to be able to help far more dogs (and dog owners)—she was thinking in the tens

Susan Garrett winning one of her many championships.

of thousands, not the dozens she was helping when she trained them in person.

When Susan first got her hands on the PLF Coaching Program, her initial goal was to make enough money to pay for her PLF tuition before the credit card bill arrived. So she took a bunch of documents that she'd already written over the years and put them into a simple ebook that she sold for $14.97. That initial launch made $27,000 in sales—considerably more than her tuition cost.

The more important thing Susan took from her first launch was that the process worked, and with her competitive background, she knew she could get better at it—a lot better. Susan got serious about creating digital training products, and she's now created a series of online courses. She opens her trainings several times per year. She always uses PLF to deliver great value during her Prelaunch—and to fill up her programs. Her launches now measure in the hundreds of thousands of dollars, and her business has grown to an incredible 16 times larger than it was before PLF. This has allowed her to build a small team that helps her continually increase the value of her trainings.

Along with the financial success of her business, Susan also has a simpler, nearly travel-free lifestyle. Now she travels only for competitions and for pleasure. Her success has allowed her to exponentially build her positive impact on the world and has taken her closer to her ultimate goal of helping all dogs and dog owners lead happier lives.

FROM COLLEGE GRAD TO RUBBING ELBOWS WITH THE STARS

Will Hamilton's path in his business is yet another example of the Business Launch Formula. He started with a $35,000 launch—a huge win that gave him a viable business after a year of struggle. And he used what he learned in that launch to set up his next three launches, which brought in a total of more than $340,000.

Those launches locked in his positioning as a leader in his market of online tennis instruction, and they dramatically built his list. No longer was he just some kid fresh out of college with a tennis website. He had become a dominant player in the tennis instruction market.

Will's launch results and his positioning from those launches helped him land deals with top professional tennis players—first the Bryan Brothers (Bob and Mike Bryan, the all-time top pro men's doubles team), and then Pat Rafter (formerly ranked #1 in the world) and Martina Navratilova (who has 18 Grand Slam singles titles and was ranked #1 in the world for 332 weeks). And that's not the end of the partnerships and deals; Will is in talks with other top pro players and is even considering moving outside the tennis niche to work with pro athletes in other sports.

LAUNCHING: NOT JUST FOR PRODUCTS ANYMORE

All four examples in this chapter show just how powerful the Business Launch Formula is. It's about building an entire business based on what you've learned in the Product Launch Formula.

The essence of PLF is giving first and asking for the sale later. You build a relationship as a trusted advisor (or even friend) before the transaction. You deliver great value, and you do it in a way that makes the sale before you've even asked for the order. In many ways, this isn't much different from what the very best salespeople have always done.

However, with Product Launch Formula you're able to do that on a scale that really wasn't possible before. It's like combining the effectiveness of a face-to-face sale with the reach of big media. No, it's not as effective as a great in-person sales presentation, and it doesn't have the reach of a huge TV network, but it brings much of the power and advantage of both.

The Business Launch Formula is a natural extension of PLF. It's a matter of taking those principles of the launch and extending them to build an entire business.

SIX KEYS TO THE BUSINESS LAUNCH FORMULA

KEY #1: Always Deliver High-Value Prelaunch Content

First, you want to deliver high value to the market with your launches. That means having great Prelaunch Content that provides value all by itself, whether your prospect buys or not. This isn't news—I've hammered this point pretty hard throughout the book.

Not all your prospects will buy from you during your launch. In fact, in almost every launch the vast majority won't buy. There are lots of reasons why, but a common one is that the timing just isn't right. If you're selling wedding dresses and your prospect isn't getting married in the next year, you're probably not going to make the sale.

However, in our current market where everyone can be a publisher in social media in a few minutes, where everyone can have an outsize voice if they so choose, the benefits of creating hundreds or thousands of raving fans is far reaching. The relationship you build during your launch can have an amplified effect. Each one of your prospects has a potentially viral impact on your business, so creating fans has never been more critical to your success.

Make no mistake—delivering real value in your Prelaunch has a lasting effect. I've had people watch me through several of my launches before they were ready to buy, but when the time was right, they remembered me. I had delivered huge value and built up a significant level of trust, and they came back and bought.

KEY #2: Always Be Building Your List and Your Relationship with That List

Once you have a warm list (even a small list of a few hundred subscribers), you realize that you are now in control of your destiny. The ability to write an email, send it to your list, and see the response within seconds will change what you think is possible. At that point, you'll get very focused on building your list.

Of course, to even use the phrase "your list" is simplistic. As I mentioned in Chapter 3 (about list building) and in Chapter 12 (on social media), you will have many lists. But in broad, conceptual terms, I'm talking about your full list universe, which will become the most valuable asset in your business. To the extent that you build your list and your list relationship, you will build your business.

Every interaction with your list will either build on or detract from your relationship with the list. That doesn't mean you should only send free content and never ask for the sale. It means providing value AND making the sale. Remember that moving someone from being a prospect to being a client will increase the value of that relationship more than anything else you can do. Once prospects buy from you, they will be more likely to buy in the future, and they'll be more likely to buy at a higher price point. They will also be more apt to refer clients to you. And they're far more likely to get results from whatever you're selling.

KEY #3: Make More Than One Offer

It happens to almost everyone who goes through the PLF process. In the midst of your first launch, you get at least one great idea for your next offer or product. That's because of the Launch Conversation—your process creates a great deal of interaction with your prospects, and you'll get lots of ideas and suggestions. And many offers will likely lend themselves to periodic launches (such as Ruth Buczynski's annual summits). Often PLF Owners will do three or four launches per year and sometimes even more.

In my various businesses, I have found the sweet spot to be somewhere between two and four launches per year. Typically one or two of those are big JV Launches (see Chapter 10) that dramatically build my list and make lots of sales. The others are smaller Internal Launches that help me refine new offers and products before I roll them out as JV Launches.

KEY #4: Use the Circle of Awesome: Seed to Internal to JV

There is a cycle of launches that works really well. I call it the Circle of Awesome™. I know that's not the most grammatically correct term, but it's something I said in a silly moment when I was with my son, and it stuck. And what it lacks in grammar, it more than makes up in, well . . . awesomeness.

It goes like this. You have an idea for a new product, so you use a Seed Launch to help birth the product. The Seed Launch (see Chapter 9) is great for getting your first few clients, making sure there's a demand, and creating a great product.

After the Seed Launch, you take the finished product and do an Internal Launch to your list. During your Internal Launch, you build out a full Prelaunch Sequence and really dial in your launch. By its very nature, the Internal Launch will usually bring you much greater financial results than your Seed Launch.

Then, if you have good results with your Internal Launch, you move onto the JV Launch. You have the data and metrics from your Internal Launch to show to potential partners, and you have your Prelaunch and Launch Sequences largely done and tested. The JV Launch has a lot more moving parts, but since you've done most of the work already in your Internal Launch, it's a lot more manageable. And the results of a successful JV Launch are often exponentially larger than your Internal Launch.

Just to bring it full circle, after you go through that sequence of launches, you'll usually have several ideas for your next product. That's when you go back and test one of your new ideas with a Seed Launch and start the entire process over again. The only difference is that this time around you'll have significantly more experience, probably a much larger list, and lots of happy JV partners who will be ready to promote your next JV Launch.

It's one big circle, and it can be pretty awesome. ☺

KEY #5: Use Relaunches and Evergreen Launches

Relaunches can be very effective—just look at the way Barry Friedman did it. As we saw in Chapter 4, he ran his Showbiz Blueprint class over and over. The small class size kept the interaction level high, which meant he could charge a premium price. It also kept the demand high, so he was able to continue relaunching the offer.

Part of the effectiveness of your relaunches will be dependent on your ongoing list building. If you have new leads coming into your list and you've developed a proven Launch Sequence, then you've got a great opportunity. You can either run periodic relaunches or use an Evergreen Launch.

Evergreen is really beyond the scope of this book, but it means that as new leads come onto your list, you will move them through their own Launch Sequence based on when they joined the list.

KEY #6: Take Care of Your Clients and Launch to Them Again

This is a universal truth of business: It's a lot easier to sell to someone who has bought from you in the past than it is to generate a new client. The exact numbers on this vary, but they are always dramatic. Based on my experience in my various online businesses, it's about 15 times easier to sell to someone a second time than it is to get a new client.

That means you want to make sure you take care of your clients. I'm a big fan of overdelivering on my promises. This is something I plan out in advance. When I'm designing a new offer, I will actually hold back on some bonus items. I won't put them in the offer, nor will I talk about them during the sale. Then, sometime after the purchase, I will surprise my clients with the extra bonuses. Even the most grizzled customer is delighted to get something that wasn't promised. In fact, it's often shockingly easy to please them—you don't have to get crazy when you're sending extra goodies.

It's not hard to impress your clients. Give them what you promised, give them great customer support, and then give them an extra surprise or two along the way. Do those things and you will be paid back 100 times. Not only will your clients be ready for your next launch, they'll be raving fans who support you during that launch.

THE FORMULA THAT LAUNCHED A THOUSAND BUSINESSES

The Business Launch Formula is too big for me to do justice to it in this chapter. Out of necessity, this is an overview from 30,000 feet, an introduction to the proven process I've seen my clients use over and over with consistent success. What they're doing is taking the Product Launch Formula and stepping it up to a higher level. Instead of a single launch of a product, it's a series of launches that create their business. Each launch builds on the success of the prior one. The list gets bigger, the offers get better, there are more past buyers to sell to, and the JV partner support gets stronger. That's the Business Launch Formula in action.

CHAPTER 15

Creating a Business You Love

A natural part of my business is that I get an inside peek into the workings of many other businesses and the entrepreneurs who create and run them. That's what the next two chapters are about. It's one thing to build a business, but quite another to build a business and a life that you truly love. I've noticed that a lot of people end up with a business they just tolerate. Worse, some people build businesses they really dislike or even hate. Either way, it's not a great situation.

It's understandable. Lots of people are like I was when I started out, desperate to get a business going and get their head above water. Any profitable business looks great when you're struggling to pay the bills and put food on the table—but for most people, once they start to get the money figured out, the business becomes about more than just profits. That's when they might ask, "Is this all there is?"

The way I look at it, if you're going to pour your heart and soul into a business, then you might as well create something you love. One of the best things about having your own business is that you get to largely make up your own rules for it, within legal and ethical boundaries, of course. So why not make up a set of rules that you can win by? Why not stack the odds in your favor?

At the risk of my sounding like the carpenter who has only a hammer in his toolbox so everything looks like a nail, Product Launch Formula is the tool that will get you the business you love. But the first step is to figure out what you want your business to look like.

YOUR "BIG WHY"

Before you have a business you love, you first need to figure out the "why" behind it. If it's just to get rich, that's fine. Making a lot of money is great. I like to think of money as stored-up freedom and energy, and I love having lots of freedom and energy. As the saying goes, there are problems with having too little money and problems with having a lot of money. I like the problems that come from having money better.

What I've noticed about money is that once people get to a certain level of monetary success, they usually start looking for other things in their life. For example, a huge driver in my life is making a positive impact in the world, primarily through helping entrepreneurs. I also love that I've been able to build a great team—my business is providing jobs and plenty of room for the people on my team to grow. Some people might be about creating great technologies. Or training people. Or reducing suffering.

I could go on, but you get the idea. At some point, there's usually a higher purpose than acquiring more money and stuff. The thing is, it doesn't so much matter what your specific "why" actually is. The important thing is that you figure it out. As the saying goes, "If you don't know where you're going, any road will take you there."

In my PLF Live workshops, I have a process to get my clients to their "big why," and this is one of the most powerful exercises in the entire event. Once you get that figured out, you become eminently more powerful.

ATTRACT THE CLIENTS YOU WANT

The reality is that not all people are created equal, and that's doubly true when it comes to clients. Some people will make great

clients for you, and some won't. There will be people who resonate with your work, your products, your offers . . . and others
who won't.

I'm not passing judgment on those people. I know some people will like me and my style, and others won't. Some will think
I'm not formal enough, that I'm too relaxed, that I should wear
different clothing or be younger or older or whatever. That's
okay, because I know that during my launch process I'll naturally
attract clients who will end up relating well to me. In fact, I have
this deep-rooted belief that I continually attract amazing people
into my life.

Now, I guarantee that some people will roll their eyes at that
last sentence or think it's a silly conceit. But that's okay, because
the odds are very strong that those are people who do NOT resonate with me. They won't be a good fit for me and my business.
See how that works? ☺

It will be the same for your business. All of us have people
we connect with better than others. In fact, that's one of the jobs
of good marketing—you want to attract the right people and
repel the rest.

That word *repel* might turn off some people, but the last thing
you want is a lot of prospects and clients who aren't a good fit
for you. I've learned this lesson over and over. It was drilled into
my head most recently when I spoke at two conferences. Both
were large conferences with many hundreds of attendees, and on
the surface, it seemed like they would have similar audiences who
would be very receptive to my training.

The first group was wildly enthusiastic; they hung on every
word I said. They participated when I asked something of them.
They were full of questions. The energy in the room was palpable.
I loved every minute I was on stage, and when I finally stepped
down I was swarmed by people asking questions for more than
two hours.

I was on fire after that talk and looking forward to the second
conference. Unfortunately, that turned out to be a very different
room. The second group was attentive and respectful, but that was

about it. I couldn't get them to participate. There were few questions. The room felt dead.

As I suffered through my presentation at that second conference, it couldn't have been more clear: the people in the first audience were "my people." Even though most of them had never heard of me before I walked on stage, they were a perfect fit for my message. On the other hand, the people in the second audience were clearly not my people. They were nice enough, but on the whole we just didn't fit each other.

The difference in those conferences was the marketing that put the people in the room. For the first conference, the marketing was very congruent with my approach to business. And, in retrospect, the opposite was true of that second conference. The marketing and messaging that put that second group in their seats was a pure hard sell, which is very different from the way I talk to my clients.

The differences didn't stop in the conference room, either, and I know this because I tracked the people who became clients after those talks. The ones from the first conference were simply better clients. They required less customer support, they had a lower refund rate, they participated in the PLF community more, they got better results, they made better case studies, and they ended up joining my elite coaching group at a higher rate.

The point of this story is this: you want to be sure you attract YOUR people into your business. Fortunately, you already have the tool you need to attract those people—the Product Launch Formula. When you follow the formula and authentically tell your story through your Prelaunch Content, you will attract your ideal clients. It's part of the process.

LOOK THROUGH THE CORNERS

When my son started racing mountain bikes, he learned an important lesson from his coach that he brought home and shared with me. He told me to "look through the corners." In other words, when you're on a bike hurtling down a steep mountain track, you don't want to look at the trail directly in front of your wheel.

That's a recipe for disaster. It means you'll always be reacting at the last second. Sooner or later you'll come to an obstacle that you won't be able to react quickly enough to.

Instead, you need to extend your vision farther down the trail. Move your horizon line as far out as you can. As you enter a corner, look through that corner to see where you're going to exit the turn. Even if trees are blocking your view, focus intently and try to see through them for a clue to what's coming next. Look beyond the corner.

Business is the same way—you need to be looking farther ahead than the next day or week or month. Don't chase every shiny object, don't be distracted by every new tactic. If you're going to change course or pursue a new direction, make sure you're doing so for a sound strategic reason.

I see too many people continually compromise their positioning, their brand, and their reputation by chasing after the latest tactic or the last dollar. It's downright sad to see people throwing away all the work they put into a business by focusing on the short term. The good news is that if you take the long view (and these days, the long view seems to be anything past the next three months), then you'll instantly stand apart in your market.

THE MASTERMIND PRINCIPLE

The idea of the "mastermind" is something Napoleon Hill wrote about in *Think and Grow Rich* all the way back in 1937, and it's an incredibly powerful concept. In fact, I wouldn't be where I am today if I hadn't actively engaged in several mastermind groups since the early days of my first business.

The way a mastermind works is simple: you get together with a group of like-minded entrepreneurs, and you support one another in growing your businesses. This isn't a networking group, although there is often some networking that naturally occurs as a by-product of being in the group. It's all about sharing, brainstorming, and holding one another accountable.

Often there will be "hot seats," and if you haven't ever been through something like that, it's pretty wild. Basically, one person presents a situation or problem that exists in their business, and then the entire group does a big brainstorm about it. If you have the right people in the group, the hot seat usually ends up being like a massive feeding frenzy among a bunch of hungry sharks. When you put 20 or 30 creative entrepreneurs into a room and then throw a business problem in front of them, well, that's like putting blood in the water. (Don't accidentally leave any arms dangling over the edge of the boat . . .) Besides, we all know it's much more fun to solve other people's problems than to work on our own issues!

I've been in a variety of formal mastermind groups over the years, starting in 1999. Some were paid memberships that were professionally facilitated. Others were groups of friends without a central facilitator. The formats varied—some were primarily email based, others phone based, and the most powerful revolved around in-person meetings.

I've also created paid masterminds for small groups of my own clients, which has given me deep insight into what it takes to create a great one. (My high-end mastermind that I've built from within my PLF community has become a band of brothers and sisters to me. I've never experienced a more powerful, tighter group.)

What I've learned over the years (from being both a participant and an organizer) is that not all groups are created equal. There is no inherent magic in putting random people together. It's all about the quality of the people and the level of community in the group.

A great mastermind has great people who are givers, people who focus on creating value for others before they look to take value. This is the very essence of a mastermind; everyone is there to focus on helping their fellow members, and they know their rewards will naturally come as part of the process.

However, being a giver isn't enough. Members need the mental horsepower and the emotional intelligence to be able to contribute to the group at a high level. You want people who do NOT want to be the smartest person in the room. The best masterminds also have a strong ethos and an almost tangible sense of community and identity, a feeling of "We're all in this together." I've been in groups where I have a real sense of loss if I miss a meeting. If I'm offline for several days, the emails from the group will be the very first thing I look at when I get back to my computer.

When you get the right people and a great community, it's pure magic. As the saying goes, "A rising tide lifts all boats," and that's exactly what happens in a great mastermind. As each member focuses on helping the others in the group, they can't help but benefit. They end up getting the ideas, connection, and accountability that drive their business and life forward.

So here's my advice: Get in a strong mastermind. Ask other entrepreneurs you know to recommend a group. There are always some self-organized free groups that may take you in, though they can be tough to find; they're almost always underground to some extent. The paid groups are usually easier to locate (and they usually have a more formal structure), or you can form a group yourself. You might have to try out a few groups before you find the one that's right for you, but the payoff is enormous when you find the right fit.

THE MOST IMPORTANT THING IN BUSINESS

At a recent PLF Live workshop, I had an attendee come up and ask me what the single most important thing in business was, the one thing that has meant all the difference for me and my success, the thing he should focus on as his business grows. That's a really tough question!

My answer was this: opportunity cost.

Wikipedia says that opportunity cost is "the cost related to the next-best choice available to someone who has picked among several mutually exclusive choices." That's a bit difficult to understand, in my opinion. I just think of it as what you have to give up when you choose between two or more options. This cost is NOT restricted to financial cost. For an entrepreneur, the biggest opportunity cost is often time.

When you start out, you will likely have limited capital, and since you'll be doing most everything yourself, you'll definitely have limited time. Picking the right opportunity is HUGELY important. Making the wrong choice can set you back weeks, months, or even years.

That's what opportunity cost is all about. You have to realize that chasing an opportunity has a greater cost than any financial expense it requires. I don't want to scare you into inaction, because taking no action has a HUGE opportunity cost itself. I just want you to realize that when you decide to go down one road, there are several other roads that you won't be able to go down—and once you start to have success, the issue of opportunity cost becomes even greater.

This is the deal: the more successful you become, the more opportunities you will have. This is what we call "deal flow." You start to have success, you build up a series of assets, you prove your worth—and all of a sudden everyone wants to do a deal with you.

Deal flow is a good thing. That's how the rich get richer. That's one of the reasons why it's easier to go from $100,000 to $1,000,000 than it is to go from zero to $1,000. But as you get into the deal flow, it's easy to get distracted. You have only so much time, energy, attention, assets, and so on, and every time you make a choice to pursue an opportunity, you are giving up something.

Usually, for entrepreneurs, that something is time.

I just heard my friend Dean Graziosi use this analogy to explain opportunity cost: It's like having a bookshelf that's completely full. If Dean finds another beautiful book he wants to buy . . . well, he can. But that means he has to get rid of one of the books already on his shelf.

So remember: having choices in your business is great. But those choices have an opportunity cost. Making the right decisions around that opportunity cost is one of the biggest factors in the success of your business.

DON'T BE TOO COOL FOR SCHOOL

If you're going to be in business and you're going to have long-term success, then you need to be a perpetual student. Your market, clients, and competitors aren't going to stand still, and you can't afford to, either. In my business, I've gotten to know a lot of super-successful business owners, and I can tell you this: Everyone at the top is a constant learner. You can't be too cool for school.

Now, that might sound self-serving since I'm in the business of teaching people about growing their business, but it's the truth. The reality is that I spend a ton of time and money on my own education. I have to. It's my job. The payoffs in business are enormous, but one of the costs for great success is that you have to stay on top of your game.

You have to go to school. And you're going to have to keep going back to school.

NO ONE CAN BE AN ISLAND

This one is simple—you need to build strong relationships in your industry. In fact, even though I used the word *competitor* in that last section, I don't really use that word in my business. I think in terms of "partners" and "future partners."

I know there are some businesses where there truly is competition. For instance, if you own a gym, the odds are very strong that your clients are going to belong to only one gym. In that case, that would make the other gyms in your local area direct competitors.

But in the current market, with more and more people becoming knowledge workers, and more and more businesses becoming knowledge businesses, there are far more opportunities to cooperate than to compete.

My current business has literally been created by doing promotional partnerships with businesses that might be considered direct competition. But instead of competing, we support each other. The end result is that we don't have to worry about splitting up the pie. Instead we work together and grow a much bigger pie.

I suggest you start thinking of ways your competitors can become your partners. Try it out for a while, because your network is your net worth.

YOU NEED TO BE IN THE INFORMATION BUSINESS

In this book, almost all of the examples I've used have been information businesses, those that deliver a product that teaches or trains people about something. It could be dog training or tennis or juggling. But not every business will be an information business. After all, we need people to sell cars or real estate or clean carpets.

However, in our current world, nearly everyone needs to be in the information business to some degree. Adding an information component to a business—either as part of the selling process or as part of the product—will become a huge element of almost every successful business.

For instance, my friend Joe Polish initially grew his carpet cleaning business by offering a free report that educated consumers on the fraudulent selling techniques that many carpet cleaning businesses use. That report ended up generating a huge amount of exposure and sales for his business. He didn't have an information business, but he used a knowledge product to build his offline service.

We live in a connected, information-rich world. People expect to be connected and to have information at their fingertips. In that environment, nearly every business should be in the publishing business at some level, either as part of their marketing or as part of their offer.

THE HUMAN TOUCH

This is something I stumbled onto when I started my first business back in 1996: it's a lot easier to sell with the human touch. I've always been happy just being me and not pretending to be some big corporation. I didn't refer to myself as "we" in my emails, and that set me apart from the very beginning. Back in the early days, everyone was trying to sound like some big, important company, but I wrote my emails to the people on my list in the same voice I would use when writing to my friends. It worked.

People want to connect with people, not faceless corporations. They don't want to get an email written in what I call "the corporate voice" or "airline speak." You know what I'm talking about: "The aircraft door is now closing. Please read the safety card that has been placed in the seat pocket in front of you." This sounds cold, impersonal, officious. Sure, there are rare exceptions; if you're in a mission-critical situation, your clients will want to know that you have the resources to back up your services. Even then, however, they'll still want to interact with a human.

The corporate voice is death to sales. People want to buy from people. Forget the royal "we" when speaking to your clients. Talk to them one on one. This will make it easier to sell your stuff, and running your business will be a lot more enjoyable. Again, the PLF process is all about creating a connection and a conversation with your prospects, communicating in a way that builds a relationship.

PLAYING BY YOUR RULES

Having a great business starts with realizing that you're in control. This might sound obvious, but so many people create a business that's modeled on existing ones that they see, or on what they think a business is supposed to look like.

Remember, you get to make the rules. You don't have to do business the way the other people in your market do it. You don't have to do business with clients you don't like. You can create a business you love. It all starts with getting clear on what that business looks like and what your life would look like if you had that business. That's what the next chapter is all about.

CHAPTER 16

A Recipe for a Big Life

After I graduated from Michigan State University with a business degree, I landed a corporate job with a really big company in Tempe, Arizona. I grew up in the Detroit area, and I had never been west of the Mississippi River, but I had always felt a pull to move out West.

It's a long drive from Michigan to Arizona. It took me four days. On the third night, I stayed in a tiny hotel in a mountain town I'd never heard of—Durango, Colorado. I had never seen mountains like that in my life, and I was impressed. In the morning I called my parents to tell them about my trip so far, and I couldn't stop talking about Durango.

After a few minutes, my dad said, "Wow, it sounds like you just want to stay in Durango and not go any farther." After all these years, I still remember him saying that, because it struck me as such a ludicrous idea at the time. The idea of my living in a town like Durango—out in the mountains—seemed about as likely as my walking on the moon.

I grew up in a wonderful, supportive family. My parents did a great job raising my siblings and me. They gave us a good start in life and made sure we went to college. The pattern for my life seemed to be set: go to college, find a "good job," and then work at that job for the rest of my life. That's what all my extended family did. That's what all my friends' families did. That's what everyone in my middle-class suburban neighborhood did.

For some reason, though, I'd always had a yearning to own a business. I have no idea where that came from, but I remember feeling that strong desire even when I was 10 years old. But I had no role models for starting and building a business. I had no frame of reference. I didn't know how people actually did something like that. It went against everything I saw in my life, so off I went to Tempe to follow that familiar pattern.

However, once I got to Tempe and started my job, I quickly learned I didn't fit in the corporate world. I was a round peg trying to fit into a square hole. It just didn't work. And that's a big reason why, just a few years later, I found myself quitting my job, walking away from the corporate world, and staying at home to take care of my two young children. I had washed out of the corporate world, never to go back.

MOVING TO DURANGO

I'm typing this to you from my hometown of Durango, Colorado. As I told you near the beginning of this book, my wife and I moved our family here 20 years ago. My dad was right all those years ago when he said it sounded like I wanted to live here. Today I do, because I can live anywhere in the world that I want.

My business is 100 percent online and my team is virtual, so that effectively uncouples my business from the constraints of geography. I can work anywhere I have an Internet connection.

Durango may not be most people's first choice, but I love it. The most beautiful mountains in Colorado are almost in my backyard, and the great deserts of the American Southwest are just a couple of hours away. I have easy access to great skiing, incredible mountain biking, and beautiful river trips. I love the people who choose to live in Durango, and it's been a fantastic place to raise our kids.

Each morning, I get up when I wake up. The only time I set an alarm is when I want to get up to the mountain early on a ski day, or if I need to catch an early flight. (I travel only when I want to—if it's for business, I'll be on my way to meet some amazing people or go to a world-class training.)

Part of the joy of living in Colorado is sharing my passion for the outdoors with my kids. Both of them are very strong mountain bikers and skiers, and they've floated down some of the greatest wilderness rivers in the world.

I don't tell you any of this to brag. I just want you to understand what's truly possible in your life. I've got a business that's helped hundreds of thousands of entrepreneurs, I've got a great team that enables me to run the business, we've got raving fans for clients, I have an income beyond anything I could have dreamed of, I get to live where I want . . . and I still have the time to enjoy the beautiful surroundings just outside my door.

Of course, sometimes when people hear this, they think it's just that I'm truly special, or maybe I have some magical powers or insider connections or I got inordinately lucky.

Unfortunately, I have no magic powers. When I started this business I had no connections whatsoever, and I certainly didn't start with any advantage or any money.

Then how did I go from a simple midwestern boy, corporate failure, stay-at-home dad struggling to make ends meet, to having the life of my dreams? It's because of the business I created with the Product Launch Formula. Sure, there's been plenty of hard work and more than a few lucky breaks, but it's all in the formula. And here's the thing—I'm not the only one who's done it. Many of my students and clients have achieved similar results. You've already read about several of them in this book.

So, how do YOU build a business and a life in which you can live where you want, work when you want, and have the lifestyle that you want?

START WITH THE VISION

When I was about to start my first business, I went through an exercise in which I created my ideal life in my mind. I read about this exercise in a training product that I had bought, and I think this helped set up all my success. The exercise didn't take long and was easy to do: I wrote down everything I wanted in my life—income, lifestyle, relationships, material things, travel experiences. The list wasn't very long because I had no idea of the possibilities back then. Compared with my lifestyle now, my vision was very modest, but that list gave me the direction I needed.

The funny thing is, as soon as I finished the exercise, I tucked the list away in the back pocket of my journal and forgot about it. Then, a couple of years later, I stumbled across the list—and realized I had achieved nearly every single goal on it. That's when I became a real believer in creating a future vision of my life in my mind . . . and writing it down.

Once my business started growing, I rapidly revised and added to the list. I wrote down everything I wanted in my future: my target income, the amount of time I could be away from my business, how I'd spend my free time, the state of my finances, what I'd be doing in my business, the impact I'd make with it, the type of people I'd work with, etc. If you choose to go deeper, you can also write down what you want in your future relationships, physical and emotional health, education, home, family, and more.

It's important to understand that there is no right or wrong answers when you go through this exercise. And what you write down is not forever; you can change it at any time. This is your ideal vision of your future life right now. You can do this exercise for any time frame you want, but I usually use three years or five years from the present. Remember, this list is a work in progress. I'm continually updating my vision for my future life, and you should do the same.

So go ahead and do it. Turn off your phone, your email, all your social media and news apps. In fact, it's probably a good idea to just turn off your Internet connection. Trust me, everything will still be there when you turn it all back on in 30 minutes. Close the door, or get out of your home and go to a coffee shop or library. Use paper and pencil, or open up a blank document on your computer. Imagine what your ideal life will look like in three years, and write down:

— What your income will be

— What kind of car you will drive

— Where you will live and in what kind of home

— Who your clients will be and how you will serve them

— What your physical and mental health will be like

— What your relationships will be like—with your friends, partner, kids, parents, co-workers, and so on

— What your spiritual life will be like

— What trips and experiences you will have

— What you will have accomplished personally and professionally

One more hint: This exercise is more powerful if you write everything down as if you've already achieved it.

Don't underestimate this process. Everything significant you create will first be created in your mind's eye.

Now that you're clear on where you're going, let's talk about some specifics of how to get there.

THE SECURITY OF BEING AN ENTREPRENEUR

To create the life of your dreams, the first thing you need is security. Lots of people who are thinking of starting a business worry about leaving the security of the paycheck world. Unfortunately, there is no longer any security in a paycheck. I'm sure you know of people who worked loyally for a company for many years, only to be laid off or have the business shut down. Perhaps this has even happened to you.

The world has changed, and the only true security is your ability to create value and get paid for that value. Once you create your own business, you understand what security truly is. Even after I lost my first business to a partnership breakup, it took only a matter of weeks until I was back on my feet and had started a new one.

The greatest investment you will ever make is the investment in your business skills. When you can create a new business from the ether, then you control your destiny. And of all the business skills you can have, the one that pays off better than any other is the ability to market and sell yourself and your business. It should come as no surprise that I think PLF is the best way to do that in this day and age.

SHARPEN THE SAW

This was one of Stephen Covey's keys to personal success in *The 7 Habits of Highly Effective People*—you need to take time away from work to recharge and refresh. You can't continually operate at a high level if you're working 100 percent of the time. No one can always be operating at peak efficiency and creativity. Unfortunately, I see lots of entrepreneurs creating a life where they do nothing but work. They literally never take a day off.

There's an old joke among entrepreneurs that the biggest benefit of owning your own business is that you only have to work half-time—any 12 hours of the day that you want. Unfortunately, it seems that's how many entrepreneurs actually work. That's not healthy, and in the long run your business and your life will suffer for it. And it's not a recipe for living a big life.

Sure, there are always going to be some long days, especially when you're starting out. But if you never have time away from your business, then you're doing something wrong.

My friend Joe Polish uses the analogy of a racehorse. If you owned a million-dollar racehorse, you would take great care in how you treated that horse. You would feed it well, make sure it was well rested, carefully monitor its workouts, give it a clean and comfortable stable, and schedule regular checkups with a vet. In your life and your business, your body is your million-dollar racehorse. Don't you deserve the same care?

I don't want to get into belief systems, but most of us would agree that we get only one shot at this life . . . at least in our current form. So how are you going to spend that one precious life? Are you going to take care of your multimillion-dollar body and mind? Will you make sure you eat healthy, nutritious food? Get enough sleep? Get outside? How about exercise? Meditation? Stretching or yoga? Regular health checkups?

Working more hours is not the answer to your problems. You need to work better and smarter, and one of the keys to doing that is continually refreshing your mind and body. You need to sharpen the saw.

WE'RE IN THE HIMALAYAS

One thing you can't avoid when you become an entrepreneur are the highs and lows in your business. Of course, highs and lows happen to everyone, whether or not they have their own business, but for most people the highs will get higher and the lows will get lower when they become an entrepreneur.

Most of us wouldn't trade this life for anything—we love the control we have over our destiny. We love not answering to anyone. We love being able to create. We love the big wins. But we know that we won't win every time; there are going to be some lows.

My friend Lisa Sasevich likes to say we live in the Himalayas— as entrepreneurs, the peaks and valleys are bigger than they are for other people. When we strap on our entrepreneur superhero outfit, life is different for us than it is for normal civilians.

That means we have to be careful to manage our mental states. It's one thing to have a bad week or two if we've got a paycheck job—in most cases, the paycheck will keep coming in. But if we're running our own business, and especially if we have a team that's depending on us, we need to be able to pull ourselves out of the funk.

Of course, I'm no different from anyone else. I have my share of ups and downs, but what I've done is create a process for handling this. I keep a list of things that will pull me up when I'm not in peak state. Everyone will have their own list, but after comparing my list with those of many of my students and colleagues, I've noticed there's often a lot of overlap.

Here's a partial list of the stuff that works for me. Take what works for you and leave the rest:

Exercise: This is at the top of the list. Nothing changes my state for the better more quickly than getting my heart rate up. It's even better if it's outside (as opposed to being in a gym).

Meditate: This is a close second to exercise. It doesn't have to be complicated; just close your eyes and focus on your breath. Five minutes is all you need, but 20 minutes is even better.

Get outside: Few things will lift me up faster than being outdoors in nature.

Have an adventure: Go on a big mountain bike ride, have a big ski day or surfing day. Go for a hike. Visit a museum. Travel.

Serve or give: Do something good for someone else. I think it's impossible to feel sorry for yourself when you're acting selflessly and helping other people.

Be grateful: Few things will lift you up faster than recognizing and feeling gratitude for all the many good things in your life, which are sometimes easy to overlook. Take time to sit down and list all your blessings. You might want to start with your breath and your life . . . they're not something to take for granted.

That's my list, or at least part of it. Yours will probably be different. What's important is that you recognize when you're in a funk and have a strategy for lifting yourself out of it.

STAY IN YOUR GENIUS ZONE

My friend Dan Sullivan talks about the concept of Unique Ability®. Another term would be your genius zone. What's the one thing (or two or three things) you were put on earth to do? What can you do so well that time seems to disappear when you're doing it? What do you do that other people find exceptional but comes so easily you can't understand why they're so amazed? Those are the things in your genius zone, or your Unique Ability.

In your business, you want to work on the things you're great at. Don't spend your time on the stuff that's difficult for you. Work on your strengths, not your weaknesses. Hire people to do the things that are not in your genius zone.

Once you get rid of activities you aren't good at, the next thing to eliminate are the things you are proficient at but still aren't in your genius zone. Again, other people are better than you at those jobs, so hire them. Eventually you will even eliminate the tasks you are excellent at—because even though you're excellent at them, they still aren't in your genius zone. Doing those things takes you away from doing your genius activities.

The more time you spend in your genius zone, the better for you, your business, your clients . . . and the world.

YOUR MOST SCARCE RESOURCE

Your most scarce resource is focus.

The world will conspire to distract you. Your phone, email, text messages, social media, and more will all pull you away from what you should be doing.

Many people wake up and instantly look at their phones. They check messages, check email, check the news, check various social media. That's a huge mistake—the only thing that's waiting in your phone is someone else's agenda. If you check your phone or your email right away in the morning, you've lost control of *your* agenda. There will be emails or messages waiting for your response, and once you start responding you've lost control of your day.

You should start the day by focusing on your highest-value activities before you get caught up in other people's agendas for you. What are your highest-value activities?

CLIENTS YOU LOVE

I mentioned this in the last chapter, so I'm not going to spend a lot of time on it, but having great clients whom you love working with and serving is a fantastic shortcut to loving your life.

I frequently hear people complain about their clients—but the thing is, they're the ones who picked those clients. If you want different clients, then change your business, change your product, change your messaging, change your marketing. You're the one attracting those clients and making the decision to work with them . . . so pick great ones.

My highest-level clients are the people in my Launch Club and my mastermind group, and I love spending time with them. Launch Club is a powerful group of my highest-level coaching students—it's an amazing community that's doing big things. The energy, enthusiasm, and level of growth in Launch Club is absolutely contagious, and the members continually push me to be my best self. I also have a mastermind with my closest students whom I meet with several times a year. Space in the group is extremely limited, and there's a rigorous selection process to get in. Once people get into the mastermind, they rarely leave.

Every time I leave a meeting with either Launch Club or my mastermind, I'm more energized than I was at the beginning of the meeting. In fact, I set up my schedule so I always have a meeting with Launch Club directly before I lead one of my big workshops, because I know the meeting will leave me on fire with energy as I head into the big event.

Of course, that's just one example. The larger point is this: you control who your clients are. You do that through your market selection, offer selection, and marketing.

Don't compromise on this. Attracting new and better clients is what the Product Launch Formula is all about. Now go get the clients you want.

YOU CAN'T GET THERE ALONE

When I started out, I had this fantasy that I could build my business all by myself. I figured my life would be a lot simpler that way, and since it was a virtual business with a virtual product, I thought I could really scale up the business without creating a team.

In fact, I didn't hire anyone or use any contractors for the first 10 years I was in business. It was just me, with my wife, Mary, helping out in the background. Not hiring help was a big mistake, and it ended up holding me back. I now see that was about as mature as a two-year-old saying, "I can do it all by myself!"

The reality is that you can't build anything great by yourself. If you even try, then you're going to be spending huge chunks of time working on things you shouldn't be working on. You'll be working outside your genius zone.

Once you start building a team, your life will get more complicated. That's inevitable—any time humans are involved, things get more complicated. You will have to learn to be a leader for your team (if you don't already have that skill), and in many ways, you will have to answer to them.

One thing that will make this process a lot easier is sticking to a policy that my friend Eben Pagan calls "stars only." In other words, you want to hire only stars—the people who are in the top 10 percent of any skill set. In fact, you should probably take this further and hire only those people who are in the top 1 percent. Stars will make your life easier. They will be self-motivated. They will require less supervision and training. They will have less drama in their life. If they're good at their skill set but they've got a lot of drama, then they're not stars.

THE MAGIC WORD

As you become more successful, there's one word that will become more important than any other. That word is *no*. As Warren Buffett said, "The difference between successful people and very successful people is that very successful people say 'no' to almost everything."

In Chapter 15 I said that the idea of opportunity cost is the most important consideration in business. That's what we're really talking about here, but on a more personal level. As you become more successful, build more personal power, and grow into the role of leader, other people will find you more attractive. It can't help but happen—it's automatic. There's a huge vacuum of leadership in the world right now, and people are looking for leaders to plug in to and follow.

The next step is that more people and more deals start to pop up in your life. Many of the opportunities will be very attractive and would have impressed you if you'd had those same opportunities earlier in your life. However, you must be very careful about what you say yes to. You have to become increasingly selective. You need to get better at saying no. Anything that doesn't advance you toward your future and your bigger vision for yourself is something that will take you off your path.

I'm not saying you can't be a friend. I'm not saying you have to abandon the people and things that got you where you are, and I'm certainly not saying you can't lend a helping hand. You just have to be very careful of your time and your energy. Every new opportunity you say yes to closes the door on a different one.

DRINKING THE ABUNDANCE JUICE

When I started publishing my free investing newsletter in 1996, there was another website publishing a very similar one. However, even though we targeted the same niche, our sites were very different. They charged for their newsletter; mine was free. They had a much more professional-looking site; mine was very amateurish. In fact, back then I couldn't even afford to buy a domain name or website hosting, so my site was hosted on a free server.

That competing site was published by a guy named Frank Collar. I would often look at his site and wander through the pages. It was my ultimate dream to have a professional site like that and publish a paid newsletter like he did. But I didn't know how I would get there. I didn't know any of the tech stuff required, and I didn't have money to hire the people who did. I didn't know how to sell. Most important, I didn't have the confidence to ask people to buy my stuff.

In any case, one day I got an email from Frank. He asked me how I put together some of the stock market charts on my website. That email gave me a shock. I was surprised that Frank even knew who I was or that my site even existed, so on one level I was flattered.

On another level, Frank was a direct competitor. It was like he was Coke and I was Pepsi (although in reality, I was more like some generic cola). We were in the EXACT same business, and those charts on my site were the only thing that was pulling in traffic to me. These days (when you can post a photo on social media from your phone in a few seconds), it's a simple thing to post an image like a stock chart to a website or blog, but it was a different world back then. I'd spent the better part of a day and more cash than I could afford figuring out how to do it. I had invested time, effort, and hard-earned money to create those charts, and I saw them as my one major asset in my business.

So as I looked at that email from Frank, I wondered what to do. Should I give him my trade secret? Should I turn him down? Or should I just ignore his email? In the end, I decided I might as well help him out. I knew that if I had figured it out, he would certainly be able to. And why put him through the day of tedious trial and error that I went through to learn how to do it?

So I took 20 minutes and typed up a complete set of instructions for how to create and post those charts, just the way I had, and I sent the email off to Frank.

Within just a few minutes I got an email back from Frank thanking me. He went on to tell me that he had many years of newsletter publishing experience in the offline world, and that he had done a lot of testing of his online newsletter. He shared a lot of great information about some of those tests—including some critical pricing tests. Then he told me that if I ever wanted to publish a paid newsletter, he would be happy to help me out with his knowledge and experience.

In that moment, when I read that email, my life changed.

I realized that we were operating in a brave new world, where in many (most?) cases, cooperation was more important than competition. Years later, I would coin the term "Abundance Juice" to describe this phenomenon. Simply put, you have the choice between an abundance-based mindset and a scarcity-based mindset. Choose wisely, because your choice will impact every area of your life. In my experience, if you pick the abundance mindset, there's a lot more joy, fulfillment, and—well, abundance.

A few months later Frank did indeed help me launch my paid newsletter. His advice and experience gave me the confidence to create that newsletter, and it became a huge success for me. (That was the $34,000 launch I told you about in Chapter 1.) Then, a couple of years later, when he was tired of publishing his newsletter, Frank actually GAVE me his list of paying subscribers. I took over servicing his subscribers and made a lot of money doing so. This was all because I had helped him out with a simple favor, all because I had shared the Abundance Juice with him.

One of my core beliefs is that you will be far happier if you drink the Abundance Juice and adopt the abundance mindset. In addition to your being happier, your business will grow faster and larger, you will attract better clients and partners, and you'll have a much bigger positive impact on the world.

So I invite you . . . go ahead, drink the Abundance Juice.

USING YOUR PLATFORM FOR GOOD

When I started out, I went through a goal-setting exercise. This was one of those exercises in which you dream as big as you can dream. Along with lots of lifestyle stuff, I wrote down "an income of $100,000 per year." That was the biggest number I could possibly imagine as an income.

Now, all these years later, I've been blessed to have had many times when I raised more than $100,000 for a charity or nonprofit—in a single day. That's purely because I've built up a big platform. And just like a Hollywood star can generate a lot of exposure and funding for a favorite cause, you'll be able to do the same as you build your business.

Everything you've learned in this book has been about building your platform and putting on promotions. Those things will give you enormous leverage to create good in the world. They give you the power to point attention and focus at whatever cause is dear to you. There are two nonprofits for which I've generated more than a million dollars in fundraising, and there are others for which I've raised or donated $100,000 or more—all because of the platform that I've built in my business. You can do the same.

A LIFE WELL LIVED

In my opinion, there is no business-building system with more amazing success stories in the last decade than Product Launch Formula. I have walked you through the entire formula in the pages of this book. In other words, I've given you the tool to create your business.

I've given you a lot of power, and as the saying goes, with great power comes great responsibility. Make no mistake—building a successful business will not automatically lead to a happy and fulfilled life. There are plenty of miserable entrepreneurs out there. The trick is to create a business AND have a great life. To get there, you need to be intentional with the business you build and the life you create. It doesn't happen by accident.

DANCING YOUR WAY AROUND THE WORLD

Sebastien Night was born in French-speaking Guadeloupe in the Caribbean, and he now lives in France. He first went through my training in 2010. Since then he's been using PLF to build his business. Initially he was in the French "dating advice" market, where he taught shy men how to approach women and ask for a date. Eventually Sebastien transitioned to teaching French-speaking people how to build their online businesses, and he's now known as "the French Marketer." Sebastien has done dozens of launches, and he's built up a serious business. In fact, he's one of the most prominent online publishers in the French-speaking world.

As with any entrepreneur, he's put in a lot of work to get to where he's at. He's also created an incredible lifestyle. A high point so far is that he was able to fulfill two lifelong dreams of his fiancée, Cecile—dancing and traveling around the world. Last year Sebastien took a six-month trip around the world with Cecile, and they danced the entire way. They visited Australia, Brazil, India, Argentina, South Africa, Thailand, Durango, and New York. While they were in India, Sebastien proposed to Cecile—and she said yes!

During the trip Sebastien worked one day per week. Like mine, his business is completely virtual, so he could work anywhere in the world. The entire trip was financed by one of his launches, and

Sebastien Night, with his wife, Cecile, and daughter, Alice.

he's also going to be paying for two great weddings—same bride for both, but one in France and one in Guadeloupe. ☺

The thing is, if you pull Sebastien aside, he'll tell you that the most exciting part is that he has friends and family who have seen his success, and they're now following his example and creating their own businesses. They're following the recipe for a big life.

To see my case study with Sebastien, as well as the video of his round-the-world trip with Cecile, go to http://thelaunchbook .com/sebastien.

CHAPTER 17

It's Your Time to Launch

So that's the Product Launch Formula.

Now it's your turn. The formula has been proven thousands of times over. All of my personal success has been created by doing exactly what I taught you in this book. I've built several businesses now, and every one of them was based on the Product Launch Formula.

What's more important is that this is the exact formula my clients have used to generate more than a billion dollars in sales. And they've done it in nearly every market or niche you can think of, with products that range from cage fighting to meditation workshops to tax preparation to marching band accessories.

THE DEATH OF LAUNCHES

Back when I first released PLF in 2005, the online marketing community was still a relatively small one. Most of the big players knew each other, and it took only a few months until some people started talking about the "death of launches." That was the exact phrase used in a major white paper that came out less than a year after I released PLF. Some of those "in the know" predicted that the PLF model was so powerful, it would collapse under its own weight. Conventional wisdom said that once everyone in the marketplace had seen a launch or two, the whole launch idea would stop working. As the old quote goes, "We have met the enemy, and he is us."

One leader in the industry went so far as to pull me aside at a conference and kindly urge me to find something new to start teaching, because the "bloom is off the rose" with this launching thing. (That was in 2006.)

The truth is, launches have only gotten bigger and better since then. A more apt quote would be "The reports of my death are greatly exaggerated." ☺

So what happened?

TACTICS COME AND GO, STRATEGY IS FOREVER

Military (and business) leaders nearly worship *The Art of War* by Sun Tzu. The book is thousands of years old, but that doesn't stop every new generation of leaders from reading it. That's because the book is about strategy, not tactics—and strategy never goes out of style.

The reason PLF keeps working is that it's based in strategy. I teach plenty of tactics as part of the formula, but those tactics are always used to serve the overall PLF strategy. And frankly, tactics come and go. For example, when I started doing launches, online video didn't exist, and live online broadcasts definitely didn't exist. For that matter, blogs and launch pages didn't exist, nor did social media or webinars. But now we use all those tools in our launches.

Tools change, tactics change. Strategy endures.

Creating a close connection with your prospect will never go out of style. Building up anticipation for an event will never go out of style. Mental triggers such as social proof, authority, community, and reciprocity will never go out of style. Building influence by delivering massive value before you ask for the sale will never go out of style. The exact way you actually deploy those things has changed and will continue to change, but the PLF strategy keeps working.

TURN YOUR COMPUTER INTO A MONEY MACHINE

Sometime around 1994—I don't recall the exact date—I received an advertisement for a product called "Turn Your Computer into a Money Machine." Now, I'll admit that's a pretty cheesy name, but it caught my attention enough so that I opened it up and started reading. I suppose I was in the perfect target market for the ad at the time—this was back when I was in my stay-at-home-dad phase. We were struggling to make ends meet, and I really needed any kind of a money machine I could get.

The ad arrived via email, and it was really long—it must have been 10 pages or more. After I read it through once, I felt I needed to read it again, so I printed it out on my dot matrix printer. Because that printer was slow and the ad was so long, it seemed to take forever.

Over the next week I read that ad over and over. It talked about creating "special reports" and selling them online. It talked about the wonders of having a publishing business and selling direct to consumers.

The idea seemed nearly unbelievable to me. However, the publishing business had been around for centuries, so I figured it had to be profitable. And I knew of small, independent publishers who seemed to be making money. For example, when I looked for books on some of my interests like whitewater kayaking and mountain biking, all the popular ones came from small publishers who were obviously grassroots, mom-and-pop businesses.

On the other hand, I had never created or published anything in my life. Even more frightening was the very idea of selling. I had no experience in sales. In fact, if I had listed the absolute most unlikely possible career choices for myself, sales would probably have been at the top of the list.

There was another big problem, too: "Turn Your Computer into a Money Machine" cost $99.50. At that time we were supporting a family of four on Mary's lone paycheck from her government-funded job. When I put together a budget for the family, we had a little more than $400 left as disposable income per year. Spending nearly a quarter of that money on something like this felt like a risky proposition.

Still, that ad made so much sense. The entire idea made so much sense, and I was desperate for a change. I spent a full week reading through that ad again and again. Every night I would lie in bed thinking about it. I would wonder if it could possibly work for me. What could I publish about? Would I actually follow through and do it? Would I be able to sell anything, or would it be another failure in my life?

Perhaps you've been in a similar place before, wondering about a potential fork in the road. Lots of times, I procrastinate when it comes to making decisions, but this was one time I acted. I suspended my disbelief, filled out the order form, and mailed it off.

THE ROAD LESS TRAVELED

Robert Frost has an elegant and very famous poem about paths taken and not taken. It seems a bit silly and a little grandiose to invoke that poem when I'm telling you about answering a direct mail ad, but that one action made all the difference.

The product was simple—it came on a single 3.5-inch floppy disk. Of course, at this point many of my readers might not know what a floppy disk was, but the training course on that disk taught the basics of direct marketing for information products. It was mostly about selling stuff on CompuServe and AOL, a couple of old online services that acted as something of a gateway drug to the Internet back in the early 1990s.

It might have been old school, but that one information product opened up a whole new world for me—the world of direct marketing and creating an online, information-based business. And that world has been amazingly good to me. Of course, the money and success didn't come instantly, or even quickly, for that matter. But they did come . . . and you wouldn't be reading this book if I hadn't answered that ad.

A number of years ago I sent an email to Sheila Danzig, the creator and publisher of "Turn Your Computer into a Money Machine." I told her what her product had done for my life and the impact it had made on my family. It was a joyful email for me to send, and I heard back from her the next day. She was thrilled to get my email and hear how she had contributed to my success.

I know that feeling, because I get notes and emails of that type from my PLF students and clients every week—and reading those success stories never gets old.

Just this morning I received an email from Franz Weisbauer, a Fulbright Scholar and a doctor in Vienna. He's an internist with a clinical specialization in echocardiography (ultrasound of the heart). In 2010 he created an online training platform (with a colleague, Dr. Thomas Binder) to teach echocardiography to doctors and sonographers. Normally this type of training would require traveling to three weekend seminars that cost $500 each. The story of this launch is not unlike many you've already read in this book. When Franz and Thomas first released the program, they did it with Hope Marketing and had few sales. They had a great product, but it wasn't selling at a level to make it a viable, ongoing business.

Then Franz heard me speak about product launches at an event. He enrolled in my PLF training at the next opportunity and relaunched his site with a full PLF-style launch. It was a huge success that completely transformed his business—and it didn't end there. The business has grown to 10 times its pre-PLF level.

But volume of sales is only one measure of the success of a business. It's an easily calculable one, but numbers don't always paint the whole picture. Another measure is the impact—the number of lives that have been saved by the doctors and sonographers who have gone through Franz's training.

It's that ripple effect that gets me so excited that sometimes it's hard to sleep at night. I taught Franz how to launch his product, then his training helped thousands of doctors to treat tens of thousands of patients (and saved lots of lives along the way). Who knows the positive effect all those patients, with a new chapter added to their life, will have on the world?

YOUR FIRST LAUNCH

The next step is up to you. My goal in this book has been to show you the process. A secondary goal has been to make you realize that you can do this. I've seen it work over and over for my students, students from every walk of life and from all around the world.

The key is to take that first step and to keep taking baby steps. If I can go from Mr. Mom with zero entrepreneurial experience to tens of millions of dollars in sales, you can certainly do it as well. If John Gallagher can go from food stamps to a seven-figure business, you can do it as well. If Tara and Dave Marino can go from heartbroken parents to a half-million dollars in sales, you can do it as well.

Don't expect to make a million dollars with your first launch. Don't expect to equal some of the outsize results I've told you about in this book. Don't compare yourself to my million-dollar launches. Compare yourself to my first launch that did a modest $1,650 in sales.

Expect to make some mistakes and learn a lot. Expect it to be a lot more work than you anticipate. Expect some frustrations and some late nights.

And expect your first launch to be unforgettable.

A LONG, STRANGE TRIP THAT'S BARELY STARTED

It's been an amazing ride. I still find my entire journey to be completely improbable and hard to believe. And every step of the way I've been forced to keep thinking bigger, to keep finding a bigger vision for myself.

I'm not sure where PLF goes from here. I continue to support my PLF Owners as they launch their businesses and products in every niche and market imaginable. My Launch Club community is incredibly strong and vibrant, and it's a gift to be able to work with the people in it. This book has been published in 12 languages, and that number continues to grow. In addition to my version in English, the PLF Coaching Program is now available through my licensees in Portuguese, Spanish, Japanese, and Italian. I now have an amazing team that helps me support my PLF Owners, and my team is now strong enough so this work should outlive me.

One big thing that drives me is hearing about YOUR launch. As I said above, hearing those personal success stories never gets old.

I long ago made enough money to take my foot off the gas pedal and coast into semi-retirement. But here I am, somewhere around 90,000 words into this book, because I wanted to reach more people. I wanted to reach YOU.

PLF is proven. It will work for you. Just follow the steps I've given you in this book. Start building your list. Tap into the extra online resources I've mentioned throughout this book. Follow along on my blog. Plug into the PLF community. Then write to me and tell me about your success story. You can reach me on Twitter at @jeffwalker or on Instagram at @jeffwalkerco.

LINKS AND RESOURCES:

Your free membership site for this book: http://www.the launchbook.com/member

My personal blog: http://www.jeffwalker.com

More about the PLF Coaching Program: http://www.Product LaunchFormula.com

GLOSSARY

Please note: Some of these terms have multiple meanings and uses. This glossary gives definitions only as they are used in this book.

Affiliate Partner—a company or person who promotes another company in return for a commission on sales. Also see: Joint Venture Partner

Algorithm—a step-by-step set of rules or instructions necessary for solving a particular problem. In marketing and advertising, algorithms are used by the big ad platforms to determine the best ads to show to the best audience.

Call to Action (or CTA)—a request made to your prospect to do something. This is when you ask for some type of commitment—whether it's subscribing to your list, leaving a comment, clicking a link, or buying your product. Typically, all communication you send to your list will have some type of call to action at the end of the piece.

Cart Close—the end of your launch, when you close down your offer.

Cart Week—the time when your launch offer is open and you're taking orders. This is typically a period of four to seven days.

Circle of Awesome™—the system of rotating among Seed Launch®, Internal Launch, and JV Launch so that the results build on each other.

Client—someone who has already bought from you (as opposed to a prospect, who is on your list but hasn't bought yet).

Cold Traffic—a paid traffic strategy in which you are advertising to people who do not know you. This is as opposed to warm traffic, which is advertising to people who are already on your email list or following you on social media.

Conversion—the event where your prospect takes action based on your marketing. You've asked your prospect to take some action, and the conversion is when they commit to it. It can refer to someone subscribing to your list, or it could be making a purchase.

Conversion Rate—the percentage of visitors who take a specific action. It can refer to your opt-in process, in which case it would measure the percentage of visitors who become email subscribers. It can also refer to sales, in which case it would measure the percentage of people who buy your product.

Creative—the material or copy in an ad.

Customer—see Client.

Email Service Provider (or ESP)—a service for hosting and sending email to your email list. For recommended services, see my Resource Guide at http://thelaunchbook.com/resources.

FAQ—Frequently Asked Question. This generally refers to a document that presents the top questions on any given topic.

Internal Launch—a launch to your email list, where you don't have any outside JV Partners or affiliates. This is the classic PLF-style launch as described in the first eight chapters of this book.

Joint Venture Partner (or JV Partner)—almost synonymous with Affiliate Partner, although this term implies a closer working relationship.

JV Launch—a launch that is driven primarily by Affiliates and Joint Venture Partners sending traffic into your launch sequence.

Launch Conversation—the interaction between you and your prospects (as well as directly among your prospects) that naturally occurs during your Prelaunch Sequence. This interaction can give you enormous insight into your market—including the big objections to your offer and what parts of your messaging are resonating with your prospects.

Launch List—the email list you build during your Prelaunch Sequence.

Launch Sequence—your overall launch, including your Prelaunch Content and your Open Cart.

Lead Magnet—something that you offer to your website visitors in exchange for adding their email address to your list. It could be a special report, an infographic, or a video tutorial. Often it will be your Prelaunch Content delivered as a workshop or master class or video training series.

List—your database of people you'll be marketing to. Lists can be based in direct mail, social media, or email. However, in the context of this book, we focus primarily on email lists.

List Host—see Email Service Provider.

Live Broadcast—a video feed over the Internet that happens in real time. The broadcast is made while the event is happening.

Live Launch—a launch in which some or all of the content is delivered via live broadcasts.

Natural Search Traffic—the visitors who come to your site through your listings in the search engines. This is also referred to as "organic" or "natural" traffic.

Objection (or Sales Objection)—the concerns that a prospect has about a possible purchase. They are the potential reasons your prospect won't buy your product or service, and they need to be answered before you can make the sale.

Offer—what you're promoting to your prospects. Your offer includes your deliverables (including bonuses), your price, your payment terms, and your guarantee.

Open Cart—the time when you release your product for sale. Open Cart can refer to the actual day and time when you start taking orders or to the entire period when your launch offer is available.

Opening Day—the day you Open Cart and start taking orders in your launch.

Opt-In Page—see Squeeze Page.

Order Page—the page where your prospects actually make their purchase. This is where they supply their contact information and payment details and click the Buy button. Typically, your Sales Page will have an Add to Cart or a Buy It Now button, and that button will lead to your Order Page.

Organic Search—see Natural Search Traffic.

Paid Search—paid placement at or near the top of a search engine's rankings. This advertising is generally sold on a quasi-auction basis.

Paid Traffic—similar to Paid Search, except it's on non-search-engine sites, such as social media pages.

PLF—Product Launch Formula®.

Pre-Prelaunch Sequence—also known as Pre-Pre, this is the warm-up period before your Prelaunch Sequence starts.

Prelaunch Content (or PLC)—the material you release during your Prelaunch Sequence. It can take a variety of formats including video, PDF report, email, blog posts, and so on.

Prelaunch Sequence—a series of high-value content released before you launch to build excitement and anticipation for your product. The content can be in a variety of formats including video, PDF report, email, blog posts, and so on.

Product Launch Formula® (or PLF)—pure awesomeness. ☺

Prospect—someone who is on your list or looking at your marketing, but who hasn't bought yet. Once they buy, they become a Client or Customer.

Rank—where you appear in the Organic or Natural Search listings for a given search term. The term can also be used in a generic global sense—e.g., "Great content can help you rank in Google."

Return on Ad Spend (ROAS) —a calculation of the effectiveness of your advertising. To calculate ROAS, you divide the amount of revenue generated by your ad by the cost of your ad. For instance, if you made $200 in sales and you spent $100 on your ads, your ROAS is 2:1.

Scarcity Phase—the period near the end of your launch, when the scarcity mental trigger comes into full effect.

Sideways Sales Letter®—a key component of the Product Launch Formula that refers to the serial, sequenced nature of the Prelaunch Sequence and the entire PLF sales process.

Sales Letter—a written message that makes the offer for a product.

Sales Page—the web page that hosts your Sales Letter or Sales Video.

Sales Video—a video that makes the offer for a product.

Seed Launch®—a simple PLF-style launch that is used primarily if you don't have a product or a list. It can also be used if you have a concept for a new offer or product and would like to market test the idea before you spend a lot of time creating the product.

Shopping Cart—the software on your website that you use to take orders. This is where terms like "Open Cart" and "Cart Close" come from.

Squeeze Page—a simple page on your website that has a subscription form for your list. Visitors to the page have only one choice—they can either subscribe to your list to see more content or they can leave the page. Also called an Opt-in Page. For recommended services for easily building squeeze pages, see my Resource Guide at http://thelaunchbook.com/resources.

Sub-list—a list that is a subset of your total list. You might have a sub-list of people who have indicated an interest in a given topic. A Launch List is a form of a sub-list.

Teleseminar—a phone call in which the host can present to a large number of people on the call. This is what we used to do before webinars and live broadcasts were a thing.

Warm Traffic—a paid traffic strategy in which you are advertising to people who are already on your email list or following you on social media. This is as opposed to cold traffic, which is advertising to people who aren't already following you.

Web Host—a service that stores all the pages for your website and makes them available on the Internet. For recommended services, see my Resource Guide at http://thelaunchbook.com/resources.

Webinar—similar to a teleseminar, but presented over the web so attendees can see the presenter's computer screen. It is most often used to display a PowerPoint or Keynote presentation. For recommended services for webinars, see my Resource Guide at http://thelaunchbook.com/resources.

INDEX

ACKNOWLEDGMENTS

The 25 years since I started my first business have been an amazing ride, and I often wonder how I got so lucky. But I didn't get here alone. I've had so many people help me on this journey that it humbles me.

This book is dedicated to my wife, Mary, who has always believed in and supported me so fiercely that it shocks me to this day, and to my two incredible children, Dan and Joan—I don't know what I did to deserve you.

To Mom and Dad, who gave me such an incredibly loving, strong foundation for my life, and to Jim, Jean Marie, and Jon. I love you and thank you for who I am.

Thanks to Virginia and especially Joe Jablonsky, who believed in me when everyone else was wondering why I was home taking care of the kids. And a special thanks to Catherine Jablonsky, who was an unwavering supporter in so many ways in those early, uncertain years.

I've got so many other amazing people to thank . . .

Reid Tracy, Brian Kurtz, and Rick McFarland gave me great feedback on this book and helped shape the early chapters. Scott Hoffman, Brendon Burchard, Michael Hyatt, and Chris Haddad helped me with feedback on the overall book concept. Thanks to Victoria Labalme for being so darn relentless with her bigger vision of this book.

Farukh Shroff gave me great input and helped fact-check the paid traffic chapter, and Siri Myhrom also gave great feedback on that chapter. Thank you!

And thanks to Rachel Miller, who helped me mold the social media chapter.

So many people helped me along my path in the early days of my business, including Sheila Danzig, Mike Reed, Frank Collar, Paul Myers, and Don Cassidy.

John Reese and Yanik Silver told me I needed to start teaching people my product launch techniques, and John named PLF for me. That advice changed my life, and it changed the world.

I've had so many incredible partners, teachers, and coaches over the years—and most of them have become close friends: Dan and Babs Sullivan, Tony Robbins, Eben Pagan, Frank Kern, Paulo Coelho, Jeff Johnson, Rich Schefren, Ryan Deiss, Dean Graziosi, Mike Filsaime, my muse Andy Jenkins (who left us way too soon), Steven Pressfield, my DWD buddy Lisa Sasevich, Tom Kulzer, Chris Knight, Brian Clark and Sonia Simone, Marie Forleo, my study buddy Dean Jackson, Joe Polish, John Carlton, Mike Koenigs, Kenny Rueter, Jason Van Orden and Jeremy Frandsen, Chris Zavadowski, Jason Moffatt, Perry Belcher, J. B. Glossinger, Randy Cassingham and all the Hotshots, the late Audri and Jim Lanford, Clay Collins, Ray Edwards, Jeff Mulligan, Ed Dale, Dave Taylor, Tim Carter, Julie Cairns, Michelle Falzon (for the poetry), Eric Wagner, Martin Howey, Greg Poulos, Jason Potash, Pam Hendrickson, my HW community, Greg Clement, Trey Smith, Michael Maidens, Ellyn Bader, the FT-Talk community, Ryan Levesque, Susan Garrett, Denise Gosnell, Will Hamilton (for my monthly photo), Brian Sacks, Stu McLaren, Mastin Kipp, Tellman Knudson, Marlon Sanders, MaryEllen Tribby, John Lee Dumas, Tom Garcia, Chris Attwood, Janet Attwood, John Jantsch, Justin Livingston, Mike Hill, Jason Friedman, Sebastien Night, Jonathan Mizel, Jay Abraham, Dan Kennedy, Gail Kingsbury, Ricardo Teixeira, Ted Pasternack, Shelley Brander, Molly Mahoney, Des O'Neill, John Gallagher (my first case study out of hundreds!), Ruth Bucyzinski, Annie Lala, Olivier Roland, Julie Helmrich, and so many more that I'm worried about all those I've overlooked.

Thanks to Erico Rocha, my amazing licensee of PLF in Portuguese for the last seven years. He's brought PLF to Brazil, and his positive impact in that country has been incredible.

Luis Carlos Flores, who is changing the Spanish-speaking world as my licensee of PLF in Spanish.

And Hideki Ikeda (my PLF licensee in Japanese), and Marco Scabia (my PLF licensee in Italian).

Special thanks to Annie Hyman Pratt for her tireless coaching on team and leadership and her gentle but pointed push to help make me a better leader.

A huge thank you to Bari Baumgardner and Blue Melnick, who have worked their magic with me backstage so I can work my magic from the front of the stage.

I wouldn't be where I'm at today, and I wouldn't be able to bring PLF to the world, without my amazing team, which has now grown to the point that I can't name all of them here in this space.

A big shout-out to my Launch Club Coaches—thank you Donna Davis, Annette James, Jon Walker, Barry Friedman, Alexa Divett, Don Crowther, Dorethia Kelly, and Ben Snelling—you've all helped me help my students. Thank you.

And Dan Walker, my producer and director in all things video and live broadcast—what an amazing gift to have his creativity and talent to lean on.

And thanks to Sharon Pivirotto, Clare Day, Corey Peiffer, Anoop Jeewoololl, J. T. Nelms and Jen Zils, who make the PLF Coaching Program sing.

Thank you to Ash Brones, Chris Saunders, Justin MacMahan, Kate Thompson, Dawn Kroom, Shereen AbuSaeedi, and Joy Collado.

FYCT: Candice Lazar and Angie Colee.

Thanks to the wonderful team at Hay House who helped me shape this book, especially Anne Barthel, Lisa Bernier, and Elise Marton.

Thank you to Diane Walker, who has helped me plan dozens of my mastermind events.

And a special thanks to Betty Sampson, my first team member (and the one with the biggest fan base among our clients). Betty set the standard for our customer service from the beginning.

And Jon Walker, whom I've been working and playing with longer than anyone.

I could not have built my company without my Chief Operating Officer, Kristen Arnold, who has been with me since 2009. Kristen is the linchpin that makes the entire team (and me) work.

And what can I say about my Launch Club and Platinum Plus, my brothers and sisters who are in the trenches fighting the good fight with me through every day—through the big wins and seemingly insurmountable challenges. I'm blessed to have you in my life on a daily basis.

A special thanks to three of my guides on the path—Jim Marsden, Jade Sherer, and Zita Xavier.

And a big sanity thanks to Billy Foster, Bryan Dear, and Mac Thomson.

Another sanity check to Jen Libera and Kelly Matthews, Chris Barnes, Paul Wheeler, and Rick Routh—and I'll never forget Jon Nicholas.

And, of course, the real stars of the show are my PLF Owners . . . who continue to inspire me every single day. Thank you.

ABOUT THE AUTHOR

Jeff Walker started his first online business in 1996, when he was a stay-at-home dad and desperate to make some money to help support his family. Now, after decades in the digital business world, he's become one of the top entrepreneurial and marketing trainers in the world, and his strategies have literally transformed the way business is done online.

His Product Launch Formula has become the gold standard for how the top experts, thought leaders, and influencers bring their products and services to market.

But his techniques are not just for big gurus: he's taught thousands of students who operate in hundreds of niches. They've generated more than $1 billion in sales, and that number grows every day.

Jeff lives in Durango, Colorado, and he loves to get outside for all kinds of adventures. He's been married to his wife, Mary, for decades. He's no longer quite as fast as his kids on skis or mountain bikes, but they still let him come along for the ride.

You can follow Jeff on his blog at JeffWalker.com, and he's easy to find on social media. You can get free training on marketing and launches at ProductLaunchFormula.com.

Hay House Titles of Related Interest

We hope you enjoyed this Hay House book. If you'd like to receive our online catalog featuring additional information on Hay House books and products, or if you'd like to find out more about the Hay Foundation, please contact:

Hay House, Inc., P.O. Box 5100, Carlsbad, CA 92018-5100
(760) 431-7695 or (800) 654-5126
(760) 431-6948 (fax) or (800) 650-5115 (fax)
www.hayhouse.com® • www.hayfoundation.org

———

Published in Australia by: Hay House Australia Pty. Ltd.,
18/36 Ralph St., Alexandria NSW 2015
Phone: 612-9669-4299 • *Fax:* 612-9669-4144
www.hayhouse.com.au

Published in the United Kingdom by: Hay House UK, Ltd.,
The Sixth Floor, Watson House, 54 Baker Street, London W1U 7BU
Phone: +44 (0)20 3927 7290 • *Fax:* +44 (0)20 3927 7291
www.hayhouse.co.uk

Published in India by: Hay House Publishers India,
Muskaan Complex, Plot No. 3, B-2, Vasant Kunj, New Delhi 110 070
Phone: 91-11-4176-1620 • *Fax:* 91-11-4176-1630
www.hayhouse.co.in

———

Access New Knowledge.
Anytime. Anywhere.

Learn and evolve at your own pace
with the world's leading experts.

www.hayhouseU.com